discovering *the* HOLy spiRit
in the New Testament

discovering *the* HOLY SPIRIT *in the* NEW TESTAMENT

Keith Warrington

HENDRICKSON
PUBLISHERS

© 2005 by Hendrickson Publishers, Inc.
P. O. Box 3473
Peabody, Massachusetts 01961-3473

ISBN-13: 978-1-56563-871-6
ISBN-10: 1-56563-871-9

Scripture quotations marked RSV are taken from the Revised Standard Version of the Bible, copyright 1952 (2d ed., 1971) by the Division of Christian Education of the National Council of the Churches of Christ in the United States of America. Used by permission. All rights reserved.

Printed in China

Second Printing — August 2006

Cover Art: The cover photo is of a stained glass window by Andrew Johnson depicting the Holy Spirit in the form of a dove. The window is is part of a larger nine-window series on the theme of the Holy Spirit throughout creation located in Holy Spirit Catholic Church, Bovey Tracey, Devon, UK.

Photo Credit: Andrew Johnson. Used with permission of Andrew Johnson Stained Glass AMGP.

Library of Congress Cataloging-in-Publication Data

Warrington, Keith.
    Discovering the Holy Spirit in the New Testament /
Keith Warrington.
        p. cm.
    Includes bibliographical references and indexes.
    ISBN-13: 978-1-56563-871-6 (alk. paper)
    ISBN-10: 1-56563-871-9 (alk. paper)
    1. Holy Spirit—Biblical teaching. 2. Bible. N.T.—Theology.
    I. Title.
        BS2545.H62W37 2005
        231'.3'09015—dc22

                                        2005007028

Contents

Preface   vii

Acknowledgments   x

Introduction   1

1. Matthew and Mark   3

2. Luke   23

3. John   35

4. Acts of the Apostles   51

5. Romans   75

6. 1 Corinthians   98

7. 2 Corinthians   120

8. Galatians   130

9. Ephesians   141

10. Philippians   160

11. Colossians   167

12. 1–2 Thessalonians   172

13. The Pastoral Epistles   180

14. Hebrews   188

15. 1 Peter   196

16. 1 John   205

17. Jude   211

18. Revelation   214

19. Listen to What the Spirit Says to the Church   221

Index of Subjects   223

Index of Ancient Sources   225

Preface

This book commenced some years ago as the result of a happy coincidence. I had been asked to teach a postgraduate course in Australia on Pauline pneumatology. The limited amount of commentary on this topic at the time drove me to study the Pauline corpus itself. One of my earliest partners in this exploration was Gordon Fee's *God's Empowering Presence,* which became a regular contributor to my thinking. At the same time, I was teaching on the Spirit in Luke-Acts, and there I benefited in particular from the writings of Max Turner, James Dunn, Robert Menzies, and, latterly, Matthias Wenk. Others have joined my collegial circle, and I have noted some of them at the conclusion of each chapter of this book. They, as well as my students, have helped sharpen my thinking and develop my conclusions concerning the Spirit in the NT.

This book has some clear perspectives in terms of readership. Over the years, many of my students have searched commentaries and other books for analysis concerning the Spirit and his work and often have been disappointed because of the limited nature of that analysis. At the same time, much emphasis, particularly in popular literature, has been placed on the charismatic gifts of the Spirit. Although such works are helpful for the healthy development of the church, exploration of the Spirit himself too often has been restricted to academic, theological volumes in which his dynamic nature gets overlooked in technical debate. This book is dedicated to the Spirit and his role in the life of the individual believer and the church. It is written with the church leader and student of the Spirit in mind, for believers who are aware of the work of the Spirit in their lives and want to know more about him.

The books of the NT were written to different audiences that, in many cases, had different needs. Thus, the authors often wrote with different agendas. The contemporary reader, therefore, should treat the books and their contents separately, with an awareness of the original settings. There is always a danger of mirror-reading when attempting to discover the setting of the original addressees of an ancient letter, and I have kept this in mind when exploring the possible backgrounds of the texts. I have tried to stay rooted in the text, focusing specifically on one main question: Why has the author included information on the Spirit? Some authors mention the Spirit more often than others do, while some books do not clearly refer to him at all.

In many ways this book follows the pattern I recommend to my students when they prepare research papers on the NT text. The text is the focus and sets the agenda, resulting in a text-driven awareness of its message to the first-century reader. A future work on the Spirit from the perspective of identifying themes of the Spirit and spirituality in the NT and offering contemporary application will, I hope, be a useful partner in this exercise of discovering more and more about the Spirit. My hope is that as a result of being exposed to the NT writers, believers will find the role of the Spirit in salvation and the Christian life more wonderful as they increasingly understand his comprehensive commitment to them.

The following points are offered as an aid to my readers:

• The issues concerning the Spirit that the authors of the NT refer to are often concerns for believers today as well. I encourage readers of this book to try to see themselves and their situations in the writings of the NT authors to their first-century readers. They might also want to identify lessons relating to the person and work of the Spirit and apply them to their own situations.

• Fundamentally, the message of the NT is that the Spirit is dedicated to the development of the life of the believer. An investigation of the varied expressions of that activity as the NT presents them is a worthwhile objective. It will emphasize the magnitude of the Spirit's commitment to the believer while also rooting that perspective in the substantial evidence of the NT.

• This book is not intended to function as a commentary on individual books (useful books, including some commentaries, are recommended at the conclusion to each chapter, and these explore wider and introductory issues while also providing in-depth exegesis relating to the NT books concerned). The commentary here relates

only to clear references to the person and work of the
Spirit.

- An accessible and balanced approach is adopted throughout. Where the text is unclear, this is acknowledged,
although possible interpretations are offered. Similarly,
where a variety of options are possible, only the main
ones are considered. Footnotes have deliberately been
kept to a minimum.

- The Spirit is the focus of attention—in particular, the
significance of the Spirit to a first-century readership
with implicit relevance and application to a contemporary readership. My goal is not to provide all the
answers, but rather to facilitate a context for thinking
and exploration.

- Each chapter deals with one or more books of the NT,
following the same structure: a brief setting; an over-
view of the main issues concerning the Spirit; an exposition of each reference to the Spirit (or block of
references if the same issue is being dealt with); and an
exploration of the significance of the reference for the
original readers. Each chapter concludes with a selected
bibliography and some study questions. The final chapter explores the relevance of the NT information about
the Spirit for the contemporary believer.

- In concentrating on the information that the NT authors
provide concerning the Spirit, I have not assumed that it ·
always had particular reference to the readers. The
information may have been incidental to the message or
part of the author's personal faith journey, with little
bearing on the lives of the readers. Nevertheless, I have
assumed that the information may have relevance to the
readers, both ancient and modern. Indeed, given the
dynamic nature of the Spirit and Scripture, that assumption must be made.

Acknowledgments

I am grateful to

- Gordon Fee for writing his highly significant book *God's Empowering Presence,* which honors the Spirit and provides an enlightening guide to the exploration of his person and ministry.

- My undergraduate and postgraduate students at Regents Theological College in Nantwich, England, and the Asian Pacific Institute in Brisbane, Australia, with whom I have had the opportunity to walk this path toward a greater appreciation of the Spirit and from whom I have learned much. With one of my postgraduate students I also have come to recognize that though Jesus has become clearer to me, the Spirit has come closer.

- My colleague Dr. Neil Hudson, who has been a fellow traveler on this journey and with whom I have teased out issues and concepts as we have explored the Spirit together.

- The editors at Hendrickson Publishers, who carefully worked through the manuscript, offering many helpful improvements to the style and presentation. I am grateful for their skill and patience.

- My wife and eternal partner, Judy, and our children, Luke and Anna-Marie. They have provided me with a remarkable context of love through which I have been released to develop my thinking. Their destinies are also determined by the same all-encompassing Spirit.

*I*ntroduction

The Spirit is referred to many times in the OT and other Jewish literature. A number of important studies have been conducted in these texts, and some conclusions, at times divergent and at other times complementary, have been reached. Most have concluded that the Spirit was referred to in association with verbal proclamation including praise and worship but also especially prophecy, while the roles of sanctification and ethical renewal have also been identified. Although we must be careful not to overly restrict the work of the Spirit in the pre-NT literature or to force it into a preconceived or narrow framework, we may safely say that these are the main areas related to the Spirit in the Jewish understanding. The Spirit is, to a limited degree, involved in miraculous phenomena, including, though to a much smaller degree, supernatural physical healings. The NT writers offer similar perspectives to their OT counterparts and thus reflect continuity with the past. However, they also explore new areas associated with the Spirit.

Although the Spirit graciously welcomes us to explore him, we should not anticipate that we will understand him. Nor is that the reason for developing a greater appreciation of who he is. The questions of importance to the NT authors are related to questions such as these: Why is the Spirit given to the church, and how can we be influenced by him? What does he do for and in believers, and how can we take advantage of his resources for our growth? What is he like, and how can that influence our response to him? Issues such as whether there is a divine hierarchy in the Godhead, how the Spirit differs from the Father and the Son, and what relationship Jesus has with the Spirit are discussed by later theologians. The NT authors were more interested in the practical application of a knowledge of the Spirit. Ours will be a similar project.

Selected Bibliography

Keener, Craig S. *The Spirit in the Gospels and Acts: Divine Purity and Power.* Peabody, Mass.: Hendrickson, 1997. Pp. 6–48.

Menzies, Ralph P. *Empowered for Witness: The Spirit in Luke-Acts.* Rev. ed. Journal of Pentecostal Theology: Supplement Series 6. Sheffield: Sheffield Academic Press, 1994. Pp. 48–102.

Turner, Max. *The Holy Spirit and Spiritual Gifts: Then and Now.* Carlisle: Paternoster, 1996. Pp. 1–18.

————. *Power from on High: The Spirit in Israel's Restoration and Witness in Luke-Acts.* Journal of Pentecostal Theology: Supplement Series 9. Sheffield: Sheffield Academic Press, 1996. Pp. 82–138.

Wenk, Matthias. *Community-forming Power: The Socio-ethical Role of the Spirit in Luke-Acts.* Journal of Pentecostal Theology: Supplement Series 19. Sheffield: Sheffield Academic Press, 2000. Pp. 56–118.

chapter 1

Matthew and Mark

Because all of the references to the Spirit in the Gospel of Mark are also found in Matthew, we will not look at the Markan passages separately. Instead, where differences are significant, we will comment on Mark in the context of the discussion of Matthew. Chapter 2 examines the material in Luke concerning the Spirit that differs from that in Matthew. Where Luke describes events similar to those in Matthew, however, we offer comments concerning his presentation here.

The Setting

As in the other Gospels, the author's name does not appear in the text of Matthew, but the believers accepted the title of the Gospel of Matthew without dispute from before the end of the second century. It appears that Matthew's aim was to declare the gospel in such a way that it would appeal to Jews. Early tradition and the Gospel's content suggest that Matthew wrote it in Palestine or Syria. The use of the OT and the Jewish emphasis intimate a Jew writing for Jews. Matthew aims to prove the messiahship of Jesus but also presents the universal application of the gospel. It is possible that Matthew intended this book to be used as a teaching manual, and the ecclesiastical teaching and material pertaining to Christian growth particularly suggest this.

Early Christian tradition strongly affirms Mark's authorship of the gospel that is associated with his name and affirm that his gospel was written in connection with the Apostle Peter. Mark joined Paul and Barnabas (his cousin [Col 4:10]) on a mission, though later left them (Acts 12:25; 15:37–40). Peter speaks of him affectionately, having worked with him in Rome (1 Pet 5:13). It is generally believed that Mark's was the earliest Gospel; the links with Peter and reliance on Mark by Matthew and Luke suggest an early date. It appears to be written for a Gentile readership, and the addressees are generally assumed to be based in Rome.

This is the Gospel of fast-moving action, one of Mark's favorite words being "immediately." Discourse and teaching material is markedly less than in the other Gospels. However, this should not be assumed to indicate a limited desire on the part of the author to teach his readers.

What Do the Texts Say about the Spirit?

The Spirit

- was involved with the birth of Jesus (Matt 1:18, 20; cf. Luke 1:35)

- was promised as part of Jesus' baptism with fire (Matt 3:11//Mark 1:8//Luke 3:16)

- was associated with Jesus (Matt 3:16//Mark 1:10//Luke 3:22; Matt 4:1//Mark 1:12//Luke 4:1)

- inspires speech (Matt 10:20//Mark 13:11//Luke 12:12; Matt 12:18; Matt 22:43//Mark 12:36)

- was associated with exorcism (Matt 12:28)

- can be the subject of blasphemy (Matt 12:31–32//Mark 3:29//Luke 12:10)

- is a member of the Godhead (Matt 28:19)

The Spirit was involved with the birth of Jesus (Matt 1:18, 20; cf. Luke 1:35)

Now the birth of Jesus Christ took place in this way. When his mother Mary had been betrothed to Joseph, before they came together she was found to be with child of the Holy Spirit. . . . But as he considered this, behold, an angel of the Lord appeared to him in a dream, saying, "Joseph, son of David, do not fear to take Mary your wife, for that which is conceived in her is of the Holy Spirit."

Exposition

The first reference to the Spirit in the Gospel of Matthew is in the context of new life.[1] It is significant that Matthew mentions the Spirit at key events in the life of Jesus, including his baptism (3:16), his first encounter with the devil (4:1), and the commissioning of the disciples (28:19). The Spirit is with Jesus before his birth and after his resurrection (1:18; 28:19).

The narrative does not intend to offer an explanation for the virgin birth, neither how it happened nor why. Rather, it seeks to establish the role of the Spirit as a central element of the birth. The angel encourages Joseph not to be fearful but to recognize the positive implications of the fact that the Spirit conceived the child.

The phrase used in both texts concerning the role of the Spirit describes the baby as having been conceived "of the Holy Spirit." The reference to the Spirit being associated with a person would remind a Jewish reader of a number of relevant truths from Scripture. The Spirit was responsible for creation (Gen 1:2) and the giving of life (Gen 6:3), and was expected to affirm and empower the Messiah (Isa 11:2). Thus, a reference to the Spirit indicated not only that the birth was divinely initiated but also that the Spirit would rest upon the one born in this way, as Isaiah prophesied concerning the Messiah.

The involvement of the Spirit in the birth of Jesus was a sign that the new age was soon to come (Isa 44:3–4). The Spirit, not Joseph or Mary, was the one who initiated the events that would lead to the birth of Jesus.

Significance for the Original Readers

The nation into which Jesus was born was desperate for help because of the hopeless despair that pervaded it. The Jews found themselves under pressure from a number of sources, and they were unable to respond with any expectation of success. Rome's subjugation of the Jews presented a critical problem. Not only did the moral, religious, and intellectual influences of the Roman Empire upset the religious standards of the Jews, but also the taxation burden, exacerbated by the tax collection system, humiliated them, reminding them of their weakness and inability to change their situation. Foreign soldiers, based throughout the country to

---

[1] See also comments on Luke 1:35 in ch. 2.

quell potential revolution and to protect the eastern borders, brought fear and insecurity as well as ceremonial and ethical contamination to the cities where they were based; in Jerusalem, the soldiers were housed in the Antonia fortress, next to the temple. The nation, though rooted in the worship of God, was bombarded by other religious voices, including the emperor cult and mystery religions. Mystery religions played an important part in the lives of people in the first centuries B.C.E. and C.E., satisfying a need that was lacking in the cult of the emperor: a personal god. These religions cut across social barriers; often, slaves and masters could belong to the same cult, and once members were initiated, class became secondary because usually anyone could be promoted to any office. Syncretistic worship also could be found throughout the land. Gaza had its local deity, the people of Ashkelon worshipped Astarte, and Caesarea was home to a temple to Augustus. There was a crying need for transformation and hope to lighten the crushing load of despair that burdened these people blinded by their own religion. Matthew's message of the birth of Jesus, ushered in by the Spirit, offered hope. The long-awaited new era had begun.

The Spirit was promised as part of Jesus' baptism with fire (Matt 3:11//Mark 1:8//Luke 3:16)

"I baptize you with water for repentance, but he who is coming after me is mightier than I, whose sandals I am not worthy to carry; he will baptize you with the Holy Spirit and with fire."

Exposition

John the Baptist speaks these words concerning Jesus, explaining that Jesus would provide a baptism different from his. Whereas John baptized with water, Jesus was to baptize "with the Holy Spirit and with fire."

Baptism

The use of the term "baptize" with reference to the Spirit probably owes more to the context of water baptism than it does to any theological understanding of the term as a description of a relationship with the Spirit. In that regard, it is better to understand baptism in terms of its watery connection—being overwhelmed or inundated with the Spirit. This is a metaphor, describing a powerful infusion of the Spirit into the life of an individual, and must always be treated as such. The use of this phrase indicates that the same people who are baptized with the Holy Spirit are also baptized with fire. There is no suggestion that one group of people are baptized with the Spirit and another with fire.

The Greek word *en,* here rendered "with," can be translated in a number of ways ("in," "by"), but the various translations do not greatly affect the meaning of the phrase. The parallel use of the word with regard to John's baptism in water helps to clarify the meaning of Jesus' baptism with the Holy Spirit. As the penitent is baptized with water by John, so the believer is to be baptized with the Spirit. The difference is that while water functions, at least symbolically, to affirm and anticipate a difference in lifestyle and commitment, the Spirit functions similarly but also resides in the life of the believer to help effect the change. The baptismal water evaporates from the believer, but the Spirit remains with and energizes the believer.

This is also an opportunity for Jesus to be exalted above John the Baptist. Not only is Jesus' baptism superior to that of John, but it also indicates the superior nature of Jesus. The addition of the pronoun *autos* ("he") to the verb *baptisei* ("he will baptize") is for the purpose of emphasis ("he, he will baptize you"). John describes Jesus' baptism with the Spirit also to identify his authority to do so.

With the Holy Spirit

The clearest fulfillment of the promise that Jesus would baptize with the Holy Spirit would be on the day of Pentecost in Jerusalem, when the Spirit filled the people who were waiting for his arrival (Acts 1:4–5; 2:4). Thus, as John prepared the way for the Messiah, Jesus prepared the way for the Spirit.

An alternative suggestion is that Jesus' baptism with the Spirit also, and specifically, relates to the issue of judgment. The following verse (Matt 3:12) supports such an interpretation, as does the reference to fire. Thus, the role of the Spirit is to affirm the identity of those who are children of God, confirming their justification by God as authentic. If this affirmation is assumed to be in association with the acceptance of the salvation offered by Jesus, this also accurately reflects the message of Paul that the Spirit functions as the one who sets believers apart to God, confirming that they are the

children of God (Rom 8:15–16). On this understanding, the anticipated baptism by Jesus would take place at the moment of salvation when the judgment of God would have occurred, evidenced
in his acceptance of the believer because of the redemption
achieved by Jesus and the repentance of the person concerned.

If this affirmation is assumed to be in association with the acceptance of the Spirit in the OT and in the creation of new life, the
commencement of the new era of the Messiah would have provided a powerful sense of expectancy for John the Baptist's
audience.

With Fire

Matthew (and Luke) add the reference to fire to the description in Mark—possibly because the helpful references to fire in
Jewish literature are more available to Matthew's readership than
to Mark's Gentile readership. The contemporary reader may identify fire with warmth, coziness, or danger. Jews, however, would
not have immediately associated fire with these things. Rather, fire
would have brought to their minds the presence (Exod 3:2) and
the protection and direction (Exod 13:21–22) of a holy God. They
would also think of the refining properties of fire—being associated with the the cleansing of sin and judgment (Isa 4:4; 29:6)—in
which the fire removes the dross while purifying the metal (Zech
13:9). Although fire has a number of such associations, its link with
judgment is the most likely reason for its connection with the Spirit
here. Both John's baptism of repentance and Jesus' baptism in fire
are related to the issue of judgment. To be saved, one needs both
baptisms: the one of personal repentance, the other of cleansing
by the Spirit. Not only does the Spirit bring the eschatological judgment forward and affirm believers at the beginning of their walk as
children of God, but he also judges sin wherever he sees it.

Significance for the Original Readers

The Jews believed that the Messiah would be endowed with
the Spirit (Isa 11:2), though the evidence that he would bestow the
Spirit is scarce (e.g., T. Levi 18:6–11). The original readers of the
Gospels would not have been expecting such an action on the part
of the Messiah. Matthew, however, presents Jesus in an exalted
way, demonstrating to his Jewish audience that Jesus is superior to
the sort of Messiah they were expecting. Not only was Jesus given
the Spirit, but he was also to give the Spirit to others. He was not

just an anointed man, albeit with supernatural powers; he functioned as God, as demonstrated by his authority to give the Holy Spirit to others.

The association with fire also would have signaled that a new era was to be born, one associated with the presence and prerogatives of God as witnessed in the OT. The Jews had experienced many bitter disappointments, but the worst of all was the apparent absence of God. The representatives of God in Jewish religion offered little hope for the future or sensitive guidance for the present. Such a religious life meant the degeneration of public and private morals. A sense of hopelessness pervaded the lives of the people. All around was despair, conscious need, and unconscious longing, and Matthew reminds his readers that into this desperate situation came a new message of change and restoration initiated by Jesus, who promised the Spirit. Matthew reminds readers of the sensational nature of this new era characterized by the presence of one who was able to give the Spirit to people—a prerogative that belongs only to God (Num 11:29; Isa 42:1). At the beginning of this Gospel story, Matthew enlightens the readers as to the superiority of Jesus, who not only is associated with the Spirit, and that from birth, but also has the capacity to bestow that Spirit on others.

The Spirit was associated with Jesus (Matt 3:16// Mark 1:10//Luke 3:22; Matt 4:1//Mark 1:12//Luke 4:1)

And when Jesus was baptized, he went up immediately from the water, and behold, the heavens were opened and he saw the Spirit of God descending like a dove, and alighting on him. (Matt 3:16)

Exposition

These verses further develop the association of the Spirit with Jesus—not just for the purpose of empowering or guiding Jesus as if he were helpless without the Spirit, but to emphasize his grandeur. His traveling companion is none other than the Spirit. Matthew's intention is to facilitate the thinking of his readers in their exploration of Jesus. Although Jesus initially looks and functions like a person, increasingly he begins to function like God.

The baptism of Jesus occurred in association with three other events: the opening of the heavens, the Spirit of God descending like a dove, and the Father speaking affirming words. Luke, more than the other writers, identifies these associated events as being more significant than the baptism itself, though this feature is not absent from Matthew and Mark. Luke notes the fact that Jesus was praying, as he does on other important occasions in the life of Jesus. In fact, Luke's presentation implies that Jesus' praying is of primary importance, for it is during his prayer that the Father speaks and the Spirit descends. Nevertheless, for each writer the actual baptism of Jesus is less important than the other events, one of which is the descent of the Spirit.

The Descent of the Spirit

Because there is no record that anyone other than John the Baptist saw the dove descend on Jesus (John 1:32–33), it is of interest that this incident is recounted for the readers. Clearly the incident is significant for all readers, besides Jesus himself. The descent of the Spirit follows the opening of the heavens. The latter is to be understood figuratively as a prelude to divine activity, as reflected in the OT (Ezek 1:1) and the NT (Acts 7:56). The Spirit then alights on Jesus' head in the form of a dove, which Luke identifies more clearly as appearing "in bodily form" (Luke 3:22).

Like a Dove

It is possible that the reference to a dove relates to the creation of the world (Gen 1:2), where, although a dove is not mentioned, there is a birdlike quality to the Spirit "moving" over the waters. Similarly, the dove sent out by Noah (Gen 8:8–12) calls to mind an association with new life. Others derive meanings from different characteristics of the dove, including its being a symbol of peace; its association with beauty (Song 1:15) and innocence (Matt 10:16); and its use as an affectionate term for a loved one (Song 2:14). Although the dove was an appropriate sacrificial offering (Lev 5:7, 11) and occasionally was used as a symbol of Israel (Hos 7:11), it is not clear that either of these latter two ideas provide relevant explanations for the dove in this text, given that the dove is associated here with the Spirit and not with the mission or person of Jesus.

Why the Descent of the Spirit?

The presence of the Spirit at this point in Jesus' life is more important than the dove itself. Although there is no reason to assume that the Spirit has not been with Jesus throughout his life, the very nature of this extraordinary appearance calls attention to the fact that something special is happening. It is possible that the Spirit inaugurated Jesus' mission here, though this could imply that his previous thirty years were not integral elements of that mission. It is more likely that an inauguration to a different stage in the development of that mission occurred at this point, after which Jesus began to preach the gospel.

It is also possible that the Spirit was empowering Jesus here, as this was an important part of the Spirit's function in the OT. This empowering may have been for the purposes of proclamation or miracles, although the OT gives significant evidence only for the Spirit's role in proclamation. However, though there is merit in this link between the Spirit and power, none of the Gospel writers stresses the role of the Spirit in empowering Jesus. For example, the Spirit is not identified as enabling Jesus to overcome the devil in the temptations that follow his baptism. Rather, Jesus combats the devil by his use of OT Scriptures, reminding him that he is testing none other than "the Lord your God" (Matt 4:7). Although it is clear that Jesus was not helpless without the Spirit—Jesus functioned with divine power of his own—the two are not completely distinct from one another. Matthew is not suggesting that the Spirit was not present in the life of Jesus before his baptism. It is simply that at the baptism the Spirit's association with Jesus was being made known—initially to John and then, through the Gospels, to others.

The Spirit's role in affirming Jesus is also significant, although Jesus was not in danger of forgetting his identity or the exalted nature of his person. In Jewish literature the Spirit functioned as a "marker," especially in terms of identifying people as leaders (Judg 6:34; 1 Sam 16:13; cf. Exod 33:15–16). To Jewish readers in particular, the presence of the Spirit with Jesus would indicate that Jesus was expected to function prophetically. In the OT, when the Spirit came upon people, they often prophesied (Num 11:29; Joel 2:28). Similarly, the Spirit is presented in association with righteous people in the OT and the Gospels. His unique involvement in the life of Jesus indicates the unique righteousness of Jesus. The descent of the Spirit upon Jesus affirms him as the appropriate and worthy vessel for the activity of the Spirit. This, of course, comes as no surprise to Jesus, for he is God incarnate, but it has value for John, as well as for the readers who are to be introduced to Jesus through the Gospels. The message is clear: If the Spirit validates Jesus, then he must be authentic.

Thus, the baptism of Jesus in general and the descent of the Spirit in particular functioned primarily to affirm Jesus and to confirm his messianic role. The presence of the Spirit acts as a powerful confirmation of Jesus' heavenly origin and divine identity. At the Jordan River, the Spirit legitimizes Jesus. While the Spirit may also empower Jesus, it is undoubtedly true that the Spirit endorses Jesus. The words of the Father, consisting of allusions to Ps 2:7, a royal psalm relating to the son and heir, and Isa 42:1, referring to the Servant, are also powerful affirmations of Jesus.

Another possibility is that the experience of Jesus at the Jordan was to parallel that of the disciples at Pentecost. The Spirit came upon the disciples in Jerusalem to confirm them in the role that Jesus had prepared for them: to be his witnesses (Acts 1:8). The Spirit mediated the power of Jesus to enable them to fulfill the divine agenda. It is important, however, to remember that Jesus' experience with the Spirit was different from the Pentecost experience of the disciples, whose mission was different from that of Jesus. It is thus more appropriate to view the experience at Pentecost as analogous, rather than identical or parallel, to the Jordan experience of Jesus. The Spirit's presence with Jesus is paradigmatic for believers in a limited sense, but Jesus' experience at the Jordan was unique, as were his person and mission.

Then Jesus was led up by the Spirit into the wilderness to be tempted by the devil. (Matt 4:1)

Exposition

That Jesus was willing to be led by the Spirit signifies his submission to the will of God. Because Jesus is the Messiah, the Spirit is leading him; the Spirit is not leading Jesus in order for him to function as the Messiah. It is not about leading and following, the superior guiding the inferior, but about the destiny of the one being inextricably entwined with the destiny of the other. It is because of the Spirit's association with Jesus that his going into the wilderness is to be understood as part of the divine agenda. He goes with the Spirit; therefore, it must be appropriate.

Although Matthew describes Jesus as being led "by" (*hypo*) the Spirit, Luke describes him as being led "in" (*en*) the Spirit (Luke 4:1). Although *en* can also be translated "by" or "by means of," it is possible that Luke intends to portray Jesus as living in the realm or sphere of the Spirit. He is the Spirit-Messiah par excellence, whose life and mission fulfill a higher agenda, that of the Spirit of God. This more clearly identifies Jesus not as subjugated to or lower than the Spirit but as living in harmony and unanimity with the Spirit.

Though Matthew, Luke, and Mark all record the same wilderness destination, Mark describes the Spirit's impetus as being much more forceful: "The Spirit immediately drove him out into the wilderness" (Mark 1:12). Matthew and Luke may have modified Mark's presentation because of the potential for misunderstanding, possibly fearing that their readers might assume that Jesus was forced to go against his will or that he was sluggish in moving in this direction. Mark's description, however, does not imply either of these but instead enables the readers to grasp something of the urgency of the next stage of the predetermined agenda. Jesus was not unwilling (after all, he was part of the precreation divine planning committee concerning the plan of salvation). Rather, Mark, with his characteristic urgency, stresses the importance of Jesus moving to the next stage of his mission by associating it with the motif of determined progress, the impetus of the act reflecting the powerful dynamic of the Spirit.

Significance for the Original Readers

The original readers would have understood from all of this that Jesus did not function with human energy and authority alone but also in the power and authority of the Spirit. They would also have grasped the importance of Jesus commencing his public ministry with the sanction, endorsement, and affirmation of the Spirit.

Furthermore, the Gospel writers are alerting their readers to recognize that wherever Jesus goes, the Spirit goes as well. Even as Jesus went through a time of testing by the devil, it would have been comforting for readers to know that he was not alone. Given their own personal experience of and relationship with the Spirit, they may have anticipated that the same qualitative companionship of the Spirit was to be their portion also. The Jews viewed the wilderness as the domain of the demonic and a place of testing, and it would have been no surprise to them to read that Jesus met the devil there. In their own metaphorical deserts or times of testing, the comfort of knowing that the Spirit accompanied them would have been a powerful encouragement. In the presence of all other spirits, the Holy Spirit was an inestimable friend.

Matthew makes the link between entering the desert and the purpose of the testing particularly clear. The testing was not an accident, but rather a specific part of Jesus' agenda. The question was not whether Jesus was willing to compete with the devil or even if he was able to conquer him. The outcome was never in doubt. Rather, the testing gave Jesus an opportunity to demonstrate his authority over the devil before he began to establish his kingdom. The Gospels introduce readers to the one who proves his authority to win the war before he completes his first skirmish with the enemy. Winning future skirmishes with the devil will be a potential reality for the readers too, and therefore they should expect the Spirit likewise to provide them with opportunities to be tested.

The Spirit inspires speech (Matt 10:20//Mark 13:11// Luke 12:12; Matt 12:18; Matt 22:43//Mark 12:36)

"For it is not you who speak, but the Spirit of your Father speaking through you." (Matt 10:20)

"Behold, my servant whom I have chosen, my beloved with whom my soul is well pleased. I will put my Spirit upon him, and he shall proclaim justice to the Gentiles." (Matt 12:18)

He said to them, "How is it then that David, inspired by the Spirit, calls him Lord?" (Matt 22:43)

Exposition

Each of these three verses (and the parallels) identifies one of the main roles of the Spirit in the lives of those who have been commissioned by him. He provides the message they are to proclaim.

The first text, Matt 10:20 (//Mark 13:11//Luke 12:12), is part of the commission Jesus gives to the twelve disciples to function in his authority on their evangelistic missions among the Jews. In the Gospel of Mark, however, Jesus offers this promise in his response to the disciples' questions concerning the destruction of the temple, in which Jesus informs them that before the end of time believers will experience terrible tribulation. Luke records the saying in the context of a conversation about the disciples' response to times of anxiety, division, and preparation for Jesus' return. Whatever their situation, Jesus guarantees that the Spirit will inspire them and empower their words when they are arrested for their message. He will not be speaking to them but through them. Although the idea of the Spirit being associated with inspiring proclamation is not unusual in the NT, the description of the Spirit as being "of your Father" in Matthew is unique in the NT (Mark 13:11 records "the Holy Spirit," as does Luke 12:12). This probably reflects Matthew's desire to encourage his readers to recognize the nature of God as their Father. Thus, he refers to God as Father twenty times (contrasted with one such description in Mark and three in Luke). Furthermore, the description of God as "your" Father emphasizes the personal relationship that believers are to enjoy with God.

In the second text, Matt 12:18, Matthew quotes Isa 42:1–4 to describe the mission of Jesus, in particular with regard to the weak and helpless, who are in need of justice. It is not of his own making; it is the authentic and ancient promise of God now being activated by Jesus. Furthermore, Matthew's citation of this quotation reaffirms that God, through the Spirit and the Servant Jesus, is concerned about matters of justice.

In the third text, Matt 22:43 (//Mark 12:36), Jesus discredits those who question his identity as the Messiah. He quotes Ps 110:1, ascribing the authorization of words that affirm him as the son of David. In doing so, Jesus points out that the Spirit inspired the words of one of the greatest Jewish heroes, King David.

Significance for the Original Readers

The first text, Matt 10:20 (//Mark 13:11//Luke 12:12), would have made a strong impression on the Gospel's original readers. As Jews, they honored God greatly, even to the extent of preferring not to use his name for fear of dishonoring it, and him. Matthew's description of the Spirit who speaks through them being associated with the Father who is also *their* Father would have encouraged them to enjoy a more intimate relationship with him as mediated by the Spirit. Jesus informs them that in situations where they may feel isolated, none other than the Father's Spirit is with them, inspiring them and empowering them. What they might once have experienced as helplessness in the face of opposition is now to be recategorized as supreme sufficiency because of the presence of the Spirit. The same Father who spoke encouraging words to Jesus in the Jordan at the beginning of his mission is the one who also will support believers in difficult times. Although their families may betray them, their Father will buttress them.

The readers of each Synoptic Gospel would have been encouraged by the promise that the Spirit would guide them in their responses to their accusers. Matthew's Jewish audience knew what it was like to be accused of betraying the ancient faith and to be marginalized by their religious constituencies. Mark's audience, probably in Rome, faced different pressures. To believe that Jesus was God was viewed as an act of folly, given that he died on a cross as a criminal. Other detractors denigrated Christianity because of its novelty—it had no history or development tested by time. The first significant persecutions would take place in Rome, and these would be of a ferocity not experienced elsewhere in the empire before that time. If ever there were believers who needed the comfort of a supernatural being who would give them the words to say and the authority with which to present them, they were the readers of Mark's Gospel.

Luke's audience, including sophisticated Gentiles, would face yet another form of interrogation from those in their communities who would find the message of Jesus unacceptable when compared with the philosophies of the day. Christianity was intellectually unsatisfying and simplistic. Believers responding to this audience would need a different set of resources from the Spirit. The verses that precede and follow this saying (Luke 12:4–10, 13–21), which highlight the importance of fearing God, of not blaspheming the Spirit, and of carefully prioritizing that which is eternal, suggest that Luke was concerned that believers might deny their faith when arrested. Thus, he offers the promise that the Spirit will be with them, not just to provide words of support and defense for their beliefs, but also to enable them to hold on to the truth and not to reject it in the face of opposition.

The second text, Matt 12:18, reminds readers that although their position is depressing because of the injustice pervading their society, they have not been forgotten. The Jews had longed for many years to determine their own destiny and govern themselves. The Maccabees led a revolt that achieved independence for a period (164–63 B.C.E.), but after the conquest by the Romans in 63 B.C.E., the hope for independence lay in ashes for centuries, except for a failed revolt in 66–70 C.E. A succession of disastrous leaders ruled the territory, including Herod the Great, who orchestrated the deaths not only of all the boys under the age of two in Bethlehem (Matt 2:16) but also of his wife, three sons, grandfather-in-law, mother-in-law, nephew, and three brothers-in-law, in addition to countless other citizens. His sons, who ruled the Jewish territories, were little better. Alongside them, the Romans instituted their own rulers, one of whom was Pontius Pilate, the man responsible for the death of Jesus and the demise of hundreds of other Jews. These politicians presided over the people during the time of Jesus and thereafter with a harsh and often savage rule. It was a period of crushing injustice, with the populace unable to effect change because of the power of the Roman authorities and the indolence of the aristocracy. The message of Matthew was that Jesus had come to address issues of injustice and that the Spirit was following the same agenda, prophetically determined in the past and to be practically delivered, albeit spiritually, in the present. Jesus' heart is for the downtrodden, and his mission is to the marginalized.

The third text, Matt 22:43 (//Mark 12:36), reaffirms Jesus' status as being even higher than the Messiah. Although the Jews anticipated that the Messiah would function with supernatural power, supported by divine authority, they did not assume that he would be God. Such a concept was an impossibility to people who believed that there was only one God. The Pharisees, in response to a question from Jesus, identify the Messiah as the son of King David. Jesus, referring to Ps 110:1, says that David identifies his son as "lord," an unusual title to give to one's son; ordinarily, a son used that title to refer to his father. The implication is clear to the Pharisees, and they choose not to respond. If David describes the son of David as his lord, then the son of David is greater than David himself. Thus, to oppose Jesus as the son of David, the Messiah, is to oppose a highly exalted person and to undermine the assessment of David; to affirm Jesus is, then, to recognize him as Lord. Again Matthew points to Jesus' identity as confirmed through the Spirit.

The Spirit was associated with exorcism (Matt 12:28)

"But if it is by the Spirit of God that I cast out demons, then the kingdom of God has come upon you."

Exposition

Jesus' statement here is part of his response to the Pharisees' accusation that Jesus achieved his ministry of exorcism by the power of Beelzebub. Apparently accepting that some Jews also cast out demons (Matt 12:27), Jesus counters that if, as they claim, he operates by the power of Beelzebub, then their exorcists must do likewise.[2] There is no reason to assume that everyone associated with the Pharisees opposed Jesus or that all other exorcists were functioning illegitimately (Mark 9:38–40). However, if they believe that their exorcists also cast out demons by the Spirit of God, then they should reconsider their rejection of Jesus. But Jesus' opponents are so eager to reject him that they are willing to run the risk of marginalizing their own exorcists.

Jesus demands, however, that a distinction be drawn between him and all other exorcists. The presence of the personal pronoun *ego* ("I") is important in Matt 12:28. The pronoun is grammatically unnecessary because the verb form *ekballo* ("I cast out") identifies the subject, so *ego* serves to emphasize the subject of the verb. Jesus is saying that although Jewish exorcists may function in the power of God with regard to exorcisms, his exorcisms are unique because they are proof that the kingdom of God has come already. Exorcisms in general do not indicate that the kingdom has come; it is *Jesus'* exorcisms that indicate this. The difference is not necessarily in the form or success of the exorcisms, but rather in the identity of the exorcist. The exorcism that Jesus performs in Matt 12:22 is important for the demonized man, but it is also important for a wider audience because it indicates that the kingdom has come.

Significance for the Original Readers

In a world in which demonic beliefs and exorcisms were familiar, the description of Jesus not just as an exorcist but also as one associated with the Spirit was important. His exorcisms, which always were successful, functioned as clear proof of his ability to initiate the kingdom and to control its development. He was not simply a successful exorcist or even the best exorcist; he was one of a different order. He was associated with none other than the Spirit of God.

---

[2] It is possible that Jesus does not believe that Jewish exorcists have such power; rather, he may be illustrating their hypocrisy and/or powerlessness, because although they criticize him, they are powerless to achieve similar results.

The Spirit can be the subject of blasphemy (Matt 12:31–32//Mark 3:29//Luke 12:10)

"Therefore I tell you, every sin and blasphemy will be forgiven men, but the blasphemy against the Spirit will not be forgiven. . . . Whoever speaks against the Holy Spirit will not be forgiven, either in this age or in the age to come."

Exposition

With these words in Matthew and Mark, Jesus concludes his response to the Pharisees who have condemned his exorcisms as having been achieved by the power of Beelzebub. Blasphemy against the Spirit is so serious a crime that it is, by definition, unforgivable. However, the blasphemy needs clarification. What is particularly heinous in this scene with the Pharisees is that despite their inability to prove him to be a fraud, they still reject him, preferring to hold to their preconceived position. It is not that they have made an honest mistake, but rather that they are determined to reject him despite the evidence in his favor. It is not that they have realized their error and have come to ask his forgiveness but Jesus has turned them away because they have committed a sin that cannot be forgiven. Rather, they persist in their mistaken belief—demonstrated by their unwillingness to follow him and confirmed by his description of them as evil (Matt 12:39, 45). Their sin is unforgivable because it attributes to Beelzebub an exorcism that Jesus attributes to the work of the Spirit. In effect, their assessment of the authority of Jesus is that it was derived from an evil source when, in reality, it was associated with the Holy Spirit. Such a predetermined stance inevitably cannot be forgiven when the people concerned are convinced of the accuracy of their assumption. The significance of that sin, as Mark 3:29 states most explicitly, is that it has eternal consequences.

In Luke, this statement is located not in the context of an exorcism but as part of a sermon Jesus delivers to his disciples, sparked by a warning concerning the Pharisees (Luke 12:2). Thereafter, Jesus speaks of the importance of recognizing that God is to be feared (Luke 12:4–5) and that the Son of Man will affirm those who follow him and reject those who do not (Luke 12:8–10). He concludes by saying that whoever blasphemes the Spirit will not be forgiven. The context here, then, is a broader one concerning verbal confession for or against Jesus.

Significance for the Original Readers

There is no evidence that the readers are in danger of committing the sin of rejecting the Spirit's activity. Rather, the Gospel writers are reminding their readers that it is a serious matter for people to reject the witness of the Spirit given either through Jesus or through them as his followers. Those who commit this sin are outside the community of believers. This is not a warning for believers who may be uncertain as to the source of a revelation or miraculous act and thus unintentionally fall into the sin of not ascribing to the Spirit that which he has achieved. Paul encourages his readers to make sure that they are not deceived by supernatural forces that are not from God (1 Thess 5:21). Matthew and Mark are referring to the danger of an unbeliever rejecting the clear work of God, as initiated by the Spirit, and ascribing it to an evil source as an excuse for not accepting its legitimacy and veracity.

The message in Luke's Gospel is slightly different, in that he records the passage in another context. Luke 12:1–3 presents the Pharisees as opponents who will be judged by God. Jesus then warns the disciples about those who have the power to kill, although he reminds them that God is on their side (Luke 12:4–7). Next, he informs them that although they will be rejected, the Son of Man will acknowledge them before God (Luke 12:8–9). Then, in the climax of the passage, Jesus' words suggest that when the disciples are rejected, the Holy Spirit is also being rejected (Luke 12:10). Inasmuch as they stand as Jesus' mouthpieces (Luke 12:11–12), if they are dismissed, then the one who inspires their witness is being rejected as well (cf. Exod 16:8). This is a powerful message of encouragement to the readers who will experience ridicule and rejection because of their beliefs, while at the same time it emphasizes the divinely inspired nature of their witness.

The Spirit is a member of the Godhead (Matt 28:19)

"Go therefore and make disciples of all nations, baptizing them in the name of the Father and of the Son and of the Holy Spirit."

Exposition

This verse contains two startling statements. First, disciples are to be made from among peoples of all nations, including the Gentiles, whereas Jesus' first commission to the Twelve was that they were to preach only to the Jews and specifically not to the Gentiles and Samaritans (Matt 10:5–6). Second, the verse presents the Spirit as equal to the Father and the Son. There has been no indication of inferiority or disharmony among the three members of the Godhead in Matthew, and now, as the author draws to a conclusion, he presents them functioning in unanimity.

Significance for the Original Readers

All of Matthew's Jewish readers believed that there is only one God. To see God represented as Father, Son, and Holy Spirit would have been somewhat disconcerting to some. Without exploring the relationship between the three or offering a systematized explanation, Matthew simply presents the fact that they may be understood as functioning together. All that Matthew has said about the Spirit and his involvement in the lives of believers is thus to be understood in the context of his being a member of the Godhead.

Also, the act of baptism, which indicates entrance into the family of God, is identified by and associated with all three members of the Godhead. The presence of the Father, Son, and Holy Spirit in the act of baptism associates it with God while affirming the complete relationship of the believer with the Father, the Son, and the Spirit.

Selected Bibliography

Bruner, Frederick D. *The Christbook Matthew 1–12 Revised and Expanded,* and *The Churchbook Matthew 13–28 Revised and Expanded.* Grand Rapids: Eerdmans, 2004.

Charette, Blaine. *Restoring Presence: The Spirit in Matthew's Gospel.* Journal of Pentecostal Theology: Supplement Series 18. Sheffield: Sheffield Academic Press, 2000.

Davies, William D., and Dale C. Allison. *A Critical and Exegetical Commentary on the Gospel According to Saint Matthew.* 3 vols. International Critical Commentary. Edinburgh: T&T Clark, 1988–1997.

Evans, Craig A. *Mark 8:27–16:20.* Word Biblical Commentary 34B. Nashville: Nelson, 2001.

France, Richard T. *The Gospel of Mark: A Commentary on the Greek Text.* New International Greek Testament Commentary. Grand Rapids: Eerdmans, 2002.

Guelich, Robert A. *Mark 1–8:26.* Word Biblical Commentary 34A. Dallas: Word, 1989.

Gundry, Robert H. *Mark: A Commentary on His Apology for the Cross.* Grand Rapids: Eerdmans, 1993.

Hagner, Donald A. *Matthew.* 2 vols. Word Biblical Commentary 33A, 33B. Dallas: Word, 1993–1995.

Keener, Craig S. *A Commentary on the Gospel of Matthew.* Grand Rapids: Eerdmans, 1999.

———. *The Spirit in the Gospels and Acts.* Peabody, Mass.: Hendrickson, 1997.

The Significance for Readers Today

1. What difference does it make in your life that the Spirit was involved in the birth of Jesus (1:18, 20)?

2. How are you, or should you be, different because you have been baptized with the Holy Spirit and with fire (3:11)?

3. How does the Spirit's association with Jesus affect your estimation of Jesus (3:16; 4:1)?

4. How can you expect the Spirit to inspire you in speaking for him (10:20; 12:18; 22:43)?

5. How does the role of the Spirit help to explain the unique nature of Jesus' ministry (12:28)?

6. What are the dangers of rejecting the Spirit (12:31–32)? How can you help others to appreciate these dangers?

7. How can you develop a more exalted view of the Spirit (28:19)?

chapter 2

*L*uke

The Setting

The author of this Gospel, who is not named, was not an eyewitness of the events he recounted but was a thorough investigator who used existing records (1:1–4). From the late second century, this Gospel and Acts have been attributed to Luke. He wrote a full, literary, orderly account for Theophilus, who probably was a Christian—although he assumes a wider, mainly Gentile, audience.

What Does the Author Say about the Spirit?

Luke records information about the Spirit that Matthew also includes in his Gospel (Luke 3:16, 22; 4:1; 12:10, 12), but Luke's emphasis is on the work of the Spirit in inspiring preaching and prophecy.

The Spirit

- inspires preaching (1:15–17; 2:29–32; 4:14–15, 18–19)
- inspires prophecy (1:41–45, 67–79; 2:25–32 [34–35])
- was involved with the birth of Jesus (1:35)
- inspires prayer (10:21–22)
- may be received as a result of prayer (11:13)

The Spirit inspires preaching (1:15; 4:14–15, 18)

"For he will be great before the Lord, and he shall drink no wine nor strong drink, and he will be filled with the Holy Spirit, even from his mother's womb." (1:15)

Exposition

In this description of John the Baptist, an angel informs Zechariah that John will be filled with the Holy Spirit.

The concept of being filled with the Holy Spirit is associated only with Luke in the NT although Paul (Eph 5:18) refers to the importance of being filled with the Spirit. In Luke 1, John the Baptist, Elizabeth (1:41), and Zechariah (1:67) are all filled with the Spirit. Luke also uses the words "fill/full" in connection with the Spirit in Acts (Acts 2:4; 4:8, 31; 7:55; 9:17), describing the Spirit's activity as overflowing through people.

What is unusual with regard to John the Baptist is that this filling with the Spirit occurred from birth or, more likely, prenatally. John therefore is unique, although God chooses other leaders in a similar way (Samson [Judg 13:5]; Israel/Messiah [Isa 49:1]). The closest parallel is with Jeremiah (Jer 1:5), who was chosen before birth to be God's servant. Although it was not uncommon in Judaism for God to choose someone from birth (Isa 44:2; 49:1), to be filled with the Spirit from birth was unprecedented and signaled the important role that John was to undertake as the one preceding the Messiah. John functioned as an OT prophet set apart by the Spirit to prophesy concerning the Messiah, although, unusually, his preparation for this task commenced before birth.

The implication of Luke 1:15 is that the filling of John with the Spirit is not an intermittent experience. This again was unprecedented, since the Spirit in the OT remained with people only until a commission had been completed (1 Sam 10:10). This is a further indication of God's affirmation of John and of the unusual nature of his anointing.

John's preaching to the people to prepare them for the coming of the Messiah (Luke 1:16–17) was the evidence that the Spirit had filled him. In this he follows other prophetic preachers in the OT who were filled with the Spirit.

Part of John's responsibility as he preached in the power of the Spirit was to live a life that reflected the truth of his message. As the Spirit fills worthy vessels such as Zechariah and Elizabeth (Luke 1:6), so also John is required to live a godly life. In the OT, the Spirit leaves those unworthy of his presence (1 Sam 16:14). The indwelling Spirit requires righteous living.

And Jesus returned in the power of the Spirit into Galilee, and a report concerning him went out through all the surrounding country. And he taught in their synagogues. . . . "The Spirit of the Lord is upon me, because he has anointed me to preach good news to the poor. He has sent me to proclaim release to the captives and recovering of sight to the blind, to set at liberty those who are oppressed." (4:14–15, 18)

Exposition

Luke describes Jesus' return to Galilee in the power of the Spirit and his teaching in the synagogues. Luke 4:16–30 then records the sermon Jesus preached in Nazareth at the beginning of his ministry, immediately after his time in the wilderness. Jesus declares good news and identifies himself as the one who will bring its fulfillment (4:21).

Jesus quotes from Isa 61:1–2 in his sermon because he wants his audience to recognize his claim that the Spirit is upon him—he is not simply referring to the fact that the Spirit was on the Prophet Isaiah. In the OT, anointing was common for those set apart for the office of prophet (1 Kgs 19:16), priest (Exod 28:41), or king (1 Sam 10:1). The implication would have been very clear to his audience: Jesus is claiming that he, too, is anointed by the Spirit. The people must then determine who this Jesus is. The Spirit's ongoing involvement in his life will be the clue; the tragedy is that most will not identify him correctly.

We need to carefully consider what we mean when we say that Jesus functioned in the power of the Spirit. The biblical material is clear that Jesus was not simply a man anointed by the Spirit. Neither was Jesus helpless without the Spirit. The reference to the Spirit, rather, points to the fact that Jesus is not functioning with a human agenda. He is commencing his public ministry by announcing his association with the Spirit. It is not that he did not have the power of the Spirit previously but now does. Luke presents Jesus ministering in companionship with the Spirit, with the power of the Spirit available to him to use at his prerogative.

The Spirit's agenda as Jesus sets it out in the sermon is important because it proclaims freedom to the marginalized. The poor, the spiritually captive, and the blind will be set free from their prisons of bondage and spiritual oppression. The Spirit supports Jesus' ministry to the outcast and the helpless. His is a ministry not to the mighty but to the marginalized, not to the rich minority but to the majority who had little hope.

The Spirit also affirms Jesus as a prophet before any prophetic ministry begins. Power, whether seen through miracles or proclamation, is not the only focus of this account; the identification and affirmation of Jesus as the bearer of this good news are also important. Jesus' prophetic ministry is unique, demonstrating proof of his person and his power. But his prophecy also declares the acts of freedom that are an integral part of the salvation he has come to achieve. The acts affirm Jesus' message, of which they are a part, while the Spirit affirms him, the messenger. Since he is the bearer of the Spirit, people should listen to him.

Jesus' unique endowment by the Spirit points to his unique mission; the uniqueness of his mission presupposes a unique endowment. While the Spirit thus affirms the uniqueness of Jesus and facilitates his supernatural ministry, to stress the influence of the Spirit at the expense of recognizing Jesus' unique status would be inappropriate.

Significance for the Original Readers

The Spirit has never functioned in others as he has in the lives of John the Baptist and Jesus, demonstrating the uniqueness of Jesus and of the one who prepared the way for his coming. As John and Jesus fulfill their commissions in association with the Spirit, so the readers of the Gospels anticipate a similar experience in their lives. The same Spirit is available and committed to enable them to complete that which God has prepared for them to do. Their responsibility is to ensure that they are appropriate vessels for the Spirit.

The Spirit inspires prophecy (1:41–42, 67–69; 2:25–32 [34–35])

And when Elizabeth heard the greeting of Mary, the babe leaped in her womb; and Elizabeth was filled with the Holy Spirit and she exclaimed with a loud cry, "Blessed are you among women, and blessed is the fruit of your womb!" (1:41–42)

Exposition

When Mary visited her, Elizabeth was filled with the Spirit and prophesied. Her prophecy of good news concerning Mary and her child was the evidence that she had indeed been filled with the Spirit.

And his father Zechariah was filled with the Holy Spirit, and prophesied, saying, "Blessed be the Lord God of Israel, for he has visited and redeemed his people, and has raised up a horn of salvation for us in the house of his servant David." (1:67–69)

Exposition

Zechariah was a priest from the countryside and not one of the religious elite based in Jerusalem. As such, he would have been reckoned as being lower in status than his urban priestly counterparts. Many Jews had deduced that God had not spoken through his urban counterparts, but here Zechariah, having been filled with the Spirit, prophesies. Again the prophecy is good news, commenting on the history of the Jewish nation followed by a promise for the future of salvation, forgiveness, and peace.

There was a man in Jerusalem, whose name was Simeon, and this man was righteous and devout, looking for the consolation of Israel, and the Holy Spirit was upon him. And it had been revealed to him by the Holy Spirit that he should not see death before he had seen the Lord's Christ. And inspired by the Spirit he came into the temple; and when the parents brought in the child Jesus, to do for him according to the custom of the law, he took him up in his arms and blessed God and said, "Lord, now lettest thou thy servant depart in peace, according to thy word; for mine eyes have seen thy salvation which thou hast prepared in the presence of all peoples, a light for revelation to the Gentiles, and for glory to thy people Israel." (2:25–32)

Exposition

The Spirit is mentioned on three occasions in association with Simeon, who is described as being righteous and devout. Given Simeon's Jewish background, it is important that the term "righteous" be interpreted in that context. In Jewish society, the righteous person was identified by his or her moral lifestyle in relationship to God and community. This righteous lifestyle was integrally linked to an ongoing relationship with God. Here, the word "righteous" does not describe Christian status, as Paul uses the word, but it is rather a definition of character, lifestyle, and attitude. Thus, Simeon is portrayed as a person worthy of the companionship of the Spirit. In the OT, as we have seen, the Spirit is associated with prophets and others similarly identified as walking closely with God. Since Simeon is in this category, it is no surprise that, inspired by the Spirit, he prophesies.

Luke also records that the Spirit revealed to Simeon that he would see the Messiah before he died and inspired him to visit the temple at the exact time Jesus' parents brought him there. These activities of the Spirit are reminiscent of the way the Spirit directs in the OT. The most important point is that the Spirit did not come to Simeon simply to give him a personal revelation or even to inspire prayer. Rather, the Spirit came to inspire prophecy concerning Jesus for the benefit of others—notably Mary, Jews, and Gentiles.

Significance for the Original Readers

Prophetic utterances once again testify to the Spirit's presence. The fact that Simeon's message is from the Spirit persuades readers that it is authentic.

Elizabeth's experience is important because it demonstrates that the Spirit chooses to work through women as well as men. The role of women in Jewish society was carefully prescribed. Although the Talmud was written well after the time of Jesus, it reflects much of first-century Jewish life and therefore is, if used discerningly, a key resource for understanding the social habits of the Jews in the time of Jesus. In the Talmud, some rabbis placed women, children, and slaves in the same category. Legally, a woman was a minor, and her husband could repudiate any agreement she made. It was generally deemed inappropriate for women to study the law or to engage in the set prayers. Rabbi Eliezer ben Hyrcanus said, "Let the words of the Law be burned rather than taught to a woman." Some rabbis would not even be seen talking to their wives in public. And yet the Spirit prophesied through Elizabeth.

The Spirit is always associated with people worthy of his presence—the Jews in Jesus' time accepted this fact, and the readers of the Gospel would have been conscious of trying to ensure that their lives were appropriate contexts for the manifestation of the Spirit.

The experiences of all those who prophesied demonstrated that the days of God's silence were over. The Jews assumed that the days of prophecy ended with Malachi. Now, however, the long-awaited prophecy of Joel 2:28–29 was being fulfilled. Both men and women were hearing God speak to them and were passing on the messages. The Spirit was initiating a new era.

The Spirit brought good news, including tidings of the birth of Messiah and the redemption of both Jews and Gentiles. Most Jews assumed, however, that if God were to speak to them, it would involve judgment. This was fundamentally based on an assumption that God had abandoned them to the control of secular political powers. In times past, when they were subjugated by enemy forces, it was because they had sinned. The fear on the part of many was that national sin was the cause of their present difficulties. If God were to speak to them, it was to be assumed that a message of judgment would precede any possible restoration of their fortunes. It is no surprise, therefore, that the first words of the angels to Zechariah and to the shepherds were "Do not be afraid" (Luke 1:13; 2:10). They assumed the worst; to be confronted by an angel of God was a fearful thing, especially since many believed that angels often were antagonistic. However, Luke introduces the Spirit of God as one associated with joy, salvation, and redemption for the people of God.

The term "filled" when referred to Elizabeth and Zechariah, is in the passive voice, indicating that the Spirit initiated this action. Although Paul speaks of the active role of the believer in response to the Spirit, Luke emphasizes the proactive nature of the Spirit. The Gospels encourage readers to recognize the Spirit's sovereignty. He is in charge of their lives.

The Spirit was involved with the birth of Jesus (1:35)

The angel said to her, "The Holy Spirit will come upon you, and the power of the Most High will overshadow you; therefore the child to be born will be called holy, the Son of God."

Exposition

Matthew (1:18, 20) also describes the role of the Spirit in the birth of Jesus, but Luke includes unique information.

Whereas Matthew describes the role of the Spirit in terms of initiating the conception of Jesus, Luke presents the Spirit as overseeing the entire birth process. Both writers affirm the role of the Spirit in the process of the incarnation: The Spirit is completely involved.

The Spirit's supervisory role in Luke 1:35 is reminiscent of how the Spirit works in the OT (Gen 1:2). The Spirit was not present in a medical capacity to ensure that the birth of Jesus was successful or to guarantee Mary's well-being; rather, the Spirit's presence demonstrated the significance of the birth. Nothing like this had happened before—and since the child to be born was God in human flesh, it was important to clearly signal the significance of the event.

The word used for this overshadowing activity (*episkiazō*) is used in the Greek OT to describe the cloud that rested on the tabernacle (Exod 40:34–35) and the protective presence of God (Ps 91:4). Luke may also be drawing from Isa 32:15–20, which describes righteousness, peace, and justice resulting from the Spirit being poured out.

Although the lives of some OT characters, especially the prophets, reflected the presence of the Spirit, Jesus, who was divinely overshadowed before his birth and dedicated as holy at birth, perfectly modeled the Spirit-led life. The Spirit did not enter Jesus for the first time at his baptism in the Jordan. According to Luke, the Spirit had been with him from the very start, preparing the way before he was even conceived (1:31, 35).

Significance for the Original Readers

The OT associates the Spirit with the concept of new life (Isa 32:15) and the new era of the Messiah (Isa 61:1–3). Jewish readers of Luke would have been able to identify with these age-old promises. However, these hopes had been shunted into the eschatological future by most people because of a belief that it was unlikely that they would be fulfilled in the present. This message and its association with the Spirit would have now signalled an exciting prospect that the fulfillment of the promise was to be in their generation.

Luke's Gentile readers would also have been familiar with the idea of gods providing new life settings. Two of their most famous writers, Homer and Virgil, had written about the amazing success individuals had achieved with the help of the gods. Homer's *Odyssey* and Virgil's *Aeneid* were the principal texts used in the schools of the era. These stories recount the lives of heroes battling against the odds to achieve their objectives, overcoming the strategies of various gods, storms, and natural enemies along the way. Through reading, memorizing, and dramatizing these stories, pupils identified principles of life and conduct desirable for becoming model citizens.

The gods proved their supremacy by their ability to empower their protégés to overcome all the obstacles facing them. Because of their worldview, many non-Jews who read Luke would be familiar with the idea that Greek legendary heroes benefited from supernatural supervision. Luke affirms that Jesus, who is of course superior to such figures, not the least because of his divinity, is overshadowed by God, who is also superior to Greek deities. For those readers who are yet to be convinced of the divinity of Jesus, Luke builds his case by demonstrating that Jesus is exalted above all others. Luke establishes this even before he records the birth of Jesus. His presentation of the life of Jesus will affirm this fact.

The Spirit inspires prayer (10:21)

In that same hour he rejoiced in the Holy Spirit and said, "I thank thee, Father, Lord of heaven and earth, that thou hast hidden these things from the wise and understanding and revealed them to babes; yea, Father, for such was thy gracious will."

Exposition

This verse is similar to Matt 11:25, although Luke introduces the saying by noting that Jesus rejoiced in the Holy Spirit. Luke uses the verb "rejoice" (*agalliaō*) four times—three of which are in the context of identifying God's acts and worshipping him because of them (Luke 1:47; 10:21; Acts 2:26). Not only does Jesus rejoice in his mission, but the Spirit also shares the moment because of his participation in that mission.

The description "in the Spirit" (*en tō pneumati*) indicates that Jesus was functioning in the context of the Spirit and in relationship with the Spirit. It was not that the Spirit exhorted Jesus to rejoice. Rather, Luke is describing here the relationship between Jesus and the Spirit. Together, they rejoice in the mission achieved thus far. Whereas the seventy disciples return with joy because they have seen demons exorcised in the name of Jesus (Luke 10:17), Jesus' joy is focused on the fulfillment of the will of God through his life. Jesus uses the word "Father" five times and the word "Son" three times in the short prayer in Luke 10:21–22, emphasizing his relationship with God as one of father and son. The Spirit is also associated with such a prayer in Rom 8:15–16.

Significance for the Original Readers

There are several significant issues for readers to grapple with here, the first of which relates to the association of joy with the Spirit. Although the OT identified the concept of joy with God (e.g., 1 Chr 16:27, 33), Jews in the first century had little expectation of divinely inspired joy. Israel's religious leaders did not offer much hope for the hard-pressed Jews and spoke of even less cause for joy. These leaders were divided and sometimes hostile to each other (the Pharisees and Sadducees opposed each other, and the Essenes despised them both), politics and hypocrisy were often linked with religion, and the centers that were created to develop the worship of God became mere ornaments of an empty religion that was based on theological concepts that Jesus would radically alter. Worst of all was the pervasive assumption that God had abandoned the Jews—the distressing conditions of their lives seemed to substantiate this belief. Luke now offers the prospect of the restoration of Spirit-inspired joy through the person and message of Jesus.

Luke's Gentile readers would not have associated joy with the worship of the ancient gods. The relationship of the gods with humankind was, rather, characterized by apathy. Luke, however, describes a different kind of Spirit, a Holy Spirit whose nature is associated with joy. This is not temporary or circumstantial happiness, but joy rooted in divine activity that is achieved for the benefit of believers.

The Spirit may be received as a result of prayer (11:13)

"If you then, who are evil, know how to give good gifts to your children, how much more will the heavenly Father give the Holy Spirit to those who ask him!"

Exposition

This verse is part of a passage in Luke (11:9–13) that is also found in Matthew (7:7–11), though with some important differences. In particular, Luke refers to the Holy Spirit, while Matthew does not ("If you then, who are evil, know how to give good gifts to your children, how much more will your Father who is in heaven give good things to those who ask him!" [Matt 7:11]). The question of which version is original or whether Jesus spoke each of these on different occasions need not detain us, as our focus is on why Luke included this saying.

The Spirit is more prominent in Luke than in Matthew and Mark. Luke includes all of the references to the Spirit found in Matthew and Mark, plus ten other references. When considered along with the dozens of references to the Spirit in Luke's second volume (Acts), it becomes clear how important the Spirit is to his overall message. When he affirms the desire of the Father to give the Holy Spirit, it is to be understood against the backdrop of all that he has identified concerning the role of the Spirit in the lives of believers.

Luke has thus far provided evidence of the Spirit's capacity to initiate new life and to inspire people to prophesy (1:41–45, 67–79; 2:25–32, 34–35), pray (10:21–22), and preach (1:15–17; 2:29–32; 4:14–15, 18–19). Luke has also identified worthy people through whom the Spirit will function. Now he records Jesus widening the promise to include all believers. The only condition is that believers request the Spirit's presence.

Significance for the Original Readers

All readers of the Gospels now have the opportunity to benefit from the inspiration of the Spirit. That which was once given to few is now to be the experience of many. Each person's experience will differ, depending on the tasks set before them, but the Spirit is available to all who ask.

In 11:5–13, Luke offers guidelines on prayer that focus on the generosity of the Father. God's children only have to ask; if they do not receive exactly what they request, the Father's response always matches their need perfectly. The Father willingly provides the best gift of all: the Holy Spirit himself.

The promise is that the Spirit will always be available to the believer who requests his presence. This does not refer to the moment of salvation, for the Spirit enters the new believer's life as part of the divine process of salvation rather than in response to a request. It is more likely that this promise reflects the Spirit's continuous support of believers, who only have to ask and find that he is there. In the OT, we find that the Spirit comes temporarily to a person (1 Sam 10:10). Now, however, there is no indication that the Spirit's presence is not permanent.

Selected Bibliography

Bock, Darrell L. *Luke*. 2 vols. Baker Exegetical Commentary on the New Testament 3. Grand Rapids: Baker, 1994–1996.

Nolland, John. *Luke*. 3 vols. Word Biblical Commentary 35A, 35B, 35C. Dallas: Word, 1989–1993.

Shelton, James B. *Mighty in Word and Deed: The Role of the Holy Spirit in Luke-Acts*. Peabody, Mass.: Hendrickson, 1991.

Stronstad, Roger. *The Charismatic Theology of St. Luke*. Peabody, Mass.: Hendrickson, 1984.

Turner, Max. *Power from on High: The Spirit in Israel's Restoration and Witness in Luke-Acts*. Journal of Pentecostal Theology: Supplement Series 9. Sheffield: Sheffield Academic Press, 1996.

The Significance for Readers Today

1. What can those who preach today learn from the examples of Spirit-inspired preaching in Luke's Gospel (1:15; 4:14–15, 18)?

2. What can we learn from the fact that one of the Spirit's major roles was inspiring prophecy (1:41–42, 67–69; 2:25–32 [34–35])?

3. What are some of the lessons to be gleaned from the fact that Luke presents the Spirit in his capacity to initiate new ventures (1:35)?

4. How can you recapture the joy of the Spirit in your life (10:21)?

5. Knowing that the Father gives the Spirit to all who ask, what will you ask the Spirit to do specifically in your life (11:13)?

chapter 3

John

The Setting

Irenaeus (120–202 C.E.) records that John was the author of this Gospel, having written it at Ephesus, where he lived until Trojan's time (98–117 C.E.). John 20:31 records the purpose of this Gospel: to encourage faith in Jesus as the Messiah and the Son of God, which results in eternal life. The fact that John presents Jesus as the Messiah excludes a purely Gentile readership, as only Jews would have completely understood the implications of the title "Messiah." Other aspects of the Gospel, however, suggest that John anticipated a Gentile readership as well.

What Does the Author Say about the Spirit?

The Spirit

- was associated with Jesus (1:32–33; 3:34; 15:26)
- is associated with salvation (3:5–6, 8; 6:63)
- is to be received (7:39; 14:16–17; 20:22)
- inspires worship (4:23–24)
- is the Counselor (14:16–17, 26; 15:26; 16:7)

The Spirit was associated with Jesus (1:32–33; 3:34; 15:26)

And John bore witness, "I saw the Spirit descend as a dove from heaven, and it remained on him. I myself did not know him; but he who sent me to baptize with water said to me, 'He on whom you see the Spirit descend and remain, this is he who baptizes with the Holy Spirit.' " (1:32–33)

Exposition

We discussed this extraordinary event in the context of the commentary on Matthew and Mark in chapter 1. John, however, offers some new information that helps explain the role of the Spirit in Jesus' life. Here we learn that John the Baptist did not recognize Jesus as the Lamb of God until he saw the dove descend upon him. Neither is there any evidence that anyone other than John saw the dove. The Spirit descended as a dove to witness to the person of Jesus, specifically for John to be able to identify Jesus as the Lamb of God (1:33).

John also describes the Spirit "remaining" with Jesus. In fact, this verb is used twice, once by John the Baptist and once in the divine message given to him (1:32–33). On the first occasion the verb is in the aorist tense (*emeinen*), describing the Spirit's definite association with Jesus, while on the second occasion a present participle (*menon*) is used, indicating a permanent and ongoing relationship. This description of the relationship of the Spirit with Jesus is significant because it is an unprecedented experience of the Spirit and exalts Jesus (and, therefore, his mission) above all others. Rabbi Aha stated, "When the Holy Spirit rests on the prophets, he rests on them only by measure" (*Lev. Rab.* 15.2). Jesus was different.

For he whom God has sent utters the words of God, for it is not by measure that he gives the Spirit. (3:34)

Exposition

This verse is part of a larger passage that emphasizes the divine authority of Jesus' message. The Spirit is included here to confirm this authority. Since the Spirit is identified with God, and Jesus has the closest relationship with the Spirit, it follows that Jesus is most likely to proclaim God's words accurately. Given that context, John describes Jesus as receiving the Spirit without measure—his words must be true because they are obviously divine. They are not the words of a mere man but of God.

Readers must not assume that Jesus is functioning here as an ordinary man into whom the Spirit has been poured in order to merely deify or divinely inspire him. The author takes it for granted that Jesus is God (1:1–5). Here, in providing evidence for this incontrovertible fact, he refers to the Spirit as verification that Jesus' words are God's words. The implication becomes increasingly obvious for the readers: Jesus is God.

"But when the Counselor comes, whom I shall send to you from the Father, even the Spirit of truth, who proceeds from the Father, he will bear witness to me." (15:26)

Exposition

This verse is significant because Jesus declares here that the Spirit bears witness to him. As we have seen, one of the roles of the Spirit is to witness to Jesus' exalted nature. Just before making this announcement, Jesus spoke of those who rejected him. His response to this rejection is to refer to the Father and the Spirit, who affirm him.

The description of the Spirit coming from the Father emphasizes the fact that Jesus comes with the support and authority of the Father. The Father and the Spirit function in unanimity of will and purpose. Therefore, if the Spirit witnesses positively to Jesus, the Father does likewise.

Significance for the Original Readers[1]

John presents Jesus as uniquely related to the Spirit. Not only was Jesus the one who baptized with the Spirit, but he also lived in constant union with the Spirit. The twofold reference to the Spirit remaining with Jesus (1:32, 33) creates a clear contrast between Jesus and all others who benefited from the presence of the Spirit in their lives. For others, the association was temporary; for Jesus, it was permanent. This fact does not merely imply that Jesus was a superior person; because the Spirit is God, the permanent association between Jesus and the Spirit points to Jesus' divinity. John is determined to demonstrate that Jesus is not merely supernatural but the Son of God himself (20:31).

In 3:34 John moves still closer to his aim of identifying Jesus as being so close to God as to warrant the conclusion that he is God. Jesus cannot receive an unlimited measure of the Spirit unless he is God. For his readers who are not believers, John provides a logical

[1]See also the comments on Matthew and Mark in ch. 1.

path to belief in Jesus as God. For believers, he presents carefully constructed evidence that Jesus is their God.

The concept of witness is important in John, and no more so than when it relates to Jesus (1:7–8, 15; 3:11, 26; 5:31–39; 10:25; 15:26). The credibility of the one who bears witness is essential. By identifying the witness as the Spirit in association with the Father in 15:26, John encourages his readers to recognize the supreme nature of Jesus and to give him due worship and obedience.

The Spirit is associated with salvation (3:5–6, 8; 6:63)

Jesus answered, "Truly, truly, I say to you, unless one is born of water and the Spirit, he cannot enter the kingdom of God. That which is born of the flesh is flesh, and that which is born of the Spirit is spirit. . . . The wind blows where it wills, and you hear the sound of it, but you do not know whence it comes or whither it goes; so it is with every one who is born of the Spirit." (3:5–6, 8)

Exposition

These verses are part of a discussion between Jesus and Nicodemus in which Nicodemus learns from Jesus how to enter the kingdom of God. Jesus says that the Spirit is the one who facilitates entrance to the kingdom.

Born of Water

Jesus states that a person must undergo a process of birth before he or she can enter the kingdom. The reference to water may indicate natural birth. Thus, to enter the kingdom, one must first be born physically. Although this seems obvious, as a Jew Nicodemus would have assumed a racial priority with regard to entrance into the kingdom. It may be, then, that Jesus is drawing him into the discussion by acknowledging the importance of one's birth before explaining that another birth is also essential—one that is not automatically granted to Jews only.[2] The problem with this interpretation is that Jesus does not associate privilege with racial identity.

---

[2] In support of this view, it is significant that rabbinic sources viewed water as a metaphor for semen, and water is naturally associated with the process of birth itself.

It is possible that Jesus is referring to the importance of water baptism as part of the process of entrance into the kingdom. John records that Jesus and his disciples baptized many in water (3:22; 4:1 [although 4:2 explains that Jesus did not perform the baptisms himself]) and that John the Baptist baptized many (3:23). However, baptism is not a prominent theme in this Gospel. John does not, for example, record Jesus' baptism. It is not clear, therefore, whether Jesus here is emphasizing to Nicodemus the importance of water baptism.

Jesus is probably using the word "water" to identify an aspect of the role of the Spirit and is therefore using it as a synonym for "Spirit." In 7:39 John informs his readers that Jesus, having spoken about "rivers of living water," was referring to the Spirit. Similarly, having spoken about drinking water that eternally quenches thirst (4:14), Jesus mentions worship in the Spirit (4:23–24). Thus, just as Matthew and Luke associate the Spirit with fire in the message of John the Baptist, so now John's Gospel links the Spirit with water—with all the connotations of cleansing related to water in the OT (Ezek 36:25). In response to Nicodemus's question, therefore, Jesus describes the birth from above (3:3) as a spiritual one, unrelated to racial identity or human endeavor but associated rather with cleansing, achieved by the Spirit and symbolized by washing with water.

Born of the Spirit

Jesus is helping Nicodemus to develop a better appreciation of the Spirit's role in the process of bringing people into the kingdom. Although Jesus does not explain the actual work of the Spirit in this regard, it is sufficient to indicate that entrance into the kingdom involves a radical course of action. One cannot initiate the process oneself—only the Spirit can do that. Indeed, the birth metaphor implies a certain passivity on the part of the one entering the kingdom. The active agent here is the Spirit.

The Spirit's role does not begin and end with transferring a person into the kingdom of God, however. Thereafter, as Jesus describes in 3:6, that person is associated with the Spirit. In fact, members of the kingdom are so closely identified with the Spirit that they can be described as "spirit." As natural birth has certain implications, mainly that the child becomes a member of humanity (flesh), so also the one born of the Spirit takes on the racial identity of "Spirit." Those born of the Spirit become members not merely of a new community and order, but of a new family and

race. They are now "Spirit people," people identified with and by
the Spirit, people of the Spirit, with all the privileges and responsibilities associated with that relationship.

The Sovereignty of the Spirit

In 3:8 Jesus uses words that can mean two different things. He
is not attempting to confuse Nicodemus. It is more likely that,
because he recognizes him as an important teacher (3:10), Jesus
speaks to him in a way that is commensurate with his training and
position. After all, these are two sophisticated minds at work, spar-
ring with each other in rabbinic style. The word translated "wind"
(*pneuma*) may also be translated "Spirit." Similarly, the word
"sound" (*phōnē*) may also be translated "voice." Jesus is likening
the wind to the Spirit in two major respects: first, the wind can do
what it wants; second, individuals can be partially aware of the
wind's activity without completely understanding it.

Jesus concludes 3:8 by stating that he is speaking about the relationship that those who have been born of the Spirit enjoy with
the Spirit. Believers can hear the sound, or voice, of the Spirit,
though they cannot control him or second-guess his plans. The
Spirit is supremely in charge in the relationship. The privilege to
hear the Spirit is not available to anyone outside the kingdom.
Jesus' words here further emphasize the importance of the role of
the Spirit.

*"It is the spirit that gives life, the flesh is of no avail; the words that I
have spoken to you are spirit and life." (6:63)*

Exposition

In the context of a conversation about eternal life, Jesus here
describes the role of the Spirit as providing life.

The most likely translation for *pneuma* here, again, is "Spirit,"
identifying the one who gives life to those who accept Jesus'
message. Jesus' words are not human concepts presented in an
envelope of human language. They are channels for life from the
Spirit (6:68).

Significance for the Original Readers

John's Gospel emphasizes the foundational importance of the
Spirit in the process of entering the kingdom. Those who enter
into the kingdom by the Spirit are then identified as Spirit people.

Although their human lives are characterized by the weaknesses of the flesh, their lives in association with the Spirit are characterized by his dynamic power, which will be fully realized in the next life but is also available now (3:36; 4:14; 5:24; 6:47, 54).

The Spirit's role is to mediate the quality of life enjoyed by God to believers. Eternal life is not simply life that lasts forever. Rather, it is descriptive of the kind of life associated with eternity. It is not simply everlasting life but fullness of life that can be experienced because one has entered into a relationship with the eternal God himself.

John encourages his readers not only to anticipate the wonder of that life to come but also to begin to live it now, recognizing that the God of eternity desires to mediate, through the Spirit, aspects of that life for their benefit. God has not only delivered them from judgment and eternal separation from God; he has also granted them a relationship with him now.

The force of 3:8 develops this concept of relationship with the Spirit. Jesus says that believers are able to hear the voice of the Spirit. The word "hear" indicates not only that believers hear the Spirit but also that they are to respond by putting what they hear into practice. Unbelievers are not even able to hear the Spirit.

Jesus' words in 6:63 emphasize that the Spirit and Jesus speak together. They are not to be separated as if they function in separate parts of the universe or with different agendas. They work together, initiating entrance into the kingdom and speaking to believers thereafter.

The Spirit is to be received (7:39; 14:16–17; 20:22)

Now this he said about the Spirit, which those who believed in him were to receive; for as yet the Spirit had not been given, because Jesus was not yet glorified. (7:39)

Exposition

John here foretells the events of Pentecost, when the Spirit would be given—initially to the disciples and thereafter to every believer. The Spirit was not generally available as an indwelling presence until after Jesus had finished his ministry and had given the Spirit to the church. Though he would not be with them in bodily form, through the Spirit he would be ever present.

John's explanation follows Jesus' quotation from the OT (the closest reference being Isa 44:3), stating that living waters would flow out of the lives of his followers. John makes the connection between this life-giving water and the Spirit explicit.

It is no coincidence that Jesus spoke these words during the seven-day Feast of Tabernacles (7:2). It was popularly referred to as the Feast of Tents because the participants camped in home-made shelters erected on rooftops or in the fields (Lev 23:34–36). It functioned for Jews as a thanksgiving for the harvest and an opportunity to remember how God had guided their ancestors during the forty years in the wilderness, especially in the provision of water (Exod 17:1–6). A water-drawing ritual took place on each of the seven days of the festival, commemorating God's provision of water from the rock. Implicit in their festivities was an anticipation of the arrival of the kingdom of God, when their "exile" would finally be over and life-giving water would be available in abundance (Isa 12:3; cf. Ezek 47:1–12; Zech 14:8 [the latter two texts were read during the festival]). Josephus described Tabernacles as the most popular festival held in the temple (*Ant.* 8.100).

Because the festival held so many associations with salvation—both remembered and anticipated—this occasion provided an ideal opportunity for Jesus to prophesy the fulfillment of this long-awaited hope. The prophecy was originally for the Jews. However, Jesus now stated that the promise was for all people, regardless of their nationality or background, and that the Spirit was presented as the life-giving source.

"And I will pray the Father, and he will give you another Counselor, to be with you for ever, even the Spirit of truth, whom the world cannot receive, because it neither sees him nor knows him; you know him, for he dwells with you, and will be in you." (14:16–17)

Exposition

Because Jesus is going to leave the disciples (14:2–3), he informs them that he will send another to take his place. This Counselor (*paraklētos* [see also 14:26; 15:26; 16:7–15]) will be their permanent companion. The fact that Jesus prays to the Father ensures that the readers understand that the Father is also involved in sending the Spirit.

There is no suggestion that Jesus is in any way inferior to the Father or that he has to pray to him to release the Spirit. In 15:26

Jesus declares that he will send the Spirit from the Father; in 14:26 he declares that the Father will send the Spirit in his name, while in 16:13 he declares simply that the Spirit will come. One must always guard against reading any divine hierarchy into the text. John 4:24 describes God as "Spirit," and there is no suggestion that the Spirit is merely an impersonal force or a lesser member of the Godhead commanded to do whatever the Father or Jesus desires. The provision of the Spirit is not a unilateral act on the part of any member of the Godhead; rather, it is central to the plan and desire of all its members. Though the Spirit existed in proximity to believers in the person of Jesus, the promise is that the Spirit will reside in them in the near future.

And when he had said this, he breathed on them, and said to them, "Receive the Holy Spirit." (20:22)

Exposition

After Jesus' resurrection, he met his disciples and, having greeted them and commissioned them as the Father had commissioned him (20:21), he breathed on them and said, "Receive the Holy Spirit." Jesus then tells the disciples that they have the capacity to forgive sins and to withhold such forgiveness.

He Breathed on Them

The fact that Jesus breathed on them does not suggest that the Spirit is some sort of material substance that can be breathed out or in. The word *emphysao* ("breathe on"), which appears only here in the NT, echoes the act of God breathing life into Adam (Gen 2:7) and into the dry bones of Ezekiel's vision (Ezek 37:9 [identified as the Spirit in Ezek 37:14]). The image of new life or restoration after a period of exile is prominent here. This act of breathing also reflects Jesus' authority to impart the Spirit to whomever he chooses.

The Result of the Breathing

It is possible that Jesus partially bestowed the Spirit on the disciples on this occasion, with the full provision being awarded on the day of Pentecost. It may also have been an acted parable of that which would occur some weeks later in the house in Jerusalem. Although it is possible that the disciples received the Spirit fully on this occasion, there are severe difficulties with this suggestion—not the least of which being that the qualifications for the Spirit coming (16:7) had not been fulfilled at this time.

The information that follows in 20:23 may provide another explanation: Jesus here transfers to the disciples his authority to grant and withhold forgiveness. The reason that they are able to access this authority, even though he is leaving them, is that they now have the ability to function in the power of the Spirit. Jesus had previously given them the privilege of offering salvation to people (Matt 16:19; Luke 9:2, 6). However, at that time they were Jesus' delegates, functioning in his authority. Before, they functioned in the sphere of the earthly Jesus; now, they do so in the sphere of the Spirit. According to this view, then, Jesus is giving the Spirit to equip the disciples in their evangelistic ministry in his absence. The Spirit then comes on the day of Pentecost for a different purpose: to indwell them permanently and to establish the church. Problems with this interpretation include the fact that the giving of the Spirit on the day of Pentecost appears to be to provide the power to witness (Acts 1:8). In view of the fact that John does not clearly identify the significance of this action by Jesus, caution is necessary in seeking to arrive at an explanation. On the basis of the evidence, the most likely reason for this act by Jesus seems to be to establish the authority of the disciples to grant and withhold forgiveness. Such authority is normally the prerogative of God, as also seen in the ministry of Jesus. Now he provides his disciples with the same capacity, their ability so to do being affirmed by the presence of the Spirit in them.

Significance for the Original Readers

These verses assure readers that, in Jesus' physical absence, the Spirit is present. Indeed, Jesus' ascension did not signify his absence, because through the Spirit he continues to offer the same quality of support that he gave to his first disciples. The same Spirit who operates in association with Jesus is now promised to them.

It is clear that the provision of the Spirit to believers fulfills the wishes of all the members of the Godhead. The description of Jesus breathing on them indicates more than the fact that he was alive. It is a very intimate way to impart the Spirit. Aspects of the Spirit that are associated with Jesus himself are being transferred to his followers.

The Spirit provides resources for evangelism. Although the disciples initially received the Spirit, it is implicit that since all believers are expected to witness to their faith, the Spirit will be available to them, too. The likening of the reception of the Spirit to living waters flowing out of a person is important for a number of reasons. The Jews expected this experience and the rabbis taught about it (*b. Sukkah* 5:55a). Not only is the Spirit identified with life-giving potential, he is also associated with refreshment and cleansing. The flowing water suggests a readily available, inexhaustible source—for the benefit of believers and overflowing to others as well. Just as Jesus receives the Spirit without measure (John 3:34), so the believer also receives the Spirit's cleansing and refreshment from an inexhaustible supply.

The Spirit inspires worship (4:23–24)

"But the hour is coming, and now is, when the true worshipers will worship the Father in spirit and truth, for such the Father seeks to worship him. God is spirit, and those who worship him must worship in spirit and truth."

Exposition

The term *pneuma* is again best translated as "Spirit" in these verses rather than "spirit." The latter term would suggest that Jesus is encouraging the woman at the well, to whom he is speaking, to adopt a "spiritual" attitude, though the identity of such an attitude is uncertain. It is more likely that Jesus is referring to the Spirit, the most common translation of the term elsewhere in John. Thus, Jesus would be understood as instructing the Samaritan woman that authentic worship is attributed not to a particular location but to a specific source, the Spirit. Although worship may be defined partly as a spiritual activity, it is more important to recognize that it is made possible because of the Spirit. As God is identified with the Spirit, to truly worship God necessitates a context in which the Spirit is present.

Jesus is saying more than that true worship is not based in error. He is not saying that there is a right way and a wrong way to worship God. Rather, he is confirming the Spirit as the one who authenticates worship. It is the Spirit who determines that worship can take place and who makes it possible. Worship takes place as a result of the Spirit's initiative as the Spirit operates an open-door policy to God for the believer.

Significance for the Original Readers

In an age when travel was often dangerous and expensive, a visit to the temple in Jerusalem was, for many Jews, something achieved once in a lifetime. For the Samaritan woman, however, such a visit was not even a possibility. The divisions between the Samaritans and the Jews were centuries old and had resulted in the Samaritans building their own temple on Mount Gerizim, which was destroyed by the Jews under John Hyrcanus in 128 B.C.E. Samaria surrendered due to famine, and the Jews celebrated their defeat with a festival.

Feelings between Jews and Samaritans subsequently became extraordinarily bitter, and later events exacerbated the situation. For example, in 10 C.E. some Samaritans entered the temple in Jerusalem at night during the Feast of the Passover. They scattered human bones in the courts, thus making them unclean. The Jews responded by excluding the Samaritans from the temple forever, even from the outer courts that hitherto had been open to them. The Jews publicly cursed the Samaritans in the synagogues and then declared them unable to participate in the messianic kingdom.

Into the midst of this animosity, however, Jesus comes and presents a new sphere of worship—one related not to a geographical location but to the presence of the Spirit. Wherever the readers were and regardless of their nationality, the only prerequisite for their involvement in authentic worship was that they be in relationship with the Spirit. Believers had already met this condition because they had received the Spirit promised to them.

The Spirit is the Counselor (14:16–17, 26; 15:26; 16:7)

"And I will pray the Father, and he will give you another Counselor, to be with you for ever, even the Spirit of truth, whom the world cannot receive, because it neither sees him nor knows him; you know him, for he dwells with you, and will be in you." (14:16–17)

"But the Counselor, the Holy Spirit, whom the Father will send in my name, he will teach you all things, and bring to your remembrance all that I have said to you." (14:26)

"But when the Counselor comes, whom I shall send to you from the Father, even the Spirit of truth, who proceeds from the Father, he will bear witness to me." (15:26)

"Nevertheless I tell you the truth: it is to your advantage that I go away, for if I do not go away, the Counselor will not come to you; but if I go, I will send him to you." (16:7)

Exposition

These four texts have one thing in common—the description of the Spirit as the Counselor. John 14:16 refers to the Spirit as "another Counselor," indicating that he is to function as Jesus did with the disciples (1 John 2:1), in close relationship to them. The term *paraklētos* may be literally translated as "one called alongside another." This term helps to describe the comprehensive nature of the Spirit's work on behalf of believers.

Thus, in addition to convicting unbelievers concerning sin (16:8), the Spirit teaches believers (14:26), guides them into all truth (16:13), reminds them of information previously heard (14:26), bears witness to Jesus (15:26), prophesies the future (16:13), and provides revelation (16:14). The Spirit provides all of this, and with an immediacy made possible by the fact that he dwells within believers (14:17). Only believers will be able to benefit from the Counselor's wisdom (14:17). Because he functions in the context of truth (14:17; 15:26), believers can be sure that this wisdom is completely reliable. The term "Counselor" includes, more widely, the concepts of supporter, comforter, encourager, and director—all undergirded by the fact that the Spirit is God. Much of this ministry of the Spirit to believers is identical to the ministry of Jesus to the disciples that John records in his Gospel.

Jesus explains that when he returns to heaven, the Spirit will come to take his place alongside believers. The term *paraklētos* is not to be understood literally as defining an exact location of the Spirit alongside the believer; John 14:17 describes the Spirit as being "in" the believer. Rather, this is a helpful description of the intimate nature of the support that the Spirit offers. At times, his role will be more like that of a legal counsel (16:8–11), while on other occasions his mediatory intervention will involve revealing the mind of God to believers (16:14). The Spirit is so close that he is able to immediately support any believer who might stumble.

It is not necessary to understand that Jesus functions in heaven on behalf of believers while the Spirit functions on earth to support them. It is not that the Spirit has taken over for Jesus, as though Jesus has now relinquished his intimate relational role with believers. Rather than assume discontinuity, it is more appropriate to acknowledge the continuity of support for believers that the Spirit and Jesus provide. Both are integrally linked with the support of, and ministry to, believers. To attempt to demarcate roles and responsibilities within the Godhead is to misunderstand the comprehensive nature of God's care for his people.

Jesus' statement that the Counselor is not able to come until Jesus goes (16:7) requires careful consideration, for it does not mean that Jesus and the Spirit cannot function concurrently. It is more likely that Jesus is explaining that believers will be unable to fully appreciate the role of the Spirit until after Jesus ascends. At that time, the worldwide ministry of the Spirit will be unmistakably evident as he continues the work that Jesus initiated. For despite Jesus' physical absence, the church will still be developing—now by the Spirit functioning through believers.

Significance for the Original Readers

These verses leave readers in no doubt that, regardless of their circumstances, the Spirit will be their Counselor. Whether they are part of a large community of believers in which teaching is readily available or whether they belong to a smaller community in which teaching is less accessible, the Spirit undertakes to provide them with that which is necessary for their spiritual well-being. As the Spirit of truth, he offers genuine guidance that is authentic and reliable.

Many in the first century sought to identify truth as a philosophical pursuit. Truth was found in authentic facts that therefore were reliable, resulting in peace of mind. Jews found that their ancient beliefs, which were associated with truth, were under pressure from beliefs promulgated throughout the Roman Empire. For the Gentiles, authentic religious activity was always difficult to determine. Some attributed occurrences such as the opening of doors or the receipt of a letter to the activities of the gods, while others identified the gods with supernatural phenomena such as thunderstorms or famine. They consequently developed countless deities with different individual functions. Devotees followed carefully prescribed rituals to appeal to them. But many such worshippers were constantly uncertain whether or not they had achieved what was needed to gain a favorable audience with the deity concerned, or even that they had been addressing the appropriate god or goddess. John, however, presents a "transparent" God, one who is desirous of sharing himself with his people in truth.

In the midst of this general cultural, religious, and philosophical confusion, John clearly presents the Spirit and his role of providing guidance to the believer. The onus is not on the believer to seek guidance and support from the Spirit, though that is appropriate. Rather, it is the Spirit who takes responsibility for providing the necessary support for the believer. This is a far cry from much of first-century religious activity—to a large degree, both Jew and Gentile believed that only following a correct ritual would bring benefit from a supernatural source. In the message of Jesus that John presents there is no ritual; instead, he offers a relationship with the Spirit. Even though the apostles would die, the church would not be leaderless, nor would there ever come a time when the church would not have access to divine wisdom. In new situations that were not addressed in previous apostolic teaching, the Spirit would be on hand to provide the necessary instruction and wisdom. The Spirit would always be there to provide insight to combat new heresies and to clarify theological nuances.

Selected Bibliography

Beasley-Murray, George R. *John*. Word Biblical Commentary 36. Dallas: Word, 1987.

Brown, Tricia G. *Spirit in the Writings of John*. London: T&T Clark, 2003.

Carson, Donald A. *The Gospel according to John*. Pillar New Testament Commentary. Grand Rapids: Eerdmans, 1991.

Keener, Craig S. *The Gospel of John: A Commentary*. 2 vols. Peabody: Hendrickson, 2003.

Turner, Max. *The Holy Spirit and Spiritual Gifts: Then and Now*. Carlisle: Paternoster, 1996. Pp. 57–102.

The Significance for Readers Today

1. What can we learn about the person of Jesus from his association with the Spirit (1:32–33; 3:34; 15:26)?
2. What role does the Spirit play in salvation (3:5–6, 8; 6:63)?
3. How would you describe the difference that the indwelling Spirit makes in your life (7:39; 14:16–17; 20:22)?
4. In what ways does the Spirit inspire worship (4:23–24)?
5. What is the significance of the term "Counselor" when applied to the Spirit (14:16–17, 26; 15:26; 16:7)?

chapter 4

Acts of the Apostles

The Setting

Acts is generally accepted as the second volume of the work by Luke, his Gospel being the first. The audience appears to be the same as that for the Gospel.

What Does the Author Say about the Spirit?

The Spirit figures more prominently in Acts than in any other NT book. A more appropriate title might be the Acts of the Spirit because of the book's focus on the supervisory and guiding role of the Spirit in the church and in the lives of believers. Acts particularly explores the manifestation of the Spirit in verbal communication, including prophecy, proclaiming the Gospel, and speaking in tongues.

Generally in Acts, the references to the Spirit are in the context of his coming into people's lives for the first time or with a new dimension, and his subsequent impact. In the Gospels, Jesus expresses the immanence of God—Jesus is a direct revelation of God to humankind; in Acts, Luke shows the Spirit operating in a similar mediatory role. It is not that Jesus is in heaven while the Spirit is on earth. They are, as always, indivisible—distinct but indissoluble partners in the development of the church.

The Spirit

- baptizes and fills, is received by, is given to, and comes on people (1:5; 2:4, 33, 38; 5:32; 8:14–19; 9:17; 10:45–47; 11:15–16; 19:2, 6)

- provides guidance (1:2, 16; 4:25; 8:29; 10:19; 11:12; 13:4; 15:28; 16:6–7; 20:22–23; 28:25)

- reveals sin (5:3, 9; 7:51; 28:25)

- affirms and empowers people for service (6:3, 5; 8:39; 10:38; 13:2; 20:28)

- inspires prophecy (2:17–18; 11:28; 19:6; 21:4, 11)

- inspires and supports the proclamation of the gospel (1:8; 4:8, 31; 6:10; 7:55; 9:31; 11:24; 13:9, 52)

The Spirit baptizes and fills, is received by, is given to, and comes on people (1:5; 2:4, 33, 38; 5:32; 8:14–19; 9:17; 10:45–47; 11:15–16; 19:2, 6)

It is best to explore the verses in this section in the context of the following groupings: (1) the Spirit's involvement in the lives of believers generally (1:5; 2:38; 5:32); (2) Jewish believers on the day of Pentecost (2:4, 33); (3) Samaritan believers (8:14–19); (4) Saul (9:17); (5) Gentile believers in the household of Cornelius (10:45–47; 11:15–16); and (6) believing disciples of John the Baptist (19:2, 6).

"John baptized with water, but before many days you shall be baptized with the Holy Spirit." (1:5)

Peter said to them, "Repent, and be baptized every one of you in the name of Jesus Christ for the forgiveness of your sins; and you shall receive the gift of the Holy Spirit." (2:38)

"And we are witnesses to these things, and so is the Holy Spirit whom God has given to those who obey him." (5:32)

Exposition

The Spirit in Believers

Each of these three verses refers to God's promise to give the Spirit to believers. Luke therefore begins his second volume by reminding readers of Jesus' promise prior to his ascension that he would baptize the apostles with the Holy Spirit (Luke 24:49; Acts 1:4). Peter, in his sermon following the fulfillment of that promise on the day of Pentecost, extends the offer of the Spirit to all who will repent of their sins and receive the forgiveness of Jesus

(Acts 2:38). He later affirms the reality of this event in a statement to the Jewish religious hierarchy (5:32).

Although the terminology differs, these verses all describe the presence of the Spirit in the lives of believers as affirmation that they are authentic members of the church. The gift of the Spirit is available to people of all nationalities (2:39). Furthermore, there is no mention that God gives the Spirit in order to enable believers to fulfill a commission. Here the Spirit is the evidence that a transformation has taken place. Luke is not suggesting in 5:32 that the Spirit is a reward for one's obedience, but rather that one's readiness to obey indicates that the Spirit is present (cf. 5:29).

Significance for the Original Readers

These verses confirm that God gives the Spirit to people on the basis of a request for forgiveness, followed by a readiness to obey Jesus. The prophecy of Jesus has now been fulfilled, and believers live in the light of this fulfillment. The Spirit is not a future prospect for them, but a present reality.

And they were all filled with the Holy Spirit and began to speak in other tongues, as the Spirit gave them utterance. (2:4)

"Being therefore exalted at the right hand of God, and having received from the Father the promise of the Holy Spirit, he has poured out this which you see and hear." (2:33)

Exposition

Jewish Believers on the Day of Pentecost Receive the Spirit
These verses describe believers receiving the Spirit on the day of Pentecost. Luke 24:49 records that believers were to wait in Jerusalem until the Spirit came, and Acts 1:4 emphasizes that they were not to leave the city during the waiting period.

The words translated "had come" (Acts 2:1) do not simply specify the date of the Spirit's coming as the day of Pentecost, thus locating it in early June. The Greek word (*sympleroo*) relates to the idea of fulfillment. Luke is telling readers that the Spirit came when the time had been fulfilled, at the right moment, at the specified time. The believers had not prayed the Spirit down; rather, the Spirit had come at the predetermined moment in order to fulfill the divine plan.

Luke often uses this description of being "filled" (2:4) with the Spirit. It is a synonym for the term "baptized" in association with the Spirit. There is no suggestion that the Spirit, having filled a believer, may not fill that same person again. In fact, after having been filled with the Spirit on the day of Pentecost, Peter and John, and others, are filled again (4:31). As with the description of the Spirit being "poured out" (2:33), the connotations of overflowing abundance are clear. Luke uses these vivid images to describe the overwhelming involvement of the Spirit in the lives of believers.

The evidence that the Spirit had indeed come upon the believers in Jerusalem is that they spoke in other tongues. That others understood what they said indicates that they spoke in known languages (xenolalia) (2:6–8). In this regard, this event differs from most, if not all, other references to the use of tongues in the NT. Here, the words spoken in tongues refer to the mighty works of God (2:11). The Spirit manifests his presence in the lives of believers by verbal communication—a characteristic that Luke often emphasizes (1:8; 4:8, 25, 31; 6:10; 7:55–56; 11:23–24; 13:9–10; 28:25).

It is possible that this supernatural ability caused the mocking reaction of some of the bystanders (2:13), although in this cosmopolitan city of Jerusalem, where many languages were spoken, there seems to be little reason for people to mock their ability to speak other languages. It is more likely that the ridicule relates to the content of their speech—that they ridiculed the believers because they were excitedly expressing all the great things that God had done. Apart from the hysterical, ecstatic worship of some pagan cults, most Jewish worship of this time was solemnly liturgical. The believers' activity of rejoicing in God would have been unusual and may thus have been treated dismissively.

Luke does not explore why the Spirit manifests his presence through verbal communication, although it was the most common evidence of the Spirit in the lives of people in the OT and would therefore have been the most understandable and most expected occurrence. Luke does not imply that speaking in tongues is a necessary proof of the Spirit's presence in the life of a believer; rather, it functions as the outpouring of the Spirit's activity through a person in mission activity to unbelievers, cutting across barriers of language. This is a major aspect of the work of the Spirit in the church as presented in the book of Acts. Here, in Acts, it is the first act of the Spirit. The fact that the Spirit enables believers to miraculously speak foreign languages reveals that one of his priorities is to ensure that cross-language evangelism takes place, resulting in the salvation of thousands. Although the words spoken praised God, they also opened the door to extend the gospel to other nations represented in Jerusalem.

The fact that the Spirit chose to come on the day of Pentecost is also significant. The Feast of Pentecost, or Feast of Weeks (Exod 23:16; 34:22), was celebrated at the end of the barley harvest, fifty days after Passover. It was a festival of thanksgiving for God's provision and was also known as the "day of the first fruits" (Num 28:26), a motif Paul used in connection with the Spirit (Rom 8:23). The Jews later celebrated the anniversary of the giving of the law at this festival. Although it may be coincidental, it is interesting nevertheless that the Spirit becomes the guiding influence for believers—an influence Paul contrasts with the law (2 Cor 3:3–6).

Acts 2:33 also emphasizes Jesus' exaltation to the right hand of God, a position symbolizing joint inheritance and authority. His ability to pour out the Spirit also demonstrates his exaltation. This does not indicate that the Spirit is in an inferior position to Jesus; rather, the picture portrays the interaction between all the members of the Godhead in providing the Spirit to believers.

Significance for the Original Readers

Most people living in first-century Jerusalem assumed that deities determined their destiny. The Jews found this idea in their history, as recorded in the OT. God had led them from Egypt to Canaan. Thereafter he had guided them through godly prophets and kings, sometimes using other nations to direct them when they were unwilling to obey him. The Gentiles also believed in providence, whereby the gods, often acting arbitrarily, fulfilled their purposes with regard to humanity. Although many debated this idea, and some offered alternative frameworks, all believed that, to a great degree, the future was out of one's control.

Luke introduces his audience to the one who has set the agenda. Indeed, the concept of divine fulfillment is a central theme of the book (1:16; 2:23; 4:28; 5:38–39; 13:29, 33; 21:14). Thus, while Luke agrees with non-Christians who thought of history as unfolding according to a divine plan, he identifies the planner and facilitator of the agenda as the Spirit. The Spirit had recorded that the events of the day of Pentecost would occur (Joel 2:28–32). Now he fulfilled his agenda. This emphasis in the book of Acts ensures its value as an evangelistic tool for people who believe in a predetermined destiny set by a supernatural force.

Now when the apostles at Jerusalem heard that Samaria had received the word of God, they sent to them Peter and John, who came down and prayed for them that they might receive the Holy Spirit; for it had not yet fallen on any of them, but they had only been baptized in the name of the Lord Jesus. Then they laid their hands on them and they received the Holy Spirit. Now when Simon saw that the Spirit was given through the laying on of the apostles' hands, he offered them money, saying, "Give me also this power, that any one on whom I lay my hands may receive the Holy Spirit." (8:14–19)

Exposition

Samaritan Believers Receive the Spirit

Having listened to Philip's message, a number of Samaritans became believers (8:5–13) and were baptized with water. Luke notes, however, that the Spirit was not initially given to the Samaritans on confession of their faith, as had been promised by Peter in his sermon to the Jews (2:38). Whatever the reason for the delay in receiving the Spirit, it appears to indicate a deficiency in the initiation of the Samaritans into the church in that they had not received the Spirit even though they had received the word of God.

In contrast to previous occasions when the Spirit filled people, the Samaritans received the Spirit as a result of the apostles Peter and John laying hands on them and praying for them. Neither the laying on of hands nor prayer should be understood as necessary elements for receiving the Spirit, as they are not present on other occasions (10:44), although Ananias did lay hands on Saul prior to his receiving the Spirit (9:17).

To assume that Peter and John could confer the Spirit in a way that Philip could not overlooks the fact that nobody confers the Spirit; he is his own master, filling those whom he chooses. Elsewhere, there is no human involvement, and the question we have to ask is this: Then why here?

The following are possible interpretations:

The Samaritans were not authentic believers and thus could not receive the Spirit. Luke records, however, that they had believed and received the word, and as a result were baptized with water. To suggest that Philip may have made a mistake concerning their belief in the gospel undermines the authority and wisdom of Philip, a man chosen because he was wise, full of the Spirit, and of good repute (6:3).[1] When Peter and John arrive, they do not identify any deficiencies in the Samaritans' faith or in Philip's message. The fact that Simon the sorcerer had been misguided does not mean that all the Samaritans were (8:9–13).

- It is possible that this verse refers to a second filling of the Samaritans with the Spirit. However, Luke writes that the Spirit had not previously fallen on the Samaritans at all.

- Some have postulated that Luke is saying that a particular capacity or gift of the Spirit had not been granted to the believers. Luke does not indicate any such lack, however, and refers clearly to the absence of the Spirit himself.

This occasion may be unique in the sense that the involvement of the apostles was necessary—not to accept the Samaritans into the church but to make the point that they, as Jews, were part of the procedure—thus establishing a framework of fellowship and harmony for the present and future. The incorporation of the Samaritans into the church was a momentous occasion. Given the animosity between Jews and Samaritans and the fact that they had been excluded from Jewish worship for centuries, it was most unusual that they should participate in what was, at the time, a Jewish church. No one could cast aspersions on the authenticity of their faith or experience, however, because they received the Spirit in the presence of the apostles themselves. This event fulfills in part the agenda set in 1:8. This understanding of the passage is possible if, because of their history, the Samaritans are a special class and therefore need to be treated differently. The fact that Philip was the first to preach the gospel to the Samaritans, followed by Peter and John (the first apostles to preach there after they had prayed for the Samaritan believers [8:25]), emphasizes the groundbreaking nature of this mission.

It is wise to be cautious in offering possible explanations for this situation and even to express uncertainty as to why it happened. It is clear that there was a delay and that it suggested a deficiency

---

[1] If the Philip in 8:5–13 is the apostle Philip, the same equation holds true because as one of the Twelve, he could, one would assume, authenticate true faith as well as Peter and John.

that was soon rectified by the arrival of the apostles. To advance beyond this is to move into speculation—a worthy and not hopeless task, but one that does not easily result in consensus.

Furthermore, if we go beyond what Luke actually states we may risk missing the point of the narrative. It is clear from this passage that the Spirit is integral to the process of salvation; without him, something is wrong and needs to be resolved. Acts repeatedly stresses the sovereign role of the Spirit, and there is no suggestion that the Spirit is at fault. Rather, the Spirit, in his sovereignty, allows the delay for his own purposes. It is important to note that the Samaritans had been welcomed into the church, and the final and public evidence of that fact was their reception of the Spirit.

It is difficult for the modern reader to appreciate the depth of animosity felt by Jews and Samaritans toward each other. This rivalry was centuries old, dating back to the return from exile of many Jews from Babylonia. It grew to a hatred, based on religious as well as ethnic grounds. The suggestion that Samaritans could be members of the church would have been a bitter pill for many Jews to accept. It is thus understandable that the Spirit should be present to authenticate the inclusion of the Samaritans into what was a Jewish church up to this time. Their reception of the Spirit is validation to Peter and John, the representatives of the apostles in Jerusalem, that the Samaritans are truly members of the church and are to be accepted as such by all others. The promise of Acts 1:8 is being fulfilled, and the Spirit is endorsed as the one who determines membership of the church.

So Ananias departed and entered the house. And laying his hands on him he said, "Brother Saul, the Lord Jesus who appeared to you on the road by which you came, has sent me that you may regain your sight and be filled with the Holy Spirit." (9:17)

Exposition

Saul Receives the Spirit

Saul received the Spirit after God chose him for service and after Ananias laid his hands on him. That Ananias addresses him as "brother" probably indicates his faith, although that term refers less frequently in Acts to someone of the Jewish race. Ananias offers no prayer but simply makes a statement rehearsing the commission he received from God. After Saul receives the Spirit, he is baptized with water.

Luke does not elaborate on the significance of Saul's being filled with the Spirit. It may be of value to note, however, that he "immediately" preached in the synagogues in Damascus, to the amazement of the people (9:20–21). To say that the Spirit is affirming Saul's salvation may be reading too much of Pauline theology into the text, although it could be the unspoken motif behind Luke's presentation of the event. As with the Samaritans, the Spirit is presented as being the catalyst for change, this time in Paul. After he is filled with the Spirit, he is miraculously healed and baptized in water. From this moment on, he commences preaching that Jesus is the Son of God. The sensational impact that the Spirit has on an individual is thus impressed on the readers, the rest of Paul's life and ministry demonstrating that the Spirit authenticates and empowers Paul to achieve the plan that God has for him. The same Spirit affirms all believers, enabling them also to fulfill the objectives set for them by God.

And the believers from among the circumcised who came with Peter were amazed, because the gift of the Holy Spirit had been poured out even on the Gentiles. For they heard them speaking in tongues and extolling God. Then Peter declared, "Can any one forbid water for baptizing these people who have received the Holy Spirit just as we have?" (10:45–47)

"As I began to speak, the Holy Spirit fell on them just as on us at the beginning. And I remembered the word of the Lord, how he said, 'John baptized with water, but you shall be baptized with the Holy Spirit.' " (11:15–16)

Exposition

Gentile Believers in the Household of Cornelius Receive the Spirit

After Peter receives a vision, he visits Cornelius, an upright and God-fearing Gentile (10:22). While Peter was preaching the gospel to Cornelius and his household, the Holy Spirit fell upon Peter's listeners, who then began to speak in tongues and worship God. This was the first occasion that the Spirit had been poured out on the Gentiles, and Peter saw no reason why they should not be baptized with water. On returning to Jerusalem, Peter described the event to the believers there. In his account he linked the Gentiles' faith in the Lord Jesus Christ with receiving the Spirit. Special events envelop the whole episode. Peter sees a vision (10:9–16) and is guided by the Spirit (10:19–20), while an angel speaks to Cornelius (10:3, 22). Clearly, Luke sees this as a momentous occasion.

The significance of these Gentiles' being filled with the Spirit has been a matter of discussion. It is possible that the Spirit affirmed their salvation or that he came to empower them for their witness as believers. In his letters, Paul speaks of the role of the Spirit in affirming salvation. There is no indication in the text, however, that Cornelius's family and friends engaged in evangelistic activity after their experience. Some have suggested that these believers received the Spirit twice. If the Spirit filled them at the beginning of the sermon ("As I began to speak" [11:15]) to affirm their salvation, the filling during the sermon ("While Peter was still saying this" [10:44]) was a subsequent experience. Although it is clear that the Spirit does fill believers more than once, there seems to be little exegetical value in this latter explanation. If Luke had intended to present a twofold expression of the Spirit, why did he not make that clear?

An alternative solution, and one in keeping with the experience of the Samaritans, is to recognize the Spirit as the one who sanctions the entrance of people-groups into the church. Thus, the fact that the Spirit welcomed Gentiles into the church both amazed (10:45) and initially scandalized (11:2–3) some of the believers. Despite the prophecy of 1:8, the idea that the church should incorporate people other than Jews was a surprise to many. It is clear from the debate in Acts 15, regarding whether Gentile believers should be circumcised or not, that the issue of nationality was crucial to many in the early church. Thus, in 15:8–9, Peter refers to the Spirit being given to the Gentiles as evidence that God makes no distinction between Gentile and Jewish believers.

Luke records that the Spirit took the initiative by baptizing the Gentiles into the church and demonstrated his presence by granting them the ability to speak in tongues. The unilateral activity of the Spirit on their behalf welcomed them into the church supernaturally. Luke does not focus on the individual salvation of some Gentiles, but rather, as with the incident in Samaria, on the fact that the Gentiles had now been welcomed into the church (11:1). Since the Spirit had affirmed them, it was incumbent upon the apostles to add their affirmation by baptizing them with water.

Significance for the Original Reader

Luke continues to enable the readers to appreciate the nature of the church in that it is presented as a multiethnic and multiracial community. Although it was significant that Samaritans were welcomed as authentic members of the Christian community, it was sensational that 'the same privilege was offered to Gentiles. After all, at least the Samaritans worshipped Jehovah as did the Jews and based their beliefs and lifestyles on the OT. The Gentiles, however, were pagans, most of whom worshipped other gods and whose lives were molded by influences other than the sacred Scriptures of the Jews. Little wonder that Peter receives a vision in which he is encouraged by God to eat unclean food prior to being asked to preach the gospel to Cornelius and his family (10:11–24). Peter needed to be convinced of the validity of this mission, and so God provided a vision to help him. As he was preaching to them, the Spirit filled the lives of those to whom Peter spoke, demonstrating that not only was it right for Peter to preach to them the gospel, but also that they were initiated into the church, their racial identity being irrelevant.

In writing the book of Acts, Luke enables his readers to realize that the gospel is for all peoples, as identified in 1:8. In this account, he demonstrates that this even included Gentiles. His is indeed an inclusive gospel.

And he said to them, "Did you receive the Holy Spirit when you believed?" And they said, "No, we have never even heard that there is a Holy Spirit." . . . And when Paul had laid his hands upon them, the Holy Spirit came on them; and they spoke with tongues and prophesied. (19:2, 6)

Exposition

Believing Disciples of John the Baptist in Ephesus
These verses describe the final occasion in Acts in which the Spirit comes upon people, namely here believers based in Ephesus who had been taught by Apollos. Apollos was an eloquent, educated, and fervent believer, but his knowledge of the Spirit was limited (18:24–25). When Paul meets these believers, they inform him that they have no knowledge of the Holy Spirit, which prompts Paul to baptize them with water in the name of Jesus. Paul then lays his hands on them, and they receive the Spirit, evidenced by their speaking in tongues and prophesying (19:1–6). After this short narrative, with no explanation, Luke moves on to describe Paul's mission to Ephesus.

There has been much discussion concerning this incident and the role of the Spirit here. Some suggest that this was a second experience of the Spirit received after salvation, while others propose that they were not believers at all or that their salvation was incomplete. However, the reference to their having believed (19:2) and the description of them as "disciples" indicate that they were authentic believers. Nevertheless, Paul felt it necessary to rebaptize them (19:3), suggesting that he was dissatisfied with their previous baptism. Luke does not explain the reasons for this event. However, he does record that, on the basis of their confession that they had not received the Spirit, Paul laid his hands on them, as a result of which the Spirit came on them. This does not mean that they would not have entered heaven if they had died before Paul's baptism. It is more likely that they would have missed the substantial benefits of the Spirit's presence in their lives on earth. To go beyond this may be to miss the point of Luke's narrative— especially since he does not explore the incident further.

The Spirit makes an immediate difference in the lives of these believers, as if to confirm that they were already missing out, by enabling them to speak in tongues and to prophesy. Although they had faith to believe and to be disciples, the Spirit wanted to give them much more.

Significance for the Original Readers

Evangelism is one of the Spirit's priorities. The Spirit initiated evangelism, enabling believers to do that which was impossible without supernatural help. Not only does the Spirit fulfill the promise of Jesus (John 15:26) throughout Acts, but he also assures readers that he is able and willing to support them in their evangelistic endeavors as well.

Luke describes evangelism beyond the borders of Israel as thousands hear the gospel and are brought to faith in Jesus. The Spirit is dedicated to welcoming people of all nationalities and backgrounds into the church. The Jews disliked and mistrusted Samaritans, and yet God incorporates them into the church. Cornelius, although described as a God-fearer, was a Gentile and a centurion who, because of his official position, had to publicly support polytheism, and yet the Spirit welcomes him too. These were radical events in the eyes of many first-century Jews, and they revealed the revolutionary nature of the Spirit, who populates the church from all people-groups.

It is also important to note the differences in how the Spirit assimilates people into the church. There is no set methodology. What matters is that he is an integral element in the process of initiating believers into the church and supporting them as they enter the wider community of believers.

Each of the events provides opportunities for new mission activities for the church. The Spirit opens new doors, and he affirms these evangelistic thrusts with sensational acts.

The Spirit provides guidance (1:2, 16; 4:25; 8:29; 10:19; 11:12; 13:4; 15:28; 16:6–7; 20:22–23; 28:25)

The discussion of this group of verses concerning the Spirit's guidance is subdivided into three sections. Each section identifies a different method the Spirit uses to guide people: (1) through the words of Jesus; (2) through the OT; and (3) in direct revelation to believers.

. . . Until the day when he was taken up, after he had given commandment through the Holy Spirit to the apostles whom he had chosen. (1:2)

Exposition

The Words of Jesus
This introductory verse reminds Luke's audience that the Spirit, who is to be the focus of his second volume, is the same Spirit who was associated with Jesus throughout his ministry.

"Brethren, the scripture had to be fulfilled, which the Holy Spirit spoke beforehand by the mouth of David, concerning Judas who was guide to those who arrested Jesus." (1:16)

"Who by the mouth of our father David, thy servant, didst say by the Holy Spirit, 'Why did the Gentiles rage, and the peoples imagine vain things?' " (4:25)

So, as they disagreed among themselves, they departed, after Paul had made one statement: "The Holy Spirit was right in saying to your fathers through Isaiah the prophet . . ." (28:25)

Exposition

The Old Testament
These verses identify the Spirit as the one who spoke through David and Isaiah. The fact that the Spirit spoke through people in the past authenticates the present experience in the lives of believers. The foretelling in 1:16 serves as a reminder that prophecy is also an aspect of the Spirit's work.

And the Spirit said to Philip, "Go up and join this chariot." (8:29)

And while Peter was pondering the vision, the Spirit said to him, "Behold, three men are looking for you." (10:19)

"And the Spirit told me to go with them, making no distinction. These six brethren also accompanied me, and we entered the man's house." (11:12)

So, being sent out by the Holy Spirit, they went down to Seleucia; and from there they sailed to Cyprus. (13:4)

"For it has seemed good to the Holy Spirit and to us to lay upon you no greater burden than these necessary things." (15:28)

And they went through the region of Phrygia and Galatia, having been forbidden by the Holy Spirit to speak the word in Asia. And when they had come opposite Mysia, they attempted to go into Bithynia, but the Spirit of Jesus did not allow them. (16:6–7)

"And now, behold, I am going to Jerusalem, bound in the Spirit, not knowing what shall befall me there; except that the Holy Spirit testifies to me in every city that imprisonment and afflictions await me." (20:22–23)

Exposition

Direct Revelation
In these verses the Spirit speaks to believers through various forms of revelation. Although Luke does not explore how the different people involved received these messages, it is clear that the Spirit provides guidance supernaturally. All of the references relate to evangelism, again emphasizing the Spirit's priority in this area.

The difference in titles for the Spirit need not detain us. Luke and Paul regularly use different titles for the Spirit without indicating different members of the Godhead.

Significance for the Original Readers

What is important to Luke's audience is that the Spirit guides believers, in particular with regard to their evangelism. The Spirit's instructions to the church to release Paul and Barnabas for their first missionary journey in 13:2, 4 highlight not only the Spirit's concern for evangelism but also his desire and readiness to support the witness of believers.

The text does not explain exactly how the Spirit guides people, but it is clear that he desires them to recognize his guidance for what it is. Thus, when Paul is planning his itinerary (16:6–7), the Spirit directs him, ensuring that he follows his agenda when it appears that Paul is uncertain as to where he should go next. The Spirit, who spoke through David and Isaiah, the most important king and prophet to the Jews, respectively, now speaks to all believers. This access to the Spirit is a privilege that carries with it a responsibility to listen and obey.

The Spirit reveals sin (5:3, 9; 7:51; 28:25)

But Peter said, "Ananias, why has Satan filled your heart to lie to the Holy Spirit and to keep back part of the proceeds of the land?" . . . But Peter said to [Sapphira], "How is it that you have agreed together to tempt the Spirit of the Lord? Hark, the feet of those that have buried your husband are at the door, and they will carry you out." (5:3, 9)

"You stiff-necked people, uncircumcised in heart and ears, you always resist the Holy Spirit. As your fathers did, so do you." (7:51)

So, as they disagreed among themselves, they departed, after Paul had made one statement: "The Holy Spirit was right in saying to your fathers through Isaiah the prophet." (28:25)

Exposition

One of the ways in which the Spirit provides guidance is through confronting sin. In 7:51, Stephen alludes to Isa 63:10. Paul, beginning in 28:25, quotes from Isa 6:9–10, referring to the fact that people can resist the Spirit. In 5:3, 9, Luke records that people can, and do, lie to the Spirit. Because of the Spirit's central role in the church, sin is personally directed against the Spirit of the community as well as against the members of the community. The Spirit's presence in believers entails certain responsibilities. Acts 4:31 describes all the believers being filled with the Spirit; in 5:1–11 we see two of those people failing to appreciate the significance of that event in their lives—a timely lesson for the whole church.

Significance for the Original Readers

Luke's readership, although some years removed from the events recorded in the book of Acts, nevertheless profited from understanding these events. The incident in 5:3, 9 reminds readers of the fact that, although the Spirit is strongly supportive of them and their mission, he cannot be treated as less than holy. He expects believers to live up to certain standards in their daily lives. Although it is not necessary to conclude that the deaths of Ananias and Sapphira resulted in the loss of their salvation, this judgment does indicate that the Spirit's desire for purity should be high on the agenda of the church. This is not an easy battle to win in a world that easily contaminates, but it must be undertaken.

The reference to the Spirit in the testimony of Stephen (7:2–53) provides another lesson. The Spirit empowered his witness (6:10), but his obedience to the Spirit resulted in his death at the hands of those to whom he witnessed. It is a painful lesson that Spirit-anointed preaching does not always result in converts. On this occasion it did not, and it was as important for the original readers to understand as it is for us today that evangelism can have a very high cost. His limited success was not a failure on his part, for at the end of the sermon Stephen is described as being "full of the Holy Spirit" (7:55) and seeing God's glory and Jesus in heaven. Furthermore, the event was not a failure, because one of the witnesses was Saul.

The Spirit affirms and empowers people for service (6:3, 5; 8:39; 10:38; 13:2; 20:28)

"Therefore, brethren, pick out from among you seven men of good repute, full of the Spirit and of wisdom, whom we may appoint to

this duty." . . . And what they said pleased the whole multitude, and they chose Stephen, a man full of faith and of the Holy Spirit, and Philip, and Prochorus, and Nicanor, and Timon, and Parmenas, and Nicolaus, a proselyte of Antioch. (6:3, 5)

And when they came up out of the water, the Spirit of the Lord caught up Philip; and the eunuch saw him no more, and went on his way rejoicing. (8:39)

"How God anointed Jesus of Nazareth with the Holy Spirit and with power; how he went about doing good and healing all that were oppressed by the devil, for God was with him." (10:38)

While they were worshiping the Lord and fasting, the Holy Spirit said, "Set apart for me Barnabas and Saul for the work to which I have called them." (13:2)

"Take heed to yourselves and to all the flock, in which the Holy Spirit has made you overseers, to care for the church of God which he obtained with the blood of his own Son." (20:28)

Exposition

One of the main aspects of the work of the Spirit, explored further in Paul's letters, is that he sets people apart for certain responsibilities and supports them in fulfilling these roles. In 6:3, 5, the seven men who are to support the apostles are chosen from those who are full of the Holy Spirit and, consequently, who are also full of wisdom and faith. Although "wisdom" is not a common expression in Acts, "faith" is. Luke uses the latter with various meanings, but here he probably is signifying a close relationship with God. Thus, as these men exhibit wisdom from the Spirit, through their close walk with God they also exhibit faith, or trust, as a result of which the Spirit is able to inspire them to certain actions. Such is the closeness of their walk with God that they may expect the guidance of the Spirit, and they respond to that guidance by faith.

The Spirit guides Philip in a more immediate way: After Philip completes his task, the Spirit whisks him away (8:39) to begin another one. The event is reminiscent of the (occasional?) experiences of Elijah (1 Kgs 18:12; 2 Kgs 2:16), and it may point to the continuity of the work of the Spirit from the OT. More important, the Spirit is depicted as the one who inspires mission activity in that Philip is shown preaching the gospel (8:40).

In 10:38, Luke records that God anointed Jesus with the Holy Spirit and power, as a result of which Jesus healed all who were oppressed by the devil, for God was with him. Although Luke may be wishing to remind his audience that the Holy Spirit is Jesus' source of power for performing miracles, we have seen that the Gospels emphasize this aspect of the Spirit's role to a very limited extent. Similarly, Luke does not refer to the Spirit in the context of the healings he narrates in Acts. It is more likely that Luke intends to remind his readers that Jesus' anointing with the Holy Spirit validates his authenticity. As we have seen, it is not that Jesus was powerless without the Holy Spirit. Indeed, the notion that Jesus could be without the Holy Spirit is meaningless since they are eternally integrated as members of the Godhead. Rather, the fact that the Spirit anointed Jesus, as evidenced by his supernatural miracles, proved beyond all doubt that Jesus was indeed the one in whose name the forgiveness of sins was to be granted (10:43).

Finally, the Spirit plays an active role in choosing Saul and Barnabas (13:2) and the elders in Ephesus (20:28). Although Luke does not reveal how the Spirit provided this guidance, the most important lesson here is that the Spirit, not leaders in the church, is the one who initiates such important decisions. The believers are not left on their own to decide who is to serve the believing community.

Significance for the Original Readers

For believers in the early church, much relating to their faith was new. Early on, Christians had no Scriptures unique to the church, as their own writings had not yet attained the status of Scripture and the OT was written by and for the Jewish community. They did not have a history of their own of worship, learning, or practice. Even their leaders were new. One of the accusations many made against the church was that it was a novelty. In a world in which pedigree and a proven track record were important, Christianity was something of an enigma. To help combat this, the NT writers regularly referred back to the OT to prove that Christianity actually has ancient roots.

The strongest influence on the stability of the believers in those early days, however, was the Holy Spirit. The Spirit helped the young leaders and members of the church to recognize that human wisdom was not guiding the development of the church. Nor was the church being empowered by natural gifts and capacities. The Spirit was in charge, controlling the selection of leaders and empowering them to complete their commissions. The manifestation of the Spirit in believers was evidence that he was involved in their community. Their church was his church.

The Spirit inspires prophecy (2:17–18; 11:28; 19:6; 21:4, 11)

" 'And in the last days it shall be, God declares, that I will pour out my Spirit upon all flesh, and your sons and your daughters shall prophesy, and your young men shall see visions, and your old men shall dream dreams; yea, and on my menservants and my maidservants in those days I will pour out my Spirit; and they shall prophesy.' " (2:17–18)

And one of them named Agabus stood up and foretold by the Spirit that there would be a great famine over all the world; and this took place in the days of Claudius. (11:28)

And when Paul had laid his hands upon them, the Holy Spirit came on them; and they spoke with tongues and prophesied. (19:6)

And having sought out the disciples, we stayed there for seven days. Through the Spirit they told Paul not to go on to Jerusalem. . . . And coming to us he took Paul's girdle and bound his own feet and hands, and said, "Thus says the Holy Spirit, 'So shall the Jews at Jerusalem bind the man who owns this girdle and deliver him into the hands of the Gentiles.' " (21:4, 11)

Exposition

One of the major roles of the Spirit in the OT is prophecy (Num 11:26–27; 1 Sam 10:10). Sometimes this prophecy took the form of foretelling, while at other times it revealed the mind of God to the people. These four texts from Acts indicate that the Spirit is operating in the church similarly to the way he functioned in the OT, although there are significant differences.

Acts 2:17–18 contains the fulfillment of a prophecy recorded centuries earlier in Joel 2:28–32. Luke records the words of Joel, although the words "and they shall prophesy" in 2:18, are added, apparently to reinforce the connection between the Spirit and prophecy already mentioned in 2:17.

Luke also affirms the OT promise that all of God's people will receive the Spirit, that the ability to experience visions and dreams and to prophesy will be available to all. The fact that Luke amends Joel to read "in the last days" instead of "afterwards" also emphasizes that these events are being made available in the present era. The future event for Joel has become a present event for Luke.

Furthermore, Luke presents the Spirit as taking special responsibility for the church. He is the gift of God for believers. Since we have no record of the content of the prophecies, we can assume that they reflected revelation from God that was of benefit to the church (1 Cor 14:3–5).

On two occasions Luke records prophecy from the Spirit foretelling future events. One speaks of a famine and the other of Paul's trip to Jerusalem. Both take the form of warnings and provide the opportunity to prepare for these events. As a result of the warning about the famine, the believers sent help to those in Judea. Not only was the Spirit inspiring believers to care for each other, but he also inspired Gentile believers in Antioch to support Jewish believers in Jerusalem (11:29).

In 21:11, Agabus prophesies concerning Paul's fate in Jerusalem, which will result in his being arrested and placed in the hands of the Gentiles. Starting at 23:16 and continuing through the end of the book, Acts explores Paul's journey to Rome and what he experiences there, largely at the hands of Gentiles. Acts 21:4 poses a dilemma in that it appears that the Spirit did not want Paul to go to Jerusalem, while 19:21 indicates that he did. It is unlikely that Luke intended to show that Paul was disobedient or that the Spirit had made a mistake. Rather, Luke is probably attempting to demonstrate the concern of the believers for Paul; because they are aware of the prophecy concerning his sufferings to come, they seek to dissuade him from going to Jerusalem, as recorded in 21:4.

In a similar vein, although Agabus in 21:11 states that Paul will be bound by the Jews, that binding is actually done by the Gentiles (22:25, 29). It may be that the Jews also bound him, though Luke chooses not to record this. However, there is no record that the Jews handed Paul over to the Gentiles either, as

Agabus's prophecy indicates. It is possible that part of the prophecy was inaccurate. If so, this incident fits very well with the advice that Paul gives to assess prophecies (1 Cor 14:29; 1 Thess 5:21) for accuracy.

Significance for the Original Readers

Luke's comments concerning the association of the Spirit with prophecy are important to the readership because they assure them that they are part of a long tradition of Spirit inspiration, traced back through the OT prophets. The same Spirit provides prophecies through the church, confirming that the believers are receiving authentic messages from God. Even though they need to assess these messages, the fact that the Spirit transmits his words through fallible human mouthpieces demonstrates his commitment to them and his desire to manifest himself through them.

The Spirit inspires and supports the proclamation of the gospel (1:8; 4:8, 31; 6:10; 7:55; 9:31; 11:24; 13:9, 52)

"But you shall receive power when the Holy Spirit has come upon you; and you shall be my witnesses in Jerusalem and in all Judea and Samaria and to the end of the earth." (1:8)

Then Peter, filled with the Holy Spirit, said to them, "Rulers of the people and elders . . ." (4:8)

And when they had prayed, the place in which they were gathered together was shaken; and they were all filled with the Holy Spirit and spoke the word of God with boldness. (4:31)

But they could not withstand the wisdom and the Spirit with which [Stephen] spoke. (6:10)

But [Stephen], full of the Holy Spirit, gazed into heaven and saw the glory of God, and Jesus standing at the right hand of God. (7:55)

So the church throughout all Judea and Galilee and Samaria had peace and was built up; and walking in the fear of the Lord and in the comfort of the Holy Spirit it was multiplied. (9:31)

For [Barnabas] was a good man, full of the Holy Spirit and of faith. And a large company was added to the Lord. (11:24)

Saul, who is also called Paul, filled with the Holy Spirit, looked intently at [Elymas]. (13:9)

And the disciples were filled with joy and with the Holy Spirit. (13:52)

Exposition

These nine texts all relate to the Spirit's role in evangelism. Acts 1:8 promises that one of the gifts the Spirit would give to believers is the power to evangelize. The other eight verses demonstrate how this power affected believers, resulting in the growth of the early church.

Their evangelism is characterized by boldness (4:13, 31) and wisdom (6:10), and although evangelism does not always result in acceptance of the gospel, nevertheless the evangelists experience Spirit-inspired joy and faith (13:50–52). Evangelism is described as being a cause of wonder (4:13; 13:12), unstoppable (6:10), associated with supernatural phenomena (6:15; 7:55–56; 13:9–11), and anticipated as having no national boundaries (1:8). In all of this, it is clear that the Spirit is the director of evangelism to the Jews, Samaria, the Gentiles, and even Rome.

Significance for the Original Readers

Luke wrote the book of Acts sometime in the second half of the first century, probably between 60 and 70 C.E. Claudius was emperor from 41–54 C.E. It was he who expelled Jews from Rome for rioting, apparently at the instigation of a certain Chrestus. If "Chrestus" is a variant of "Christ," this incident may have stemmed from a breakdown in relations between Christians and Jews, resulting in the expulsion of the latter (Acts 18:2). Claudius was succeeded by Nero (54–68 C.E.), who persecuted the Roman Christians in 64 C.E., arranging for them to be thrown to wild animals while covered in animal skins, or crucified, or burned alive to serve as a column of lights at the entrance to his palace. Nero's reign was followed by a year in which four emperors vied for the throne—eventually Vespasian, who crushed the Jewish revolt in 70 C.E., became emperor.

In this era of change and insecurity, believers felt increasingly vulnerable because of the cruelty and inhumanity of their leaders. In 95 C.E., Domitian executed Flavius Clemens, who was his first cousin and a consul, on the charge of atheism—possibly because Flavius Clemens was a God-fearer or a Christian. For believers, increasingly excluded by Jew and Gentile alike, the support of the Spirit from the moment they became Christians was a welcome encouragement and gave them hope for the future.

To witness to one's faith in Jesus in the first-century world was to risk facing ridicule, opposition, and even death. Evangelism, therefore, was not for the fainthearted. The promise of the Spirit was not that the situation in which one witnessed would change, but that the Spirit would provide the resources necessary to witness—regardless of the situation. Thus, the examples of others in the church encourage believers to believe the promises concerning the supportive role of the Spirit and to engage in evangelism. Although there was no guarantee of success, believers could always count on the resourceful presence of the Spirit.

Selected Bibliography

Barrett, Charles K. *A Critical and Exegetical Commentary on the Acts of the Apostles.* 2 vols. International Critical Commentary. Edinburgh: T&T Clark, 1994–1998.

Keener, Craig S. *The Spirit in the Gospels and Acts.* Peabody, Mass.: Hendrickson, 1997.

Menzies, Ralph P. *Empowered for Witness: The Spirit in Luke-Acts.* Rev. ed. Journal of Pentecostal Theology: Supplement Series 6. Sheffield: Sheffield Academic Press, 1994. Pp. 48–102.

Mittelstadt, Martin W. *The Spirit and Suffering in Luke-Acts.* London: T&T Clark, 2004.

Penney, John M. *The Missionary Emphasis of Lukan Pneumatology.* Sheffield: Sheffield Academic Press, 1997.

Turner, Max. *Power from on High: The Spirit in Israel's Restoration and Witness in Luke-Acts.* Journal of Pentecostal Theology: Supplement Series 9. Sheffield: Sheffield Academic Press, 1996.

Wenk, Matthias. *Community-forming Power: The Socio-ethical Role of the Spirit in Luke-Acts.* Journal of Pentecostal Theology: Supplement Series 19. Sheffield: Sheffield Academic Press, 2000.

The Significance for Readers Today

1. In what ways have you experienced the filling of the Spirit in your life (1:5; 2:4, 33, 38; 5:32; 8:14–19; 9:17; 10:45–47; 11:15–16; 19:2, 6)?
2. How does the Spirit provide guidance (1:2, 16; 4:25; 8:29; 10:19; 11:12; 13:4; 15:28; 16:6–7; 20:22–23; 28:25)?
3. In what ways does the Spirit reveal sin (5:3, 9; 7:51; 28:25)?
4. How has the Spirit affirmed and empowered your service for him (6:3, 5; 8:39; 10:38; 13:2; 20:28)?
5. How does the Spirit inspire prophecy (2:17–18; 11:28; 19:6; 21:4, 11)?
6. How has the Spirit inspired and supported your witness (1:8; 4:8, 31; 6:10; 7:55; 9:31; 11:24; 13:9, 52)?

chapter 5

Romans

The Setting

Paul wrote this letter (1:1) prior to his visit to Jerusalem (15:25), having completed a significant evangelistic journey in the northeastern region of the Mediterranean (15:19, 23). The readers lived in a city that housed around one million people, some forty to fifty thousand of whom were Jews. It appears that Paul's readers were a mixture of Jewish and Gentile Christians (1:16; 2:9–10; 3:9, 29; 9:24; 10:12; 11:13–32; 15:7–12), with the latter being the majority, and that they congregated in as many as five different house churches (16:5, 10–11, 14–15).

What Does the Author Say about the Spirit?

The letter, which provides a comprehensive description of the work of the Spirit in the believer, contains many references to the Spirit's various roles. Some of this material concerning the Spirit is unique to Paul.

The Spirit

- is set apart and sets believers apart (1:4)

- provides spiritual gifts (1:11; 12:6–8)

- provides a balance to the law (2:29; 7:6, 14; 8:2, 4)

- is the channel for the love of God (5:5; 15:30)

- opposes the flesh and identifies and empowers believers as God's children (8:5–13)

- affirms adoption for believers (8:14–17)

- is the "firstfruits" for believers (8:23)

- prays for believers (8:26–27)

- empowers the believer (14:17; 15:13, 16, 18–19)

The Spirit is set apart and sets believers apart (1:4).

Designated Son of God in power according to the Spirit of holiness by his resurrection from the dead, Jesus Christ our Lord.

Exposition

As a result of his resurrection, Jesus is affirmed as the Son of God. Although Jesus functioned in authority while on earth, his authority was necessarily limited—partly because of the restrictions of his being in human form. After the resurrection, he was free of such restrictions. The Spirit is said to play a part in this resurrection.

The phrase "Spirit of holiness" is unique in the NT, and it is worth considering why Paul uses it here. The concept of holiness is to be understood as meaning more than sinlessness; its fundamental meaning is of being set apart. Here, Paul is either further defining the title "Holy Spirit," emphasizing that the Spirit is different, or set apart, or he is pointing out that one of the things the Spirit does is to set people apart. In support of the first option is the fact that elsewhere Paul describes the Spirit as being holy (5:5; 14:17; 15:16). The second option is also a possibility, because the terms translated "holy" and "hallow, consecrate" are found elsewhere in the Bible to describe what is set apart and thus to be distinguished from others (sacrifices [Exod 29:33–37], priests [Exod 19:22], the temple [1 Kgs 9:3], and the Jewish people [Exod 19:14]). The second option finds further support in 8:15, where Paul refers to the Spirit of adoption, the Spirit who initiates the process of adoption for the believer.

Which of these two interpretations is more appropriate in this context? It is possible that Paul is purposefully ambiguous here, using "Spirit of holiness" with both connotations. The Spirit is, by definition, set apart, and he sets believers apart to God. The use of the term "saints" (*hagioi*, "ones who are set apart, consecrated, holy") in 1:7 to describe the community of believers in Rome is significant in this respect. God calls believers to be holy, "saints" who are set apart from the rest of society.

Significance for the Original Readers

Just as the Holy Spirit is set apart, so the Spirit has set believers apart from within a pagan society. For Gentile believers this is all the more remarkable, given that they were not part of God's people in the OT. Furthermore, this setting apart does not result from any action on their part; the Spirit has achieved it for them.

The Spirit provides spiritual gifts (1:11; 12:6–8)

For I long to see you, that I may impart to you some spiritual gift to strengthen you. (1:11)

Exposition

In 1:11–15, Paul expresses his desire to come to the believers in Rome. In 1:11, he uses this unique combination of the terms *charisma* ("a gift") and *pneumatikos* ("spiritual, relating to the Spirit"), rendered as "spiritual gift," to describe what he wishes to impart to them when he visits them. Since elsewhere Paul uses each of these terms independently to refer to "spiritual gifts," he may be combining them in 1:11 for emphasis; in other words, he seeks to impart a spiritual gift of great significance.

It is also possible that the gift relates to his desire to teach them or preach the gospel to them, since the gospel is the greatest gift of God to humanity and the clearest sign of God's grace. Regardless of the form this gift takes, Paul anticipates that it will be for their benefit.

Having gifts that differ according to the grace given to us, let us use them: if prophecy, in proportion to our faith; if service, in our serving; he who teaches, in his teaching; he who exhorts, in his exhortation; he who contributes, in liberality; he who gives aid, with zeal; he who does acts of mercy, with cheerfulness. (12:6–8)

Exposition

Paul lists the gifts here in the context of an analogy that reminds the readers of the various functions in the human body.

Apparently, some believers were demeaning others in the Christian community (12:3b). Paul reminds his readers that all of the ways in which believers serve in the church are gifts from God, granted for the benefit of all. They need to consider this fact in order to best appreciate their own status and contributions (12:3c).

The purpose of 12:6–8 is not simply to provide a comprehensive list of gifts, to promote diversity, to establish universality of opportunity, or even to identify the Holy Spirit as the source of the gifts. Rather, this passage encourages believers to use their gifts and guides them in that use. Possessing the gifts is useless unless those who have them also use them.

Paul states that prophecy, the first gift mentioned, must be used "in proportion to our faith." It is possible that with "*our* faith" he is emphasizing Christian faith and thus reminding readers that they must use all of their gifts in accordance with the fundamental characteristics of the Christian faith (including loving sensitivity to others, accountability to others, and humility). When using gifts, it is also important to acknowledge that every believer is part of the body (12:3–5), a membership that carries certain privileges and responsibilities.

Although it is possible that Paul is encouraging them to develop self-confidence to use a particular gift that they feel they have been given, there is little in Paul's writings to support this view. Rather, the guidelines that follow suggest that he is fundamentally indicating that just as one who has been provided with the gift of serving should serve, so also the one provided with the gift of prophecy should prophesy. The reference to faith could thus relate to the awareness of recipients that they had been given a gift by God, their faith being identified as the belief that God had given them a gift.

Significance for the Original Readers

Rome was a diverse city, with many different cultures, languages, people groups, and religions. The majority populace in Rome felt oppressed by the ruling minority, the privileged few who were in possession of most of the wealth and power. Many, perhaps most, believers belonged to this underprivileged majority—a group that lacked a sense of self-value.

Paul is reminding believers here of their value, particularly the value placed on them by God, who has given them the power to benefit others both within and outside their community. However,

they need encouragement to use the resources that have been
granted to them and to do this with enthusiasm and commitment.

The Spirit provides a balance to the law (2:29; 7:6, 14; 8:2, 4)

*He is a Jew who is one inwardly, and real circumcision is a matter
of the heart, spiritual and not literal. His praise is not from men but
from God. (2:29)*

Exposition

This verse is part of a long section in which Paul explores the
roles of the law and the Spirit in the life of the believer. Paul often
refers to the OT law as the standard that God prescribed for the
Jewish people. Their failure to meet this standard was covered
by the sacrificial system. In 2:29, Paul acknowledges that the law
confirms the racial identity of the Jew, particularly demonstrated
by a physical surgical operation (circumcision). Since the death of
Jesus, however, it is the Spirit who marks the spiritual identity
of the "Jew" with spiritual internal surgery (to the heart, the place
of emotion and direction [1:21; 2:15; 5:5; 6:17]). Paul declares here
that the Spirit confirms the identity of believers, irrespective of the
law (as prophesied in Jer 31:3–34; Ezek 11:19).

The terms translated "spiritual" (*pneuma*) and "literal" (*gramma*)
are best understood as relating to the Spirit and the law. Paul is
contrasting the life influenced by the Spirit with the one dominated
by the law—a life in which the Spirit affirms salvation on the
believer's behalf. What determines the validity of one's claim to be
a true Jew (child of God), says Paul, is not something outwardly
observable, such as circumcision. What is important is the internal
change within the person. It is not what has been done *by* an individual that determines one's place before God, but rather what has
been done *for* an individual by the Spirit. Believers cannot commend themselves (2:29), therefore, nor do they need to, because
what confirms and sets them apart is the work of the Spirit.

*But now we are discharged from the law, dead to that which held
us captive, so that we serve not under the old written code but in the
new life of the Spirit. (7:6)*

Exposition

Here in 7:6 Paul notes that believers have been "discharged" (released) from the law, having died to it. This death results in the possibility of a new, fulfilling life of the Spirit. These concepts are complex and raise some important questions for consideration.

The Identity of the Law

Although this text may be alluding to the legalistic excesses of some Jewish religious groups, such as the Pharisees, Paul is probably referring again to the OT law as a whole. And while it is possible that he is referring to the mistaken belief that the law can lead to salvation, it is more likely that he is refuting the view that the law can be the main guiding influence for believers. It is not that the law no longer offers guidance, but that a better guide, the Spirit, is now available. This does not mean that the Spirit will offer advice contrary to the OT law. It does mean that the Spirit's advice is contemporary; relevant to the lifestyle and context of the believer; available apart from a code or handbook of laws; not confined to ancient Jewish ceremonial issues; and the result of the Spirit's internal influence. At the same time, the Spirit reveals the consequences of sinful behavior to believers while providing them with the power to obey his promptings.

How Did the Law Make People Captive?

Even though the Jews may not have been aware of it, the law was the controlling influence in their lives. It was the standard for their behavior, consistently pointing out their failings and assigning their punishment (separation from God). But it could not provide power for them to improve. Thus, because of their inability to keep it, the law locked them in a cycle of captivity that led only to condemnation.

How Have Believers Been Released, or Discharged, from the Law?

In 7:4, Paul states that believers have "died to the law through the body of Christ." He is referring to Jesus' death on the cross and identifies believers with that death and its consequences. His analogy is of a marriage relationship in which one partner has died. He argues that because of the believers' union with Christ, it is as if they died when he died. As a result, their relationship with their previous partner, the law, has changed. They are now free to engage in a new relationship with a new partner, Jesus. As the law was an integral element of the old covenant, so the Spirit replaces the law in the new covenant. The believer no longer needs the law to set the standard; the Spirit sets the standard now.

How Do Believers Serve in the New Life of the Spirit?

Paul describes the believer carrying out his or her service "not under the old written code." As well as drawing attention to the fact that a new guide is in place, he draws a contrast between the old law, consisting of words and letters (and which is therefore, to a degree, external, impersonal, and lifeless), and the new life of the Spirit, which is internal, personal, and vital. Paul is not advocating the abandonment of a righteous lifestyle (6:1–23); rather, he is explaining that a new covenant, along with a new law and a new lawgiver, the Spirit, bring freedom from the OT law and its covenant.

We know that the law is spiritual; but I am carnal, sold under sin. (7:14)

Exposition

In 7:14, Paul describes the law as being spiritual, or of the Spirit (*pneumatikos*). Elsewhere, he contrasts the law and the Spirit (2:29; 7:6; Gal 5:18). Here, he refers to the law as being of the Spirit; it comes from God. He describes the law in this positive way in order to help believers appreciate that he is not demeaning it. On the contrary, the sinful state of humanity is not the fault of the law; the real culprit is sin, which renders people unable to keep the law.

The problem is simply this. God gave the law not only to establish that there was a gulf between God and humanity but also to point out its immensity. The law was never intended to be the means of establishing a relationship with God. The concept of a relationship with God, based on the belief that God exists and desires such a relationship, predated the law—as exemplified in the life of Abraham (Gal 3:17–18).

The law was unable to bridge the gulf between God and humanity, and any attempt to keep the law in order to achieve such an aim was, and is, doomed to fail for two reasons: (1) it is impossible to keep the law (and God never expected anyone to be able to do so); (2) even if someone did keep the law, it would not achieve salvation, because salvation is God's gift to helpless humanity and cannot be earned.

For the law of the Spirit of life in Christ Jesus has set me free from the law of sin and death. . . . [he condemned sin in the flesh] in order that the just requirement of the law might be fulfilled in us, who walk not according to the flesh but according to the Spirit. (8:2, 4)

Exposition

In 8:2, 4, Paul again explores the relationship between the law and the Spirit. He uses the term "law" in a number of ways. In 8:2, he says that a new law has set the believer free. He plays on the term "law" to develop the theme, though the word is best understood here as meaning "principle" or "sphere of being." The believer now lives and operates in a different sphere with a different framework for life. The believer has been freed from the power of the law that Paul associates with "sin" and "death." It is not that the law was sinful but that it revealed sin; the law is not identified with death, but it condemns the sinner to death. The believer experiences freedom when the Spirit brings him or her into relationship with God, releasing the believer from the punishment of death for breaking God's laws. This action by the Spirit also guarantees the completion and full realization of that freedom for the believer in the next life.

In 8:4, Paul says that the Spirit enables the believer to fulfill the law. It is not that, with the Spirit, the believer can keep the law better than he or she could without the Spirit's help. Paul has already established that the believer is not to look at the law as that which is to be obeyed; rather, the believer is to obey the Spirit, who is the believer's guide. Paul is not saying that the requirements of the law are to be fulfilled (by obedience) but that those requirements laid down by the law have already been fulfilled in the believer. They have been fulfilled in the sense that believers base their relationship with God on faith that Jesus has done everything necessary. Believers realize that they cannot keep God's laws; rather, they come in faith to receive God's grace and forgiveness and to live in the freedom associated with the Spirit.

Significance for the Original Readers

Paul is speaking to a largely non-Jewish readership who may feel like intruders into what was originally a faith dominated by

Jewish people, whose founder was a Jew who came to minister to the Jews and whose chosen leaders were Jews. These Gentiles probably felt that they lacked the credentials to participate in this faith that was so closely identified with the Jewish culture and beliefs presented in the OT. Paul chooses to use the key marker of Jewish identity (circumcision) to help his audience realize their position as believers. As circumcision set the Jews apart from other nations, so the Spirit now performs a different form of "circumcision" on the hearts of the Gentiles that sets them apart to be included among God's people. God no longer requires physical circumcision. All believers are now admitted to God's family based on the Spirit's circumcision of their hearts—not on something that they themselves do.

As a result, the Spirit provides a relationship with God and empowers believers to lead an increasingly righteous lifestyle. The law, which kept the Jews in a state of bondage, always reminding them of their sin but never enabling them to escape from it, no longer governs the lives of believers. The law has served its purpose and the time has come for the next stage in the plan of salvation: the Spirit comes to live in the believer.

The law demanded holiness; the Spirit makes believers holy by giving them the gift of salvation achieved by Jesus on the cross. The Spirit is thus the alternative to the law and the powerful antidote to the weakness of the will (the flesh [8:3]). Those who walk with the Spirit (i.e., believers) have met God's standard not on their own merits but on the basis of faith in Jesus. They have passed the exam without having to take it. Had they taken it, they would have failed, but God passed them at the cost of the sacrifice of his Son, who passed it for them. It seems unfair, but God has made the rules. The believer's response is a sense of awe, especially because the ongoing requirement to live according to God's standards is made possible by the presence and empowerment of the Spirit within the believer.

The Spirit is the channel for the love of God (5:5; 15:30)

Hope does not disappoint us, because God's love has been poured into our hearts through the Holy Spirit which has been given to us. (5:5)

Exposition

This is the first time that Paul mentions love in Romans, and it is in the context of the Spirit. The Spirit has an important part to play in channeling God's love to believers. Unlike human hope, which sometimes is illusory and unstable, their faith is assured. The proof that believers have not misplaced their faith comes through their experience of the love of God. This love is directed through the Spirit, who takes up residence within them.

The outpouring refers to lavish generosity (cf. Joel 2:28 and Mal 3:10, where God pours out his Spirit and blessings on his people). Paul explains the love of God more as an experience than as an intellectual perception and acknowledgment. The fact that love is located in the believers' hearts further expresses the emotional nature of God's love. Paul expects the believer to feel God's love. The verb translated "has been poured" (*ekkechytai*) is in the perfect tense; in Greek, this tense implies that an act done in the past has ongoing significance. The experience of the love of God, therefore, beginning with salvation, is intended to be an ongoing reality for the believer. Furthermore, it is the Holy Spirit who pours out the love of God in the life of the believer.

I appeal to you, brethren, by our Lord Jesus Christ and by the love of the Spirit, to strive together with me in your prayers to God on my behalf. (15:30)

Exposition

In 15:30, Paul mentions the Spirit for the final time in Romans, again in the context of love. Here, Paul is appealing for united prayer on his behalf. He does this because of the love that the Spirit initiates among believers. It is not love for the Spirit but love motivated by the Spirit that he seeks. Since it is the Spirit's role to stimulate love, he expects to see the believers being prompted by the Spirit to love.

Significance for the Original Readers

The context of the reference to love in 5:5 is one of suffering (5:3). Paul's message to readers here is that the presence of suffering does not indicate an absence of God's love. The Spirit continuously manifests God's love to believers, reminding them that they are in a relationship with God.

The concept of God loving ordinary individuals was an unusual one for the Romans. They had long attempted to maintain a peace with the gods (*pax deorum*) by placating them with rituals, sacrifices, and prayers. They had no expectations of friendliness from the gods, let alone love. In addition, by the time Paul wrote his letter to the Romans, the *pax deorum* focused largely on the protection of the emperor by the gods. It was assumed that ordinary humanity was of little significance to the gods. Nevertheless, many sought for an ecstatic relationship with the gods through the mystery religions[1] of the day or through magical forces.

In this context, Paul's message would take some digesting, and it makes sense that he accompanied promises of God's love with the reflection that the Spirit who resides within them is the guarantee of this amazing truth. Here Paul emphasizes that a loving relationship with God that is based on experience, and not merely on intellectual belief or doctrinal assent, is the norm for believers.

The Spirit opposes the flesh and identifies and empowers believers as God's children (8:5–13)

For those who live according to the flesh set their minds on the things of the flesh, but those who live according to the Spirit set their minds on the things of the Spirit. To set the mind on the flesh is death, but to set the mind on the Spirit is life and peace. For the mind that is set on the flesh is hostile to God; it does not submit to God's law, indeed it cannot; and those who are in the flesh cannot please God. But you are not in the flesh, you are in the Spirit, if in fact the Spirit of God dwells in you. Any one who does not have the Spirit of Christ does not belong to him. But if Christ is in you, although your bodies are dead because of sin, your spirits are alive because of righteousness. If the Spirit of him who raised Jesus from the dead dwells in you, he who raised Christ Jesus from the dead will give life to your mortal bodies also through his Spirit which dwells in you. So then, brethren, we

---

[1] Mystery religions were popular cults in which devotees celebrated the life of a deity and adopted lifestyles related to the principles of the cult. Each religion incorporated beliefs and worship relating to the deity concerned. These religions competed with early Christianity because they met many of the needs of the people, including a personal relationship with a deity, a structure that incorporated a sense of belonging, and a hope for the future as well as a spiritual and practical framework for the present.

are debtors, not to the flesh, to live according to the flesh—for if you live according to the flesh you will die, but if by the Spirit you put to death the deeds of the body you will live.

Exposition

In these verses Paul contrasts the Spirit with the flesh, identifying the incompatibility between the two and the resulting tension. He is not describing an internal struggle in the life of the believer; rather, he is identifying his readers as people of the Spirit and not of the flesh. Thus, the life characterized by the word "flesh" is inappropriate for them. Elsewhere, he has used the term "flesh" to mean human flesh (1:3) and human effort (Gal 3:3). Here, he uses the word to describe a lifestyle that is not influenced by the Spirit. Such a life may be grossly immoral or not, but that is not the issue in focus; a life that is devoid of the Spirit cannot please God (8:8), however moral the person concerned may be. Indeed, whether they realize it or not, such persons are in a state of enmity with God (8:7) because their lives are devoid of the presence, influence, and power of the Spirit.

In 8:5, Paul simply notes that different concerns dominate the contrasting lives. Thus, a life influenced by the Spirit focuses on those aspects of life that are important to the Spirit. The results of the two lifestyles are also different (8:6). A life devoid of the Spirit results in (spiritual) death, while a life lived with the Spirit results in vitality and peace (temporal and eternal).

In 8:9, Paul addresses his readers directly and describes them as being "in the Spirit." He also refers to the fact that "the Spirit of God dwells in" them. These apparently contradictory phrases are to be appreciated not in spatial terms but as metaphors emphasizing the intimacy of the relationship between the believer and the Spirit, initiated by the latter. The fact that this is the first occasion in Romans where Paul refers to the Spirit as being "of God" is significant. It is none other than God who resides within the believer. The sense of privilege and challenge that this fact brings is remarkable. The term "dwells" further indicates Paul's anticipation of a tangible experience of God, beyond acknowledging truths concerning salvation and confessing belief in Jesus. Intimacy of relationship, not merely intellectual response, is what Paul intends when he refers to the Spirit inhabiting the life of the believer.

Paul makes this distinction in order to establish this relationship as proof of being a Christian. The word translated "if" in

8:10–11 may be translated "since," which emphasizes Paul's certainty. Retaining the sense of "if" challenges any of his readers who are not Christians to become Christians. Paul is not casting doubt on whether the Spirit is present in the lives of believers; rather, on the basis of the presence of the Spirit, he establishes their identity and security as children of God. The Spirit is their identifying mark that they are children of God.

Paul emphasizes this security by stating that Christ is also in them, through the Spirit, who is "the Spirit of Christ." This description helps Gentile readers to better appreciate the identity of the Spirit. They were used to the idea of spirits, but it was difficult to identify aspects of the Spirit. Knowing that the Spirit is "of Christ" enables them to understand that as Jesus lived and ministered, so also the Spirit is expected to function. Similarly, Paul identifies for his Jewish readers the Spirit (of God) of the OT who now empowers people as being in partnership with Christ. The Spirit manifests Christ to the believer; believers know Christ through the Spirit. The Spirit is the presence of Christ in the life of the believer.

Paul tells them (8:10) that, although their bodies die because of sin, the Spirit of life is in them, granted as a result of righteousness (bestowed upon them at salvation). On the basis of this fact, Paul encourages readers to realize that their resurrection is affirmed since (rather than "if") the same Spirit who raised Jesus from the dead also guarantees to raise them from the dead. Thus, Paul is confirming their position as believers in the context of eternity. He is not encouraging them to take advantage of the power of the Spirit to improve their lifestyles (he will come to that in 8:12). Here, he focuses on the glory of the position of the believer. The Spirit comes into the life of the believer at salvation and does not leave, but at the death of the believer transforms him or her as Jesus was transformed. The contrast is between death and resurrection, the latter being achieved by the same Spirit who elevated Jesus to his new life at his resurrection. Paul does not explore how this happened; he simply notes that it did happen and that the same awaits the believer. Given this certainty and the lavish provision of the Spirit, Paul reminds readers that because of the presence and the commitment of the Spirit, they must live righteous lives (8:12–13).

Significance for the Original Readers

In these verses Paul describes the Spirit in a number of ways (the Spirit, the Spirit of God, the Spirit of Christ). He is not seeking to confuse his readers or to suggest that there is more than one Spirit. Paul is less interested in explaining the mystery of God and more interested in exploring the role of God—Christ, the Spirit of God, or God—in the believer's life. Roman readers would have been used to the idea that a "divine spirit" resided in every person. With vivid picture language Paul demonstrates the quality of the Spirit residing within believers. Because believers are set apart, they should not exhibit characteristics of a life devoid of the Spirit. Rather, their lives should reflect the presence and influence of the Spirit. Although they are weak due to sin, believers are to continually take advantage of the Spirit's power to reform their lives in accordance with the will of God.

The Spirit affirms adoption for believers (8:14–17)

For all who are led by the Spirit of God are sons of God. For you did not receive the spirit of slavery to fall back into fear, but you have received the spirit of sonship. When we cry, "Abba! Father!" it is the Spirit himself bearing witness with our spirit that we are children of God, and if children, then heirs, heirs of God and fellow heirs with Christ, provided we suffer with him in order that we may also be glorified with him.

Exposition

Paul has been declaring the difference that the Spirit makes in the lives of believers (8:1–13). Now, he explains that the activity of the Spirit results in sonship. The term translated "sonship" is found five times in the NT, all in Paul's letters (Rom 8:15, 23; 9:4; Gal 4:5; Eph 1:5). There is no equivalent term in the OT. This relationship of "sonship" is certain because the Spirit is none other than the Spirit of adoption, who, after coming into the lives of believers, places them in God's presence.[2]

Consequently, Paul encourages believers not to live as if they were slaves, but to enjoy the confidence that comes with being children of the Father (8:15). He also reminds them that the one who arranges this transfer of ownership is not a spirit of slavery Paul uses the concept of "slavery" to refer to this present age (8:19–25), which he contrasts with the eternal life to come. The

---

[2] See commentary on Gal 4:6 in ch. 8.

Spirit beckons believers into the future and enables them to experience it in the present. Paul declares that the Spirit will lead them not into fear but into freedom—not freedom from their responsibilities as children of God but freedom to be children of God.

"Abba! Father!" may be either a cry of joy in response to their relationship with God or a cry in time of need. Regardless of their circumstances, the Spirit continuously affirms believers. Only the Spirit can provide this assurance, because only he knows the mind of God (since he is God).

Believers need a great deal of confidence in order to refer to God as "Abba." This confidence comes from the Spirit, who exerts a direct influence on their minds and emotions, assuring them that they truly are that which they hardly dare to believe: the adopted children of God. The Spirit acts as a reliable friend who affirms that such a relationship is valid and not presumptuous.

Furthermore, believers are to participate in the inheritance that belongs to the children of God. Thus, the word "if" in 8:17 is best translated "since" or "because" ("since children, then heirs, heirs of God"). Paul's description of believers as also being joint heirs with Christ emphasizes that they have been exalted to this position and are able to benefit from the resources of God just as Jesus does. Although they will receive the full benefits of this promise only in the next life, the guarantee is certain because of the quality of the guarantor, the Spirit.

Finally, Paul assumes that Christians are willing to suffer. He exhorts them to consider this suffering in the light of the fact that, as the children of God, they will be glorified with Christ hereafter (cf. 2:7, 10; 5:2; 8:21; 9:23).

Significance for the Original Readers

The concept "children of God" would have struck a familiar chord with Jewish readers. They knew that the OT referred to Jews as being the inheritance of God (Isa 63:17; Jer 10:16). Non-Jewish readers would also have been familiar with the concept because of the spark of divinity that they assumed resided within every person, accounting for one's strengths, talents, and capacity to achieve good. Because of this, they thought, they were children of God. Here, however, Paul applies the concept to believers, with no reference to their pedigree or skill. It is simply a divine act that the Spirit affirms.

Many of the believers would not have been able to easily identify with the positive familial relationships Paul describes because
they came from deprived backgrounds, including slavery (in Rome,
slaves comprised some twenty to thirty percent of the population).
This would have been especially true of the Jews, many of whom
came to Rome as slaves.

Although some believers who were slaves were not able to
leave their servitude, nevertheless Paul affirmed their destiny as
freedom, initiated and guaranteed by the Spirit. Paul encourages
them not to live with their minds so occupied with the present that
they are unable to gaze into the future and recognize that they have
been called to an eternal future. The Spirit resides within them to
affirm them as people whose destinies lay beyond this life on earth.

The promise that the Spirit will not lead them into fear (8:15)
seems strange until we see it in the context of the Jews' constant
fear of displeasing God by breaking his law. Gentile readers were
also familiar with fickle gods who often reacted disproportionately
and arbitrarily to human actions that, whether done inadvertently
or intentionally, displeased them. Paul declares that the Spirit affirms love, not fear, as characterizing God's relationship with believers as his adopted children.

Adoption, as a legal act, was not a Jewish institution, and Paul
is probably referring to Roman adoption. In Roman practice, adoption terminated the relationship to one's biological parents (including the cancellation of any debts). The new father provided the
adopted child with his family name and the promise of an inheritance. Similarly, from the moment that the individual becomes a
believer, he or she becomes an heir of God.

The concept of adoption was particularly significant to Gentile
readers. Adopted children enjoyed an exalted relationship with a
father, equaled only by that of biological children. Adoptees were
released from previous relationships, welcomed into a new family,
and legally protected in their new relationship. In addition to these
promises, when God adopts believers, he places himself in the
vulnerable position of being open to being hurt and even rejected
by his children.

Believers must consider suffering in the context of adoption.
Paul is not declaring that believers must suffer in order to receive
their adoption. Rather, he is reflecting on the fact that while his
readers may well suffer for their faith (Nero's persecution of Christians, in 64 C.E., was only a few years away), in doing so they will
follow in the footsteps of their Savior. This is only the preface to a

life characterized by glory. Present sufferings do not undermine their right to be called children of God. God determines adoption, and the Spirit assures it, for believers to enjoy eternally.

The Spirit is the "firstfruits" for believers (8:23)

Not only the creation, but we ourselves, who have the first fruits of the Spirit, groan inwardly as we wait for adoption as sons, the redemption of our bodies.

Exposition

Paul introduces this verse by establishing that creation looks forward to being released from the bondage imposed by sin (8:18–22). This provides the background for understanding that God will also release believers and reveal the destiny he has predetermined for them. In the context of final redemption, Paul describes believers as having the "firstfruits," identified as the Holy Spirit. The term "firstfruits" regularly referred, in a sacrificial sense, to the first of the flock or the first of the fruits of the harvest that worshippers gave to God (Exod 23:19; Lev 2:14). Here, Paul uses the term to describe a down payment or guarantee of something to come. The gift of the Spirit is the foretaste of what is to come.

Significance for the Original Readers

We need to interpret the metaphor "firstfruits" carefully. The reference does not indicate that the believer receives only part of the Spirit at salvation. Rather, Paul is emphasizing the significance of salvation and, in particular, establishing that it is not restricted to life before death. On the contrary, death is the gateway into life as it was intended to be. Although believers will experience full redemption only in the next life, the guarantee of that experience is the presence of the Spirit in the present. The Spirit provides a glimpse and an insight into the life that believers will know in its fullness when the resurrection occurs. The Spirit is a flavor, a whisper, a breath of what is to come.

The Spirit prays for believers (8:26–27)

Likewise the Spirit helps us in our weakness; for we do not know how to pray as we ought, but the Spirit himself intercedes for us with sighs too deep for words. And he who searches the hearts of men knows what is the mind of the Spirit, because the Spirit intercedes for the saints according to the will of God.

Exposition

Paul develops the theme of weakness by commenting on the weakness of believers with regard to prayer. He does this not simply to emphasize the weakness of believers, but rather to demonstrate the commitment of the Spirit, who undertakes to provide complete freedom in the next life as well as resources to compensate for the weakness of believers in the present. The prayer here may refer to the weakness of believers living in this present age, which demands constant prayer, or to a particular situation in which one may be uncertain how to pray. Paul is not suggesting that the Spirit will ensure that God will always answer the prayers of believers according to their desires, though he may be suggesting that the Spirit will provide wisdom with regard to how one should pray.

More important is the fundamental recognition that the Spirit is doing something *for* believers. Recognizing the weakness of believers, the Spirit operates on their behalf. Rather than emphasizing that the Spirit helps the believer so that together they can achieve a particular aim, this fact undergirds the Spirit's lavish commitment to the believer.

The term used in 8:26 to describe the response of the Spirit, "intercede" (*hyperentynchano*), occurs nowhere else in the Bible, although a similar verb (*entynchano*) means "to obtain an audience with" or "to appeal to" (Acts 25:24; Rom 8:27, 34). Here, the term's prefix (*hyper-*) emphasizes the intensity of the help that the Spirit offers.

The form that help takes is prayer. We must not lose the principle of this truth in an attempt to unravel the mystery of how it is that the Spirit, who is God, can pray. To whom is the Spirit praying? Can the Spirit pray to himself? We need to carefully unwrap the image of the Spirit praying. Paul is declaring a truth that is precious and therefore to be appropriated, but it is also a mystery and therefore cannot be completely understood (although certainly it should be explored intellectually and experientially). The picture is of the Spirit, who is God, relating so intimately to believers that for a moment it is as if he is closer to them than to God. However, since he is God, his support of believers will always be successful, enabling him to pray for them.

Significance for the Original Readers

Some interpreters maintain that Paul is describing the opportunity for believers to speak in tongues (glossolalia). Thus, the believer prays in tongues, assuming that the utterance in tongues articulates the desire of the individual (1 Cor 14:14–15). The problem with this view is that it assumes that all believers have received the gift of tongues, which is not reflected elsewhere in Paul's writings (1 Cor 12:30). Neither is there any evidence in the NT that the Spirit operates through the gift of tongues, although tongues are viewed as a prayer/praise language (1 Cor 14:2, 14). This interpretation would also imply that the Spirit acts on the believer's behalf only when he or she is speaking in tongues. The text does not reflect this limitation of the Spirit's advocacy.

The term translated "too deep for words" (*alaletos*) is significant. It may be translated "without words" or "unable to be expressed." Paul may, therefore, not be seeking to identify the Spirit's intercession on behalf of believers. Rather, he may simply be clarifying that the Spirit is interceding and that believers may depend on the sincerity and meaning of his intercession, even though they may not hear it. It may be silent, but the Spirit's intercession taps at the very heart of the issue and expresses the most complete advocacy on behalf of believers. The significance of the Spirit's involvement is that he will seek to ensure that God's will is enacted. This is a foregone conclusion, since the Spirit is God.

The Spirit empowers the believer (14:17; 15:13, 16, 18–19)

This group of verses is subdivided into three sections, each of which identifies a different element of the Spirit's empowerment: (1) to change and be changed, (2) to hope, and (3) to achieve signs and wonders.

For the kingdom of God is not food and drink but righteousness and peace and joy in the Holy Spirit. (14:17)

[Because of the grace given me by God] to be a minister of Christ Jesus to the Gentiles in the priestly service of the gospel of God, so that the offering of the Gentiles may be acceptable, sanctified by the Holy Spirit. (15:16)

Exposition

To Change and Be Changed

The larger context of 14:17 (vv. 14–23) concerns the issue of eating certain foods. It appears that some Gentile believers allowed their perceptions of freedom to drift, if not into license, then into unwise insensitivity. Some Jewish believers who were overly sensitive about dietary and calendrical matters (14:5) misunderstood their actions and were offended and even scandalized by their behavior (14:13).

Paul encourages them to exercise their freedom (14:13–16), but to do so cautiously and sensitively. He graphically puts things in perspective by reminding them of the core values of the kingdom of God as reflected in the Spirit. Those are the issues that determine a life pleasing to the Lord (14:18). What matters is not so much adherence to rules as developing relationships with one another. If believers live with the Spirit as their guide, they will display characteristics that reflect the kingdom.

Though Paul usually uses the term "righteousness" to describe the state of acceptance that God grants at salvation, here he refers to a morally upright lifestyle. He anticipates that a person influenced by the Spirit will live a righteous life and demonstrate peace and joy. These are natural fruits of the Spirit in the lives of the believers.

Having identified the Gentile believers as those whom God has set apart by his grace to be members of his family, Paul mentions a secondary role of the Spirit in 15:16—to empower them to live according to the standards of that family. Having set them apart, he enables them to live in a way that is different from that of their unbelieving peers.

This verse is found in a passage that reminds readers of the valid place that Gentiles have in the family of God (15:8–18). The evidence of this is that the Holy Spirit has sanctified them (set them apart). In particular, Paul describes the Spirit making the Gentiles an acceptable "offering" to God. For the Jewish audience in particular, this description denotes the acceptability of the Gentiles to God, for the law demanded that offerings to God be pure. If the Gentiles are an offering acceptable to God, it must be because God himself has declared them acceptable. God now brings Gentiles, who were not allowed any closer than the court of the Gentiles in the temple area (Acts 21:28), in and incorporates them as a pure offering (Rom 12:1).

May the God of hope fill you with all joy and peace in believing, so that by the power of the Holy Spirit you may abound in hope. (15:13)

Exposition

To Hope

This text relates to Paul's encouraging Jewish and Gentile believers to accept each other as valid members of the family of God (15:7). As other passages in the NT reflect, the potential for disharmony between Jewish and Gentile believers was ever present and often related to lifestyle as well as to the controversy over God allowing non-Jews to receive his mercy and love. Paul therefore prefaces the prayer in 15:13 with four OT texts that promise that Gentiles will share in God's promises. As a result of these promises and the presence of the Spirit in their lives, the Spirit's power will exhilarate believers. The word translated "abound" (*perisseuo*) expresses abundance to the point of excess.

For I will not venture to speak of anything except what Christ has wrought through me to win obedience from the Gentiles, by word and deed, by the power of signs and wonders, by the power of the Holy Spirit, so that from Jerusalem and as far round as Illyricum I have fully preached the gospel of Christ. (15:18–19)

Exposition

To Achieve Signs and Wonders

In 15:13, Paul anticipates the power of the Spirit leading to a surge of confidence. In 15:18–19, he associates the Spirit with an expectation of signs and wonders in the context of evangelism. Paul writes of the combined role of Christ and the Spirit. On the surface, it appears that Christ achieves what is necessary to bring faith to the Gentiles through the power of the Spirit. Rather than trying to extricate the ministry of Christ from that of the Spirit, however, it is better to appreciate why Paul writes what he does. The work of Christ and the work of the Spirit are interdependent, and it is unnecessary to separate them into mutually exclusive areas of ministry. Paul mentions both in order to show readers that Christ, who lives in heaven, is not absent from their evangelism (or from other aspects of their lives). Christ is present by the Spirit, who lives among them in community because he dwells in them as individuals.

Significance for the Original Readers

Like Paul, Paul's readers were aware of the privileges that came with being a Roman citizen (Acts 16:37–38; 22:25–29). Roman citizenship enabled them to own property, get married, have legitimate children, and make wills, and it also protected them from certain punishments. When Paul declares that believers are set apart to be citizens of God's kingdom, the implications are clear. However, the privilege of such citizenship also brought with it significant challenges.

The Spirit, who has set them apart, has the capacity to make them practically holy. Believers, with the help of "the Spirit of holiness," are to develop a lifestyle different from that of those around them. Just as the lifestyle of the Jews who were obedient to the law set them apart from the surrounding nations, so also the Roman believers, influenced by the Spirit, are to be living testimonies to God in their world.

It is characteristics inspired by the Spirit that will influence the secular society in which they live. Those with true liberty demonstrate a readiness to love while helping to correct behavior in the context of fellowship with other believers. Paul continues to reveal here the integral role of the Spirit in empowering believers to exhibit characteristics of the kingdom in their lives.

The theme of hope, based on the power of the Spirit to inspire believers, dominates Paul's prayerful benediction in 15:13. We need to understand the term "hope" in its Jewish context. Gentile usage of the word in contemporary society identified hope with uncertainty, fear, and insecurity. The Jewish use of the word identified it with certainty, confidence, and assurance (4:18). The presence of the Holy Spirit in believers' lives is the guarantee that this hope will be realized.

Finally, Paul encourages his readers to realize that just as Jesus manifested signs and wonders when preaching the message of the kingdom, so also they have the authority, through the Spirit, to achieve signs and wonders in the proclamation of the gospel.

Selected Bibliography

Cranfield, Charles E. B. *A Critical and Exegetical Commentary on the Epistle to the Romans.* 2 vols. 6th ed. International Critical Commentary. Edinburgh: T&T Clark, 1975–1979.

Dunn, James D. G. *Romans*. 2 vols. Word Biblical Commentary 38A, 38B. Dallas: Word, 1988.

Fee, Gordon D. *God's Empowering Presence: The Holy Spirit in the Letters of Paul*. Peabody, Mass.: Hendrickson, 1994.

Moo, Douglas J. *The Epistle to the Romans*. Grand Rapids: Eerdmans, 1996.

The Significance for Readers Today

1. What are some implications of the Spirit setting you apart for God (1:4)?
2. What gifts that God has given you can you use today (1:11; 12:6–8)?
3. In what ways has the Spirit set you free (2:29; 7:6, 14; 8:2, 4)?
4. What is the evidence of God's love for you (5:5; 15:30)?
5. In what areas do you need the Spirit's help to reform your lifestyle so that it reflects godly characteristics (8:5–13)?
6. What are the implications of the fact that you have been adopted into God's family (8:14–17)?
7. What are the consequences of the Spirit being the "firstfruits" in your life (8:23)?
8. How does the Spirit's praying for believers relate to you (8:26–27)?
9. What practical results can you expect from the Spirit's empowerment (14:17; 15:13, 16, 18–19)?

chapter 6

*1 C*orinthians

The Setting

The church at Corinth was established on Paul's second missionary journey. Corinth was an ancient city rebuilt as a Roman colony after its destruction by the Romans following a rebellion in 146 B.C.E. People from many different cultures lived there, and it grew to be one of the wealthiest cities in the empire, boasting the most ornate theaters, palaces, and temples. Its wealth came from pottery and brass industries and the commercial activities of its ports. It became a military base, controlling the land and sea routes, and it was popular with the emperors as an alternative home to Rome.

Paul was there for eighteen months (Acts 18:1–18) with Aquila, Priscilla, Silas, and Timothy. Opposition from the Jews was strong and resulted in Paul being brought before the Roman tribunal. Fanatical Jews beat Sosthenes, the leader of the synagogue, after the case collapsed. The congregation appears to have been a mixture of Jews and Gentiles (1:22–24; 7:18), most of whom were poor and uneducated (1:26–29), with a few wealthy folk (1:11, 14) but also some slaves (7:21–23).

What Does the Author Say about the Spirit?

The first letter to the Corinthians contains a great deal of information relating to the Spirit, much of it concerning what the Spirit does through believers rather than for them.

The Spirit

- provides gifts (1:7; 12:4–7, 11, 27–31; 14:1, 12)
- empowers the believer (2:4)

- reveals wisdom (2:10–15; 7:40)

- creates a corporate body (3:16–17)

- is involved in the salvation of believers (6:11; 12:3, 13)

- inhabits a believer's body (6:19–20)

The Spirit provides gifts (1:7; 12:4–7, 11, 27–31; 14:1, 12)

So that you are not lacking in any spiritual gift, as you wait for the revealing of our Lord Jesus Christ. (1:7)

Exposition

The term translated "spiritual gift" is *charisma*. This, the first use of this term in 1 Corinthians, is important in terms of helping readers to understand supernatural phenomena. Paul wants them to recognize that any ability they have is a gift, and indeed the word *charisma* derives from the verb *charizomai,* which means "give, grant, bestow upon." These are gifts of grace granted to the undeserving; they are not rewards or rights. Therefore, it is expected that the recipients in turn will administer these gifts gracefully, graciously, and for the benefit of others.

Given the charismatic chaos in Corinth, it is unlikely that Paul is congratulating them concerning their possession and use of these gifts. Furthermore, it is improbable that he is being ironic in his use of language; the perversity of the Corinthians was such that they probably would not have identified irony, but would more likely have assumed that Paul was affirming them in their giftedness. He defines their potential as believers to function with gifts of the Spirit, having already noted the gifts at which they excel: speech and knowledge (1:5). The latter is something of a backhanded compliment, given that other gifts with more beneficial consequences for the community of believers are missing. Nevertheless, in what will be a corrective list of their many irregularities in belief and practice, Paul concentrates on the positive things that he finds in the church before he moves on to deal with the negative.

Finally, Paul places the gifts in the context of the era that is waiting for the return of Jesus. Many of the Corinthians probably assumed that their gifts indicated that the return of Jesus was imminent or even that in some mystical way the end had already occurred, that the final consummation was close at hand. Paul clarifies that these gifts are for the present era, not the life to come.

Significance for the Original Readers

Paul has much to say by way of correcting and guiding his readers, some of which results in sobering reading. Before he begins to deal with some of the major problems in the church, he thanks God for these believers and for the potential that lies within them (1:4–7). Paul tells them that their gifts do not result from their progress as believers. They have no reason to boast or assume superiority over others as if they had deserved these gifts. God has provided them with gifts because of his graciousness, not because of their worthiness (1:4).

Paul is careful not to marginalize or disappoint his readers too quickly. Many of them had come from deprived settings, from the lower socioeconomic strata of society (1:26–29). They were not accustomed to having anything that would have given them prestige and self-worth. He is mindful of the need not to destabilize them, while at the same time he realizes that if they too quickly assume reasons for their gifts that will lead to pride, the church will descend into selfish disharmony.

Now there are varieties of gifts, but the same Spirit; and there are varieties of service, but the same Lord; and there are varieties of working, but it is the same God who inspires them all in every one. To each is given the manifestation of the Spirit for the common good. . . . All these are inspired by one and the same Spirit, who apportions to each one individually as he wills. (12:4–7, 11)

Exposition

These verses commence a long section that explores the role of gifts in the Christian community. Before Paul identifies specific gifts, he establishes a number of basic principles essential to the correct use of the gifts. Again, the word he uses for "gift" is *charisma*. To reinforce that he is describing donations that God generously supplies to the church, not rewards that believers deserve, he incorporates a number of clarifications and explanations in these verses.

- He associates the gifts with the words "service" (12:5) and "working" (12:6). Gifts are not for personal or selfish use. They are for the purposes of service and working for the benefit of others.

- Each member of the Godhead is involved in giving the gifts to the church (12:4–6). The Spirit, the Lord (Jesus), and God (the Father) all participate in delegating gifts to the church.

- Every believer is gifted (12:6–7, 11). Some may receive a permanent capacity to function in a particular way. It is possible for anyone to have any gift, depending on the sovereign design of God, who delegates the gifts when and to whom he wishes.

- The gifts are manifested according to the will of the Spirit (12:7, 11). Paul is not necessarily assuming that this is the sole responsibility of the Spirit, thereby separating the members of the Godhead so functionally. Nevertheless, given the specific role of the Spirit in the life of the church and the individual believer, it makes sense that the focus in the distribution of gifts is on the Spirit.

- The gifts are varied (12:4–6). Paul lists the various gifts in 12:8–10 (see also Rom 12:6–8; Eph 4:11; 1 Cor 12:28; cf. 13:1–3; 14:6, 26). He does not intend any of these lists to be comprehensive; rather, they are representative (cf. 7:7, which refers to the gifts of celibacy and marriage). These lists demonstrate the diversity of gifts available to believers.

- God grants the gifts for the benefit of the group (12:7). Believers are to use them selflessly, not selfishly; for the benefit of others, not for personal gain.

Significance for the Original Readers

Many of the people in the church were poor, and some were slaves. Although it is difficult to ascertain the number of inhabitants of Corinth (the population must have been in the low hundreds of thousands), there were more slaves than free citizens. Many of these slaves were treated poorly by others, even by fellow slaves. People who were used to being treated this way would not automatically assume that God would give them a supernatural

gift. Paul's perspective is that, in God's design, all are equal benefi-
ciaries of God's gracious activity.

The fact that the gifts are provided freely by God, their diversity, and the emphases in usage contrast sharply with the selfish-
ness and individuality among the believers. It appears that some of
the believers were boasting because of their gifts (4:6–7), and so
Paul reminds them of the fundamental nature of the church. The
church is to function corporately, as individuals take responsibility
for the welfare of one another. If they fail to recognize that they
are a loving body of believers, they will fail to exist as a church, for
the privilege of being part of the Christian community carries with
it the responsibility of living in harmony. The information in these
verses concerning the use of the gifts is intended to help them recognize the incongruity of administering the gifts selfishly without
appreciating the reason why they were given in the first place.

Paul is asserting not uniformity within the church, but rather
harmony in diversity; not individuality, but a dynamic relationship
with the Spirit resulting in deep relationships among the members.
The fact that the Spirit gives these gifts should increase the sense
of responsibility among those who administer them. This fact
should also compel them to administer the gifts in keeping with
the nature of the one who gives the gifts. At the same time, Paul
encourages them to see that no believer need wait forlornly, assuming that the Spirit has not given him or her a gift. Indeed, Paul
explicitly states the opposite. Individual believers, within the community of the church, are responsible to help identify gifts received, to use their own gifts effectively in the community, and to
encourage others to use their gifts as well.

*Now you are the body of Christ and individually members of
it. And God has appointed in the church first apostles, second
prophets, third teachers, then workers of miracles, then healers,
helpers, administrators, speakers in various kinds of tongues. Are
all apostles? Are all prophets? Are all teachers? Do all work miracles?
Do all possess gifts of healing? Do all speak with tongues? Do all interpret? But earnestly desire the higher gifts. And I will show you a
still more excellent way. (12:27–31)*

Exposition

These verses contain a second, though slightly different, list of
gifts in the same chapter. The identity of the gifts and the fact that

some of them are different from those Paul mentioned earlier are not central issues. The chapter began by stating that there are many gifts; it ends with the recognition that they are diversely distributed. Specifically, Paul notes that not all believers should expect to receive any particular gift.

The answer to all of the questions that Paul asks is no. There is no need for anyone to feel deficient because he or she does not function in one of the gifts in particular. As he demonstrated earlier, the Spirit sovereignly distributes the gifts. Therefore, the absence of any particular gift in a believer is not due to some fault in the individual concerned; rather, it is according to the will of God. Paul's focus is not on the particular gifts he mentions here or even on their diversity; rather, his point is about the diversity of distribution.

Three other issues demand attention. The first relates to the imperative "earnestly desire the higher gifts" (12:31). It is possible to translate this phrase as an affirmation of their current practice: "you are earnestly desiring the higher gifts." However, this translation is unlikely because there is no evidence that this is what the Corinthians were doing. It is more likely that Paul is encouraging them to earnestly desire the greater gifts, and the present tense of the verb indicates that they should continuously be striving in this direction.

The second issue relates to the identity of higher, or greater, gifts—what are they? Paul provides an immediate answer when he says that he will demonstrate a more excellent way. He then launches into a description of love as the superlative way of demonstrating the presence of God in one's life. However, it is also possible that the factor that determines whether one gift is higher than another relates to how beneficial the gift is for others in the community. Thus, after he sets the gifts in the perspective of love, he illustrates his point by contrasting uninterpreted tongues with intelligible prophecy (chs. 13–14). Whereas the former benefits no one other than the speaker, the latter benefits everyone who hears it. In that equation, prophecy is the higher gift because it benefits the community, while tongues without interpretation does not. Paul is not seeking to establish a hierarchy of gifts, for all of them, as gifts of God, are intrinsically equal. Rather, he identifies the important underlying principle that believers need to administer the gifts for the greater good of the community. When believers follow this principle, the gifts are highly beneficial.

The third question to consider is whether 12:28 indicates a hierarchy of gifts. This appears not to be the case. Although the gift of miracles precedes the gift of healing in this list, the opposite is true in 12:9–10. Paul presents the first three items in the list in 12:28, however, in a hierarchical manner. They retain the same order in Eph 4:11 (though evangelists and pastors are placed between prophets and teachers). It is possible that Paul is affirming the fact that these gifts have particular importance in the development of the church.

What is of central importance is that God distributes gifts, as he pleases, to different people for the benefit of the church. It is this mutual interdependency and diversity that Paul celebrates.

Significance for the Original Readers

Although the church in Corinth was not very large numerically, clearly it contained a number of dominant individuals (4:6; 8:1–13; 11:21), and division was rife (1:10–13; 3:3, 21; 6:1–6). The preceding section (12:12–26) deals with issues of appreciation and sensitivity among the members. Here, Paul focuses on how believers are to apply these qualities in the area of gifts. It appears that some had been attempting to manipulate others into believing that all should function in one or more of the gifts, no doubt leading to pride on the one hand and guilt and insecurity on the other. Paul's assessment is clear. The gifts of God are for all. He is not saying that God may never use some believers in a particular way, but rather that they need not feel marginalized if they are not, since the decision is God's. Insofar as they are able, they are to focus on expressing their gifts in the best way possible, especially for the benefit of others.

Paul contends that no one should expect to function in any gift other than that which God has given him or her. Diversity, not uniformity, is the norm of the Spirit.

Finally, believers need to understand Paul's encouragement to seek the better gifts in the context of his stress on the fact that the Spirit bestows gifts; it is not up to the individual to obtain them. As we have seen, too, there is little to suggest a hierarchy of gifts. He is not even suggesting that tongues is an insignificant or the least important gift. All gifts are important. Paul's central point here refers back to what he mentioned in 12:7, a concern that underlies much of the letter: the need for harmony and fellowship in the church. A lack of corporate responsibility has caused many of the church's problems, and he returns to this underlying issue with reference to the use of spiritual gifts in the church. Thus, believers must always use their gifts for the edification or the benefit of others. In doing so, they demonstrate a higher, better use of the gifts. The context for this superior form of the administration of one's gifts is the way of love. If believers are using their gifts in love, they will be using their gifts in the best way possible.

Make love your aim, and earnestly desire the spiritual gifts, especially that you may prophesy. (14:1)

. . . since you are eager for manifestations of the Spirit, strive to excel in building up the church. (14:12)

Exposition

The word translated "spiritual gifts" in 14:1 is *pneumatika,* a substantive adjective meaning "spiritual, pertaining to the spirit." Although the word "gift" is technically not part of the Greek word, given that the following verses describe the operation of two of the gifts, "spiritual gifts" is a suitable rendering. Paul probably intends, however, to place the emphasis on the Spirit, not the gifts. Thus, he encourages the believers to focus on the Spirit's agenda in developing the church. When Paul concluded his discussion on the gifts as provisions of God in 12:31, he referred to them as *charismata.* He probably uses the different term here to change the emphasis. While in the previous context he was concentrating on the gifts of the Spirit, here he is concentrating on the Spirit of the gifts, who manifests himself through his gifts. In order to reflect the Spirit faithfully, recipients need to exercise their gifts according to his principles, as outlined in the guidelines following this introduction in 14:1.

In 14:12, the translation of *pneumaton* as "manifestations of the Spirit" places the emphasis on the Spirit's activities rather than on the Spirit himself. Although it is difficult to separate the person of the Spirit from his work, it is helpful to be aware of the possibility that Paul is seeking to maintain a nuanced emphasis on the Spirit who acts rather than on the acts of the Spirit.

Significance for the Original Readers

The Corinthians have regularly missed the Spirit in their zeal to receive his gifts. Consequently, when they have used the gifts of the Spirit, they often have failed to reflect the Spirit. Instead, they have mocked the Spirit by their egocentric and selfish behavior. Paul encourages them to maintain their zeal but to harness it and direct it toward fulfilling the wishes of the Spirit. The Spirit provides gifts for the Christian community, but believers need to recognize that those gifts function most appropriately, and only achieve their objective of edifying the church, when the individuals concerned allow the Spirit of the gifts to work through them.

The Spirit has determined the objective of building up the church and has established his agenda of using believers to accomplish it. However, the Corinthians have shut the Spirit out of the development of that plan, instead instituting their own models of behavior and initiating their own programs. In particular, this chapter reveals that they have decided that speaking in tongues suits their selfish purposes. Paul argues that they will best accomplish the purpose set by the Spirit—strengthening the church—by the gift of prophecy. As always, the Spirit knows best, and believers need to learn this lesson.

The Spirit empowers the believer (2:4)

My speech and my message were not in plausible words of wisdom, but in demonstration of the Spirit and of power.

Exposition

The first specific reference to the Spirit in 1 Corinthians is found in the context of power and proclamation. It appears from what Paul has written in 1:17–31 and later in the letter that the believers are allowing themselves to be dominated by the belief that they should achieve the goal, regardless of the cost, of being wise. The prevailing mind-set of the first century would have encouraged them in this regard.

In response, Paul declares that he too operates in wisdom (1:18–25; 2:6–16). But this wisdom is radically different from that of the secular world. Paul also proclaims that he functions in power that is evidence of, and demonstrated by, the Spirit. Thus, although his preaching style and content may not have met secular expectations with regard to oratory and philosophical content, his preaching, nevertheless, is associated with a power that reveals the presence of the Spirit.

It is not a simple matter to identify the results of the manifestation of the power of the Spirit; the word "demonstration" (*apo-*

deixis) is used only here in the NT, which makes it difficult to be certain of its meaning. It is possible that Paul is referring to miracles of healing and/or exorcism; both happened in his evangelistic missions. He is probably referring to the power demonstrated in the Corinthians' believing the gospel, despite its "foolish" contents (1:18), its "foolish" recipients (1:27), and its poor presentation (2:2–4). The Spirit demonstrates his power in human weakness; it is this that distinguishes Paul's message and God's salvation from secular philosophies.

Significance for the Original Readers

In the Greco-Roman world, education was largely for the rich, who paid fees for education at home, with tutors, or in a private school. Romans highly valued practical subjects for study—pragmatism, not philosophy. They saw education as a means of preparing children for the practicalities of life. For the Greeks, however, education was more about broadening the mind, exploring truth, and questioning absolute certainties. Philosophy was the noblest subject, and they investigated issues of life and death, values and beliefs, and God and suffering. Education was a journey to be enjoyed, with detours along the way to gather more information. It is this Greek understanding of wisdom, which placed less emphasis on practicality and more emphasis on philosophy, that influenced the Corinthians.

Paul refuses to employ the style of philosophers, to engage in speculation, or to preach in an erudite way that may in itself have convinced people of the truthfulness of his message. Instead, while not dismissing the value of carefully teaching the gospel, he relies on another source of conviction: the Spirit. It is the activity of the Spirit, convicting and convincing those who listen to Paul's message, that results in their coming to faith in Christ. No secular wisdom can compete against that kind of powerful conviction and empowerment. That is Paul's aim, as he reveals in 2:5: Their faith must rest not on human wisdom but on the power of God.

The Spirit reveals wisdom (2:10–15; 7:40)

. . . God has revealed to us through the Spirit. For the Spirit searches everything, even the depths of God. For what person knows a man's thoughts except the spirit of the man which is in him? So also no one

comprehends the thoughts of God except the Spirit of God. Now we have received not the spirit of the world, but the Spirit which is from God, that we might understand the gifts bestowed on us by God. And we impart this in words not taught by human wisdom but taught by the Spirit, interpreting spiritual truths to those who possess the Spirit. The unspiritual man does not receive the gifts of the Spirit of God, for they are folly to him, and he is not able to understand them because they are spiritually discerned. The spiritual man judges all things, but is himself to be judged by no one. (2:10–15)

But in my judgment she is happier if she remains as she is. And I think that I have the Spirit of God. (7:40)

Exposition

In these passages Paul again is combating the pervasive suggestion that the wisdom undergirding the message of the gospel is insubstantial and inferior to the framework that the Corinthians employ for determining wisdom. The features of the Corinthians' wisdom are not clear, but Paul calls it "a wisdom of this age or of the rulers of this age" (2:6), which would indicate that it is either a secular form of reasoning or one influenced by forces antagonistic to God, whether human or demonic. Adherents of this wisdom probably saw the message of the gospel as primitive or quaint, sincere but not sophisticated, and lacking in intellectual challenge and maturity—not just simple, but simplistic. In contrast, the Corinthians saw their own wisdom as refined and cultured, polished and fashionable.

Paul provides an alternative and distinctive wisdom, the fundamental difference being its source—the Spirit. Thus, 2:10 does not record the details of his wisdom, but simply that the Spirit has revealed it—that is what matters. Because the Spirit is the fountain of wisdom, Paul does not need to specify its contents to establish that his wisdom is supreme. His wisdom is of a different quality; it is derived from the Spirit.

Unbelievers cannot understand or receive the wisdom of the Spirit (2:14), though believers are able to appreciate its value and live by it (2:6–9, 13, 15) because the Spirit who imparts the wisdom resides within them (2:12). This wisdom determines the plans arranged by God. God's wisdom is unimaginable (2:9), benefits those who love him (2:9), and was a mystery for a long time until he revealed it through his Spirit (2:7, 10). Because this wisdom is divine, it is therefore, by definition, superior to human thought.

Paul's description of imparting wisdom to believers is set within the context of Jesus (2:2, 16b), the Spirit, and God. Rather than attempting to ascribe individual responsibilities to members of the Godhead in the transmission of wisdom, it is better to recognize that Paul's focus is on the divine interaction with the human in the message of the gospel. The members of the Godhead function interdependently and harmoniously to delegate divine wisdom to the church. The crucial issue for Paul is that, in contrast to any other human form of wisdom, the wisdom of God is of a different order and belongs uniquely to God.

The message of the gospel is that this exceptional wisdom has conceived the plan of salvation for humankind. Furthermore, the Spirit has dedicated himself to transmit this wisdom—the gospel and all it contains—continuously to believers and to enable them to understand some of its mysteries. One example of the wisdom that the Spirit imparts is found in 7:40, with regard to the possibility of remarriage for widows. Paul's suggestion is that they should stay single—a conclusion that he believes the Spirit has prompted. As with many other life issues, there was no specific guidance regarding this particular question in the OT. It is in this respect that the Spirit's involvement in a believer's life is unique. In situations in which the text does not provide specific divine guidance, Paul anticipates that the Spirit can still offer direction.

Significance for the Original Readers

It was commonly said that one could not walk down a street in Corinth without bumping into a philosopher. Many schools of philosophy were based in the city, and a highlight of any day was to listen to an orator presenting a lecture according to the ancient rules of rhetoric or to a philosopher expounding a belief. People enjoyed theorizing and discussing issues and beliefs. It was part of the entertainment and culture of the day. It is with this background in mind that Paul responds to the clamor by the Christians for a gospel that they can bring into the ideological setting of Corinth.

Paul, however, while accepting the notion that his message is based on wisdom, does not countenance the possibility that his wisdom can be compared with others. Indeed, his emphasis on the facts that it comes from the Spirit and is available only to believers isolates it from all other wisdom. The believers have the

Spirit available to them. The Spirit not only introduces them to God's wisdom in the form of the gospel, but also provides himself as the inexhaustible source of wisdom for all areas of life. The implications of this are remarkable. The one whose wisdom is inexhaustible is present in the life of the believer to provide direction and to facilitate growth. The tragedy was that the Corinthians were not achieving this potential, since they did not take advantage of the Spirit and his wisdom. Seeing this situation, Paul described them as people living as if the Spirit did not exist or, worse, living in opposition to the guidelines offered by the Spirit (3:1, 3). The wisdom of the Spirit was available to them, but they tried to develop their own wisdom.

The Spirit creates a corporate body (3:16–17)

Do you not know that you are God's temple and that God's Spirit dwells in you? If any one destroys God's temple, God will destroy him. For God's temple is holy, and that temple you are.

Exposition

Paul uses the image of a temple here and in 6:19 (cf. Eph 2:21–22). The context here relates to the development of the church that Paul established in Corinth. His plea is that it be built carefully (3:10), on the foundation of the person and mission of Jesus (3:11), and with integrity (3:12–15). In his final exhortation on this matter he identifies the church in Corinth as God's temple, in which the Spirit dwells. Anyone involved in the development of the church, therefore, must be sensitive and conscientious. Paul writes these words not so much to encourage his readers regarding their association with the Spirit as to remind them of the implications of that relationship. Paul uses the introductory phrase "Do you not know that . . ." elsewhere when he has strong words to say (5:6; 6:2, 3, 9, 15–16, 19).

The word for "temple" here, *naos*, often refers to the innermost part of the temple, the holy of holies (as opposed to the temple precincts, for which a different term, *hieron*, is often used, as in 1 Cor 9:13). In the OT, God dwelled in the temple; now, the Spirit is said to dwell in the community of believers, the church. In English, the word "you" can be either singular or plural; we can see the force of Paul's declaration more clearly by looking at where the Greek indicates the plural "you": "Do you [pl.] not know that you [pl.] are God's temple and that God's Spirit dwells in you [pl.]? If any one destroys God's temple, God will destroy him. For God's temple is holy, and that temple you [pl.] are."

Paul is not stating here that the Spirit indwells every believer, though he does affirm that elsewhere. The significant point here is that believers, as a community, comprise a dwelling place of God. Together they form a temple in which the Spirit dwells; they are not individual temples of the Spirit. This means that they cannot exist as if other believers do not matter. Each person has an important part to play in the corporate community, and they best reflect the Spirit when they all live in harmony and unity. Similarly, they cannot live as if their actions do not matter to the Christian community. Not only do they need to bear reputable witness to the secular community, but they also need to remember that the church is a mystical entity, a sacred society, an association of the Spirit. Private actions, whether good or evil, may make waves throughout the church. Finally, believers cannot live as if their actions do not matter to God. Paul concludes by noting that negative activity toward the church, God's temple, will result in serious consequences from God: destruction. While he does not give specifics of such destruction, the warning is forthright.

Significance for the Original Readers

Corinth was home to a number of temples. In addition to the temples to the emperors, to Asclepius the healing god, to Melicertes the god of sailors, and dozens of shrines, there were two temples that dominated the city. The temple to Aphrodite, the goddess of love, sat atop a mountain called the Acrocorinth, which overlooked the city, while the temple to Apollo stood just meters away from the shops and marketplace. Both temples provided opportunities to indulge in heterosexual and homosexual activity with the priestesses and priests, as participants believed they were engaging with the respective deities. The temples in Corinth, therefore, were associated with the inappropriate worship of false gods, as well as with illegitimate activities.

Similarly, the temple in Jerusalem was associated with the abuse of power and corruption. Political deliberations, not spiritual matters, dominated the activities therein, and accusations of injustice and bribery were common. A description of the temple in the Talmud (b. Pesah. 57a) sheds some light on its condition:

Woe is me because of the house of Boethus; woe is me because of their staves!

Woe is me because of the house of Hanin; woe is me because of their whisperings!

Woe is me because of the house of Kathros; woe is me because of their pens!

Woe is me because of the house of Ishmael the son of Phabi; woe is me for their fists!

For the High Priests and their sons are [Temple] treasurers and their sons-in-law are trustees and their servants beat the people with staves.

It is interesting to note that the believers met next door to the synagogue (Acts 18:7). The irony and the tragedy are that God dwelled among the believers who had been ejected from the synagogue, the very place in which the Jews saw God's presence as being particularly significant.

Paul's words, therefore, are poignant for Jews and Gentiles alike. Both are acquainted with other temples that offer worship and dictate lifestyles. Paul reminds them that they function as a temple in Corinth and are to worship and live distinctively, and in a way that is acceptable to and initiated by the Spirit who dwells within.

Herod's temple was a monument of artistic and architectural grandeur, taking over eighty years to complete (long after his death) and measuring about one hundred by two hundred meters. The Temple Mount itself was expanded to some thirty-six acres and could hold about seventy-five thousand people. The temples in Corinth were also grand affairs. The church in Corinth—the temple of the Spirit—could never compete with them in terms of stately architecture and lavish settings. However, the church was expected to reflect a reality that was indestructible and far more amazing—the Spirit of God within. The tragedy was that the worship and lifestyles of its members were not accurately reflecting the Spirit. Their individualism and lack of mutual care harmed not only their witness in the community but also the church itself. They were living without the crucial elements of fellowship and unity. Furthermore, they did not recognize that they needed to mend their ways—revealing either an assumption that the Spirit was pleased with their lifestyles or, worse, indicating that they did not care. The communal nature of the church is crucial to Paul's understanding of its identity. If it exists in disunity, it loses an integral element of its raison d'être.

The Spirit is involved in the salvation of believers (6:11; 12:3, 13)

And such were some of you. But you were washed, you were sanctified, you were justified in the name of the Lord Jesus Christ and in the Spirit of our God. (6:11)

Exposition

Having expressed his displeasure at the behavior of church members who have been taking each other to court, Paul concludes his response by reminding them of the roles of Jesus and the Spirit in their lives. In particular, he reminds them that they have been washed, sanctified, and justified. The meaning of these verbs is relatively straightforward. Having been washed clean of their sinful lives, they have been set apart to live a different kind of life and justified in their new situation. In all of this, the believers are passive recipients.

The question is which of these actions has the Spirit undertaken and which has Jesus undertaken. This text does not provide a clear answer, and so it is important to look to other texts for guidance. The death of Jesus has brought forgiveness and justification to believers, which includes their being set apart to God. However, several texts also describe the Spirit's involvement in the same events (Rom 15:16; Titus 3:5). If there is any distinction in responsibilities, it probably lies in the Spirit's capacity to effect the changes and to appropriate the benefits to believers. In all of this it is also clear that the members of the Godhead function in harmony and in equal authority.

Significance for the Original Readers

This information is not so much for the purpose of creedal formulation as it is for practical theology. The behavior of the Corinthians is unacceptable to Paul for a number of reasons, which he outlines in 6:2–8. However, the most telling argument against their practice is that it is illegitimate in light of the activity of the Spirit on their behalf. Despite the fact that they have been washed, set apart to God to be different, and made right before God, they are indulging in practices that indicate their disunity and undermine all that has happened to them thus far. Despite their newfound position, they are living as they did before, with the attitudes of their old lives dominating their lifestyles and determining their actions. The Spirit has marked them and changed them; they are expected to take note of what the Spirit has done for them and to respond accordingly.

Therefore I want you to understand that no one speaking by the Spirit of God ever says "Jesus be cursed!" and no one can say "Jesus is Lord" except by the Holy Spirit. (12:3)

Exposition

Here Paul commences a long section related to spiritual gifts with reference to the sources of supernatural phenomena. The Corinthians would have been acquainted with such phenomena because of the variety of religious experiences available to the first-century worshipper. They need guidance in identifying legitimate spiritual forces. Paul provides them with two tests to help them in this respect.

The tests are relatively straightforward. No one can state that Jesus is cursed and also claim to be functioning as the mouthpiece of the Spirit. Similarly, no one can declare that Jesus is Lord unless the Spirit has inspired that confession. The assumption is that to say that Jesus is Lord involves more than merely uttering words.[1] Rather, the claim is to a relationship-based commitment to the Lord, demonstrated by a lifestyle of obedience. For a believer to make such a statement and to work it out throughout his or her life is to make a decisive break with the past and probably to make some personal sacrifice.

The Spirit and Jesus function in harmony and in shared purpose. Those who confess that Jesus is Lord and live by that belief experience the presence and inspiration of the Spirit.

---

[1] The slave woman in Acts 16:16–18 correctly identified Paul and his companions as servants of the Most High God, but she was not a believer. She had a "spirit of divination," and her words, though correct, were demonically inspired. She did not know the influential presence of the Spirit in her life. The implication of Paul's message here is that if she did, she would have known a complete change of lifestyle.

Significance for the Original Readers

People who were familiar with ecstatic and frenzied behavior in worship would have feared being deceived and forced back into that way of life by demonic spirits. Paul does not want them to experience this uncertainty, and he distinguishes the Spirit from the spirits associated with their earlier lives.

At the same time, to state that Jesus is Lord was a major step for first-century people, often resulting in their being cut off by family, friends, and neighbors. To become a Christian was a sacrificial act, because it meant a decisive break with the beliefs of contemporary society. Paul assures believers here that the Spirit has inspired them in such a courageous decision. It has not been a mistake, nor the result of deception or force. The same Spirit who will provide them with the gifts he describes in the following verses is the one who initiates their Christian walk.

For by one Spirit we were all baptized into one body—Jews or Greeks, slaves or free—and all were made to drink of one Spirit. (12:13)

Exposition

Having explored the fact that the Spirit provides gifts to every believer (12:4–11), Paul begins a section exploring the concept that they form a body (12:12–31). Paul employs the metaphor of baptism to describe the reality of being united into a body, that is, being baptized into the body (of Christ) by the Spirit. It is possible that he is making a rare reference to the act of water baptism, which is associated with, though not the same as, regeneration. He does not, however, use the word "water" in the description.

It is more likely that he is using the concept of baptism in the way he uses it elsewhere—to refer to a decisive break with the past and a commitment to a new destiny. Thus, in 10:2, he describes the Jews as having been baptized into Moses as an illustration of their identification with Moses' destiny and leaving the past behind. Paul is not necessarily referring to the act of baptism itself here, but rather to what it represents. There is an OT precedent for such a metaphor in Ezek 36:25, and the word "baptize" does evoke thoughts of a deluge of the Spirit into a believer's life. In John's Gospel, Jesus identifies water with the Spirit (7:37–39), as well as with the reception of eternal life (4:10, 14).

Clearly, the concept of drinking of one Spirit is a metaphor, and it probably relates to receiving the Spirit at salvation, given the aorist verb *epotisthemen* ("we were made to drink"), indicating a point in time when an action took place. However, there is no reason to conclude that the action does not continue throughout the life of a believer.

Significance for the Original Readers

Not only does the Spirit treat believers as individuals, affirming their roles and gifts, but he also places them in fellowship with other believers. In a city such as Corinth, with its populace ranging from wealthy citizens and intelligentsia to slaves and beggars, the quest for camaraderie was ever present. For example, people gathered to form guilds related to their occupations, to hold banquets identified with a particular temple or cult, and to participate in the activities of the gymnasia. A sense of belonging brought peace of mind, stability, and self-worth. Paul demonstrates that the Spirit also recognized the importance of this social dimension by incorporating individual believers into a group, with attendant privileges and responsibilities.

The concept of drinking would have brought to mind the refreshment of water and its life-giving and life-enhancing properties and preciousness in a time and place in which it was less accessible than in the modern West. The experiential nature of the Spirit's involvement in the life of believers is also important, and these metaphors remind them of the tangible relationship with the Spirit that is available to them. The Spirit is so committed to believers that while the Spirit takes the initiative they are passive—placing them in the body with other believers and providing himself as their everlasting resource.

The Spirit inhabits an individual's body (6:19–20)

Do you not know that your body is a temple of the Holy Spirit within you, which you have from God? You are not your own; you were bought with a price. So glorify God in your body.

Exposition

The context dictates that the meaning of these verses is different from that of 3:16–17, where Paul refers to the Spirit's indwelling of the corporate community of believers. Here, however, he refers to the Spirit's indwelling of the individual believer. Here is another example of how far the Corinthians have strayed from faithfully reflecting God in their lifestyles. Some members were arguing that certain bodily activities did not necessarily affect one's spirituality. They deemed physical actions to be unimportant, restricted to this passing age. What someone did in the body, they said, was irrelevant in an eternal context. They therefore deduced, for example, that gluttony affected only the body and could not harm one's spirituality or eternal destiny, because the body was to perish (6:13).

It appears that some had developed this argument to such an extreme that they were engaging in activity with prostitutes, concluding that it was acceptable because it only involved the body, which will perish anyway (6:15–16). Although it is obvious that the body will perish, Paul is not prepared to accept the validity of the equation. One of the logical conclusions of such thinking is that any sin could be deemed as unimportant or even irrelevant to one's Christian walk.

Paul responds by reminding readers that not only is the body created for the Lord, not immorality (6:13), but it is also the temple of the Holy Spirit. To engage in improper activity, be it sexual or otherwise, implicates the Spirit, because he has committed himself to be present in the life of a believer.

Paul catalogues a number of important points that emphasize the illegitimacy of the action. He identifies the Spirit as being in them, as being holy, and as being from God. They should, therefore, glorify God in their bodies. This is a sobering and challenging message. The Spirit has dedicated himself to live with individual believers, and yet they are living as if he is not there. His presence in their lives does not appear to make a difference.

The Spirit, who is holy, is the unfortunate witness of unholy activity. He who inspires holiness is being ignored in this respect. He who is God has to entertain ungodly acts. The Spirit lives in the believer's body, which Paul characterizes as the Spirit's temple with its images of consecration and dedication, and yet the believer practices immorality in that temple. The question is not how the Spirit indwells a body or where the Spirit lives in a body. Paul is emphasizing the incongruity of such behavior in such close proximity to the Spirit. It is illegitimate, inconceivable, unbelievable—a crime against the Spirit and all he stands for. It is tragic that Paul has to spell it out so graphically.

Significance for the Original Readers

"While the tongue swears, the heart does not" was a popular proverb from the era that helps to explain the thinking of the Corinthians. The principle behind this maxim is that physical activities do not affect the most important part of a person: the spirit that exists forever. With this view, it was possible to engage in all kinds of illicit activity and remain convinced that it affected only the body and not the central part of a person. It appears that the Corinthians have willingly or unwittingly been contaminated by such thinking. So pervasive and persuasive is this idea that Paul rebuts it forcefully and refers to the Spirit again as the conclusive aspect of his argument.

The notorious immorality of the city exacerbated the situation. The verb *korinthiazesthai* meant "to live like a Corinthian" and described an immoral person, while the depiction of a prostitute in the theater was represented symbolically by a woman from Corinth, such was the general perception of the morality of Corinthian women. Examples from the temple of Asclepius, which was dedicated to healing diseases, also testified to the immorality of the city. Those seeking healing left clay representations of the affected body part. The numerous clay sexual organs presented to the god for healing indicate widespread sexually transmitted diseases in the city. Corinth, a major port and the third major city in the empire after Rome and Alexandria, was populated by a wide variety of cultures and peoples who had originally brought with them a diversity of practices and perversions.

For Paul, the most unsettling aspect of the sin of the Corinthian believers is the Spirit's presence and witness. While the Spirit is not contaminated by the sin, because he indwells the believer, he becomes an unwilling and close witness to that which is diametrically opposed to his person and mission. The Spirit is present in the bodies of believers in order to affirm their importance as vehicles for the glory of God, and the role of the Spirit is to ensure that this potential becomes actualized. The actions of the Corinthians are most regrettable, though only Paul and the Spirit appear to feel this regret.

Selected Bibliography

Fee, Gordon D. *God's Empowering Presence: The Holy Spirit in the Letters of Paul*. Peabody, Mass.: Hendrickson, 1994.

Garland, David E. *1 Corinthians*. Baker Exegetical Commentary on
the New Testament. Grand Rapids: Baker, 2003.
Thistleton, Anthony C. *The First Epistle to the Corinthians: A Commentary on the Greek Text*. New International Greek Testament Commentary. Grand Rapids: Eerdmans, 2000.

The Significance for Readers Today

1. How can believers identify the gifts that the Spirit provides
   (1:7; 12:4–7, 11, 27–31; 14:1, 12)?
2. How does the Spirit empower believers (2:4)?
3. When has the Spirit provided you with wisdom (2:10–15;
   7:40)?
4. What benefits and responsibilities result from the fact that the
   Spirit has created a corporate body (3:16–17)?
5. How is the Spirit involved in the salvation of believers (6:11;
   12:3, 13)?
6. Practically speaking, how should the fact that the Spirit inhabits a believer's body impact your lifestyle (6:19–20)?

chapter 7

2 Corinthians

The Setting

The second letter to the Corinthians is a defense of Paul's apostolic authority in which he explains his ministry (chs. 1–7, 10–13) and reminds the Corinthians about the need to collect money for the Jerusalem church (chs. 8–9).

What Does the Author Say about the Spirit?

Although he is addressing the same believers he wrote to in 1 Corinthians, a different situation motivates Paul to write this letter. Outsiders have infiltrated the church and are undermining his work (2:17; 3:1; 4:2), and he contrasts his authority, ministry, and message with theirs. His is dominated by the influence and person of the Spirit, theirs by the letter of the law. His mission is based on the new era of the Spirit, theirs on the old era of the law. His focus is on the theocentric influence of the Spirit, theirs on the egocentric keeping of the law.

The Spirit

- seals the believer (1:21–22; 5:5)

- gives eternal life (3:3, 6)

- transforms the believer (3:16–18)

- enables the believer to live a godly life (6:6–7)

- provides fellowship (13:14)

The Spirit seals the believer (1:21–22; 5:5)

*But it is God who establishes us with you in Christ, and has com-
missioned us; he has put his seal upon us and given us his Spirit in
our hearts as a guarantee. (1:21–22)*

Exposition

In the larger context surrounding 1:21–22, Paul is seeking to establish the validity and integrity of his ministry among the Corinthians. To do this, he turns to the Spirit for affirmation and records that
the Spirit has been given as a "guarantee" (*arrabōn*). This word is
found in ancient papyri detailing commercial activities and, in particular, as a technical term for a first installment or guarantee. The
Spirit is God's down payment and, as such, he acts as a guarantee.[1]

Paul uses the first-person plural "us" to identify those who
have received the Spirit. They have been commissioned and have
received the seal of the Spirit.[2] It is because of what the Spirit has
done for Paul that he can appeal to him as the one who will vali-
date and authenticate his ministry among the Corinthians. Paul's
mission strategy has always been under the controlling influence
of the Spirit, who commissioned him in the beginning and who directed his footsteps thereafter.

Significance for the Original Readers

The verses leading up to this declaration contain plenty of information to help the readers realize that Paul was not uncaring in
his absence from them or insensitive to their situation. Thus, he reminds them of his own sufferings (1:5) on their behalf (1:6) and of
their partnership in suffering (1:7). He graphically describes the intensity of his past afflictions (1:8–9) and informs them of his reliance on their prayers for him (1:10). He then addresses the
suggestions that his behavior toward them has been inappropriate
and insincere (1:12–14), reminding them that his love for them had
motivated him to attempt to visit them first (1:15–16). However,
the idea that any insincerity on his part would adversely affect the
message that he brought (1:17–20) increases his concern. It is this
fear that the Corinthians may assume insincerity on his part that

---

[1] See commentary on Eph 1:14 in ch. 9.
[2] See commentary on Eph 1:13 in ch. 9.

causes him to affirm that the Spirit has entrusted him to this mission (1:21–22). He can be trusted, and therefore the gospel he preached can be trusted.

He who has prepared us for this very thing is God, who has given us the Spirit as a guarantee. (5:5)

Exposition

In 5:1–4, Paul has been referring to the fact that life in the human body is temporary and that a new, immortal life form awaits the believer. He does not anticipate an interim when he will function without some form of body, believing instead that the new will replace the old. The presence of the Spirit, who again functions as a guarantee, specifically affirms that fact. The Spirit guarantees this new life.

Significance for the Original Readers

Life for the Corinthians and all first-century people was fragile. Concerns about health were often on their minds, though for the vast majority it was not an area over which they had much control. Many people had a poor diet, resulting in malnutrition and diseases, and medical care often was available only to the wealthy and was of uncertain quality. Postnatal infant mortality rates were very high, perhaps as high as 25 percent in the first year of life. Life expectancy was around thirty years of age. The Mishnah identifies the best of physicians as destined for Gehenna.[3]

Similarly, the range of pharmaceuticals available and the danger of the surgery practiced led to confusion and frustration. When medicine was inadequate, people saw the gods as an alternative source of healing.

Asclepius was renowned as a healing deity, and many temples were established in his name throughout the empire, dispensing the hope of healing. Asclepius was a doctor, and after his death people began to ascribe divine characteristics to him. People who had needs (physical, financial, emotional) visited the temples, often staying overnight in the hope that their problems would be resolved. Worshippers viewed the many harmless snakes that inhabited the temples as his earthly representatives, and so they be-

---

[3] *m. Qidd.* 4:14; see also Philo, *Sacr.* 69–71.

lieved that to be touched by one of the snakes was equivalent to a touch by Asclepius himself. Many claimed to have received a visit from him in their dreams and to have received answers to their prayers, including physical healing.

If health issues were uppermost among the concerns of the people, however, life after death was even more uncertain. Paul is convinced of his eternal destiny and encourages his readers to be as confident about theirs, concluding with the fact that the presence of the Spirit in their lives acts as a constant reminder of their eternal security.

The Spirit gives eternal life (3:3, 6)

And you show that you are a letter from Christ delivered by us, written not with ink but with the Spirit of the living God, not on tablets of stone but on tablets of human hearts. (3:3)

[God] has made us competent to be ministers of a new covenant, not in a written code but in the Spirit; for the written code kills, but the Spirit gives life. (3:6)

Exposition

In 3:3, Paul contrasts stone tablets, on which the law was written (Exod 31:18), with human hearts, on which the new covenant was inscribed (Jer 31:33). He describes believers as a "letter from Christ"; because the Spirit is part of their lives, they function in the role of transmitting the messages of the Spirit. Furthermore, he describes the Spirit as "the Spirit of the living God." Paul wants his readers to understand the significance of the fact that their faith is alive and enlivening. Thus, his description of the Spirit emphasizes the fact that he represents life—the life of God.

In 3:6, Paul continues the theme but adds that whereas the Spirit is life and gives life, life based on the law (the written code) kills. Whereas the law is negative, the Spirit is positive. Whereas the law identifies and points out sin, warning of the consequences of sin and guaranteeing that sin will not go unpunished, the Spirit helps believers practically overcome sin by empowering them in the process. The Spirit thereby gives life to the believer.

Paul may simply be speaking against a misuse of the law or against following human traditions based on the law that are illegitimate. It is probable, however, that he is contrasting the law that cannot give eternal life with the life-giving message of the Spirit. The law was unable to fulfill its purpose because people were unable to keep it. While the law prompted people to obedience, it did not empower them to obey; instead, it condemned them as failures.

The Spirit, on the other hand, while likewise moving people to obey, additionally empowers them to do so. The Spirit has already established the people as adopted children of God for whom forgiveness is available when they fail. The Spirit does not function like a written code to be consulted when temptation looms; rather, he is an ever-present guide who influences the decisions of the believer while also providing wisdom on the many issues that the law does not address.

Significance for the Original Readers

Because the readers are in danger of drifting toward reliance on the law, Paul stresses the role of the Spirit in salvation. These Corinthians are no different from many other believers who think it better to live their Christian lives by a set of rules. Paul, however, prefers that they live in relationship with the Spirit. Rules are easy to identify but not so easy to obey. They can lead to condemnation and excess guilt and can convince the believer that all that matters to God is complete obedience rather than a wholehearted desire to obey God coupled with a desire to love him. Paul's message from God, however, is that rules are a poor runner-up to a relationship.

The role of the Spirit is to walk with believers, seeking to influence and empower them toward a godly life. Believers in turn need to listen to the Spirit's guidance, which is not always easy; indeed, at times it may seem easier to follow a set of rules than to commit to developing a relationship with God. Putting check marks in the boxes can sometimes be easier than touching base with God—but the latter is the purpose of the Spirit. His presence in the life of believers does not simply make it possible for them to keep rules. He enables them to walk with the giver of the rules as they benefit from his presence, influence, and power.

The Spirit transforms the believer (3:16–18)

When a man turns to the Lord the veil is removed. Now the Lord is the Spirit, and where the Spirit of the Lord is, there is freedom. And we all, with unveiled face, beholding the glory of the Lord, are being changed into his likeness from one degree of glory to another; for this comes from the Lord who is the Spirit.

Exposition

Paul Contrasts the Believer with Moses

Paul is still in the process of developing the significant difference between trying to live by the guidelines of the law and being influenced by the Spirit. He raises the stakes considerably by quoting from the OT in order to prove the supremacy of the Spirit-directed life. Furthermore, he adapts Exod 34:34 to clarify his argument in 2 Cor 3:16. Whereas Exod 34:34 describes Moses entering the Lord's presence and removing his veil, Paul describes believers turning to the Lord and having the veil removed from them. The contrast is clear. Not only does Paul alter the words and their tenses to indicate a conversion experience (the imperfect of *eisporeuomai* ["go in"] in Exod 34:34 becomes the aorist of *epistrephō* ["turn"] in 2 Cor 3:16), but he also presents the believer as the passive recipient in the veil's removal. Whereas Moses was active in the process, the believers are passive as the work is done for them. Furthermore, whereas Moses removed the veil temporarily while in the presence of God, the veil is removed permanently for believers—because they are constantly in the presence of God (as a result of the Spirit).

The Transformation of the Believer Is Greater

Paul goes on to say that, as a result of this experience, the believer knows freedom, the revelation of God's glory, and transformation into his likeness. The freedom that Christ achieved and the Spirit affirmed comprises the ability to enjoy the benefits of the new covenant. These benefits include the boldness and liberty (3:12, 17) to enjoy an unrestricted relationship with the Lord and all the resources of God through the Spirit, as well as freedom from the bondage of a life lived in the impossible attempt to keep the law.

Whereas Moses had to veil his face so that the people could not see the reflected glory of God, Paul declares that believers experience the opposite. The word Paul uses here can mean "reflect on" or "radiate" (*katoptrizomai*). Thus, it is possible that he anticipates believers being able to reflect on God to a greater degree with the help of the Spirit and/or to radiate God through their lives with the help of the Spirit. There seems little reason to deny either option.

The Spirit Effects the Transformation of the Believer

It is the transforming process of the Spirit that substantiates the supremacy of the Spirit over the law. Believers do not improve or become Christlike simply because they are Christians. There is nothing automatic about the development of one's spirituality. Paul declares that the Spirit has the capacity, the desire, and the determination to transform the believer into the likeness of the Lord. He is not describing the activity of the believer in transformation, but rather the action of the Spirit. It is not clear exactly how this happens; indeed, it is possible that Paul is employing poetic analogy in an attempt to articulate the inexpressible and the unimaginable. Whatever the process anticipated, Paul is certain that it will be a glorious one and the end product will be Christlikeness.

The Transformation of the Believer Results in Glory

The concept of glory is not easy to define. It is a superlative describing something or someone superior to all others. The Bible uses the word "glory" (*doxa*) to describe people who have influence (Gen 45:13), riches (Gen 31:1; Eph 1:18), or power (Isa 8:7; Col 1:11). It describes someone or something that makes an impression. The term "glory" describes, for example, the fact that God is impressive. The cloud that signified the presence of God's glory weighed down upon the tabernacle (Exod 40:34), expressing his supreme importance. He has glorious presence. He has weight, influence, and authority. In this regard, the word "glory" is best used of God. He is superior to all, and the word "glory" represents his deity. What best defines God is that he is glorious, and in that regard he is unique. It is the privilege of the believer to increasingly explore that glory and to radiate it to others.

The message is clear. The Spirit has now granted the wonderful experience that the Lord provided for Moses to all believers, and to an even greater degree.

Significance for the Original Readers

Paul's Jewish readers were familiar with the heroic figure of Moses. He rescued the Jewish people from slavery, he brought them the law, and he led them for forty years, guiding them to the promised land and mediating between them and God in the context of divine providence.

In Corinth, some who had infiltrated the church and who were undermining Paul's message of grace were now advocating a life of obedience to the law. To combat this, Paul presents the very special relationship that Moses enjoyed with God as being unique among his contemporaries in order to demonstrate that believers can enjoy a superior relationship with God as a result of the Spirit in their lives. Moses' experience, though wonderful, was always temporary, partial, and preparatory. Now that Jesus has come, the Spirit is able to provide all believers with a superior, relational, and empowering experience with God. Rather than being restricted to occasional visits to the tabernacle, this relationship is constantly available because the Spirit dwells in believers, giving them unrestricted access to God.

The Spirit enables the believer to live a godly life (6:6–7)

[As servants of God we commend ourselves in every way] . . . by purity, knowledge, forbearance, kindness, the Holy Spirit, genuine love, truthful speech, and the power of God.

Exposition

The larger context of this verse is a list of qualifications and experiences that function as evidence of the authenticity of Paul and his colleagues as servants of God. As such it includes sufferings (6:4–5, 8–10), in the middle of which is this list of godly attributes (6:6–7). A reference to the Spirit is central here. Although it is possible that Paul is referring to a holy spirit as evidence of his godliness, along with the other attributes, he is probably referring to the Holy Spirit, who makes it possible for him to live in this way.

Significance for the Original Readers

Paul is exhorting his readers to develop their faith in Christ and not miss out on the benefits that are integral to salvation. Paul reminds them that he and his colleagues were able to respond to suffering for the faith with grace and godliness. The pressure did not cause them to break; rather, they exhibited a supernatural response, demonstrating the power of the Spirit, who makes it possible for believers to live according to his standards.

The Spirit provides fellowship (13:14)

The grace of the Lord Jesus Christ and the love of God and the fellowship of the Holy Spirit be with you all.

Exposition

This benediction, which is unique in Pauline literature, mentions each member of the Godhead. It is unlikely that Paul is formulating a Trinitarian creedal declaration; church councils would explore such matters much later. For Paul, God is inexplicable and not to be circumscribed or pedantically defined. God is a mystery who functions as a Trinity—and it is not Paul's aim to demarcate individual responsibilities within the Godhead. How God functions and how he is to be experienced are much more important matters than being able to comprehensively understand him. Thus, in this verse Paul is focusing on the fellowship (*koinōnia*) associated with the Spirit.

Significance for the Original Readers

The concept of fellowship is central in the Corinthian correspondence. Without it, they have shown themselves to be a poor testimony to the city, an inadequate reflection of God, and an embarrassing representative of God's nature. With the Spirit's help, Paul shows them that they can improve their fellowship with God and their relationships with each other.

Selected Bibliography

Barnett, Paul. *The Second Epistle to the Corinthians.* New International Commentary on the New Testament. Grand Rapids: Eerdmans, 1997.

Belleville, Linda L. *2 Corinthians.* IVP New Testament Commentary 8. Downers Grove, Ill.: InterVarsity, 1996.

Fee, Gordon D. *God's Empowering Presence: The Holy Spirit in the Letters of Paul.* Peabody, Mass.: Hendrickson, 1994.

Martin, Ralph P. *2 Corinthians.* Word Biblical Commentary 40. Dallas: Word, 1986.

The Significance for Readers Today

1. What difference does it make in your life that the Spirit has guaranteed you (1:21–22; 5:5)?
2. How does a relationship with God, rather than obedience to the law, give life to a believer?
3. In what specific areas is the Spirit transforming you, your life-style, choices, and attitudes (3:16–18)?
4. In what areas of your life do you need the supernatural power and grace of the Spirit to respond in difficult circumstances with godly attributes (6:6–7)?
5. What difference could an improved fellowship with the Spirit make in your relationships with God and with others (13:14)?

$g$alatians

The Setting

Galatians 1:1 identifies Paul as the author of this letter. Paul and Barnabas established churches on their first missionary journey in Galatia in the cities of Pisidian Antioch, Iconium, Lystra, and Derbe (Acts 13–14; 16:6; 18:23). Paul wrote this letter in large part because some people, probably Jewish Christians, were trying to persuade the believers that they were illegitimately overlooking the law.

What Does the Author Say about the Spirit?

The Spirit is an important theme in this letter, and Paul mentions him nearly twenty times. The Spirit functions as the proof that Christ has completed the process of justification, contrary to the teachings of some that believers needed to achieve more, especially in regard to a greater adherence to the law. For Paul, the gift of the Spirit introduced the new covenant and signaled the end of the old era (3:19–4:7). Furthermore, Paul demonstrates that the Spirit can do what the law cannot: effect the righteousness that God demands.

The Spirit

- initiates salvation (3:2–5)

- is a promise received by faith (3:13–14)

- affirms that we are children of God (4:6)

- guarantees our future (5:5; 6:8)

- guides the believer (5:16–18)

- provides fruit for the believer (5:22–6:1)

The Spirit initiates salvation (3:2–5)

Let me ask you only this: Did you receive the Spirit by works of the law, or by hearing with faith? Are you so foolish? Having begun with the Spirit, are you now ending with the flesh? Did you experience so many things in vain?—if it really is in vain. Does he who supplies the Spirit to you and works miracles among you do so by works of the law, or by hearing with faith?

Exposition

In 3:1–5, Paul begins his teaching concerning the relationship between the flesh, the law, and the Spirit. When he speaks of "flesh" here, he is not referring to the physical body of a person; rather, he is using the word to describe activity that an individual undertakes in his or her own strength. The flesh does not necessarily refer to an evil lifestyle and can simply define a life in which the Spirit is not the controlling influence. When Paul speaks of the law, he is referring to the OT law, the guiding influence of the Jews.

In a series of questions, Paul reminds the Galatians of all of the factors present in their salvation. They began their relationship with God by accepting the gospel by faith. The Spirit came into their lives as the evidence of their new status (4:6), not as a result of human effort or keeping the law (3:2). He reminds them that miracles accompanied their salvation, and he asks them rhetorically whether these miracles were a result of their own efforts (3:5). The answer is obvious. The miraculous work of the Spirit in salvation is due to the initiative of the Spirit, not the believer. It is therefore foolishness to try to continue one's walk with God by human effort instead of benefiting from the resources of the Spirit.

Paul expresses concern that these believers may be developing a lifestyle that is not influenced by the Spirit. Instead, they have come to believe that pleasing God depends on human effort and keeping laws—and so they live lives dominated by the flesh (3:3), trying to develop their Christian walk by their own effort. This attitude is both inappropriate and unnecessary, for the Spirit is with them to guide and empower them. Furthermore, human effort becomes an illegitimate action if it means that they are attempting to achieve what the Spirit has already achieved on their behalf.

Significance for the Original Readers

Paul wants the readers to understand a number of different principles here. To attempt to become a child of God by one's own actions is inappropriate for at least three reasons. First, it is an impossible, and therefore foolish, undertaking. Second, even if the status of child of God could be achieved, it would mean that one would do so by earning that privilege through one's own efforts rather than receiving it as the gift of God. That would mean the status of being a child of God would be granted as a payment or a reward for one's own actions rather than as a gracious gift from God. Third, any attempt to earn this relationship is offensive because it rejects what the Spirit has done on the believer's behalf and undermines the completed nature of the salvation achieved by Jesus on the cross.

Paul's readers are in danger of losing their sense of security as children of God. They are forgetting that the Spirit has established them, once and for all, with this status. They are also in jeopardy of losing touch with the pure simplicity of their experience with God. God wants them as his children, and there is nothing they can do to improve their acceptability before he welcomes them into his family.

Some had suggested that the believers needed to obey certain aspects of the law in order to be certain that they were children of God and to please God. Believers should follow the written law, they said, instead of the guidance of the Spirit. Paul needed to undermine those who wanted to make salvation complicated by adding rules. He reminds them, therefore, that the Spirit has indwelled them from the time of their conversion to Christy. He emphasizes the point by asking them when the Spirit came into their lives: Was it when they were trying to obey the law, or was it after they believed the gospel of salvation in Jesus Christ? It is clear which answer he expects. The presence of the Spirit in a person's life is thus the evidence of entrance into the Christian life.

The fact that Paul refers back to the presence of the Spirit in their lives as evidence of a dramatic personal transformation assumes that they had experienced the Spirit dynamically. The Spirit's work is not secret, silent, or unnoticed. They had felt his impact on their lives.

The Spirit also enables believers to achieve their goals and works miracles among them (3:5). It is the Spirit who has initiated their relationships with God, and it is the Spirit who will maintain and guarantee those relationships. To attempt to achieve by human effort what the Spirit has done is to treat the Spirit's work as insubstantial and ineffective. Paul refers to such an attempt as being of "the flesh" (i.e., achieved by one's own effort). He wants his readers to be aware that, although it sounds too good to be true, their relationship with God is indeed based entirely on the Spirit's work on their behalf.

The Spirit is a promise received by faith (3:13–14)

Christ redeemed us from the curse of the law, having become a curse for us—for it is written, "Cursed be every one who hangs on a tree"— that in Christ Jesus the blessing of Abraham might come upon the Gentiles, that we might receive the promise of the Spirit through faith.

Exposition

The blessing of Abraham, which is now available to Gentiles as well, relates to his having been reckoned righteous through faith (3:6). Abraham's readiness to trust God flowed out of a relationship established with God before the law was even given. Paul now builds on this truth as he explains that believers also receive the Spirit by faith—and not on the basis of having fulfilled any laws or achieved, by human effort, any level of holiness. Thus we are to understand Paul's reference to "the promise of the Spirit" (3:14) as "the promise that is the Spirit."

Significance for the Original Readers

Since the Spirit has already been given to believers, Paul wants his readers to recognize their folly in attempting to keep the law in order to receive the Spirit. Not only were many of Paul's readers Gentiles, but they also represented many different people-groups. The Greek geographer Strabo describes Galatia as being populated by very mixed peoples whose ethnic backgrounds were uncertain. This mongrel people had been granted the same privilege of a relationship with God based on faith that Israel's hero Abraham experienced.

The Spirit affirms that we are children of God (4:6)

And because you are sons, God has sent the Spirit of his Son into our hearts, crying, "Abba! Father!"

Exposition

Just as God sent his son (4:4) to make adoption possible, so also he sent the Spirit of his Son (4:6) to activate it. God simultaneously adopts us and sends the Spirit; both occur at salvation, and Paul wants his readers to understand that the two events are intertwined. Paul uses this descriptive phrase "Spirit of his Son" only here. By linking the Spirit with the Son, Paul is emphasizing that the Spirit in believers is none other than the Spirit of the Son of God, who loved them and secured sonship for them. The cry "Abba! Father!" was Jesus' address to the Father; now, it is also the cry of believers. Theirs is a shared sonship.[1]

Paul is not anticipating a theological inquiry regarding the overlap between the Spirit and the Son. Instead, he is anticipating a faithful response to the intellectual perception that the sonship Jesus enjoyed with the Father is now a reality for the believer also. Can you and should you completely understand it? No. Should you enjoy and explore it? Yes.

Paul describes the Spirit coming "into our hearts" (4:6), fulfilling the prophecy in Ezek 11:19 concerning a future time when God promised to "put a new spirit" in his people. It is no surprise that Paul describes the Spirit entering the heart of the believer. For people in the first century, the heart was the seat of the emotions and the center of one's moral, spiritual, and intellectual life; it represented the central core of one's life.

It is uncertain whether it is the believer or the Spirit through the believer who utters the cry that Paul refers to. Perhaps it is better not to attempt to separate them. Paul probably wants the readers to recognize the Spirit's essential role in initiating and affirming the adoptive relationship between the believer and God. The Spirit inspires believers to acknowledge that it is valid for them to refer to God as "Father." Although believers may be disowned by many, they know with certainty that they are owned by the Father.

The term "Abba" defines the relationship between the Father and his children. Children, including adult children, used this intimate form of address. Jesus uniquely used it to address God as his Father and, in the Lord's Prayer, he encouraged the disciples to address God as "Father."

---

[1] See also commentary on Rom 8:14–17 in ch. 5.

Significance for the Original Readers

In response to the insistence by some Jews that a relationship with God was based on circumcision, Paul focuses on adoption and the gift of the Spirit as the mark of a relationship with God. As a result of Jesus' death, believers did not need to look to the law for guidance in life or for evidence that they were God's children. Paul affirms that the presence of the Spirit in the believers' lives is evidence of their salvation and proof of their redemption from the law (4:5–6). This is remarkable not only because Gentiles are now part of the family of God but also because the Spirit enters every child of God. This marks another extraordinary contrast to the experience of believers in the OT, when the Spirit entered the lives of only the privileged few (mainly prophets and kings) and did so only from time to time.

Paul exhorts believers not to regress into slavery to the law, for they are now in a permanent, life-changing position with God. He is now their Father, and they are his children, whether they are Jews or Gentiles, irrespective of whether they even know any of the law, let alone whether they are attempting to obey it. Paul anticipates that the Spirit will make a significant impact in the life of every believer. Paul describes the Spirit as a very real and personal friend who touches, and is touched by, those he inhabits.

The original readers would have been very surprised by the concept of a God who readily accepts them. Although our knowledge about the Galatians to whom this letter was sent is sketchy, the general picture of the Galatian people is not encouraging. The ancient historian Polybius described them as the most formidable and warlike nation in Asia, renowned for their lawlessness (*Histories* 2.22, 23, 33). When King Attalus of Pergamum conquered them (230 B.C.E.), it was celebrated as a victory over barbarianism. Now, however, a people who were known for their lawlessness have been welcomed into a community that does not take their previous lives into consideration, lawless or not. Acceptance into this community comes through a gracious God who provides them with salvation as a gift, affirmed by the presence of the Spirit.

The Spirit guarantees our eternal life (5:5; 6:8)

For through the Spirit, by faith, we wait for the hope of righteousness. (5:5)

For he who sows to his own flesh will from the flesh reap corruption; but he who sows to the Spirit will from the Spirit reap eternal life. (6:8)

Exposition

As we have seen, some were teaching that the Galatians could only achieve a right relationship with God by keeping the law. This is both inaccurate and impossible. The Spirit, who is given by faith at the moment of salvation, demonstrates that the believer is in a valid relationship with God. Furthermore, Paul refers here to the fact that believers, on the basis of faith, await the final and public confirmation of their righteousness, which has been guaranteed by the Spirit. The word "hope" does not communicate any sense of uncertainty, which is often associated with it in contemporary usage.

Attempting to keep the law by one's own efforts, which Paul defines as an act of the flesh, does not provide righteousness. Paul instead identifies the Spirit in a person's life as the necessary factor whose influence will result in a life of righteousness and whose presence will assure the final outcome, when that righteous state will be publicly declared (6:8).

Significance for the Original Readers

The readers lived in an uncertain world. The Galatians had been controlled by three different empires during the previous 350 years. The future was not in the hands of the individual member of society; it was determined by superior powers. Paul speaks of the one who is the supreme power, who guarantees their future in association with the Spirit.

The Spirit guides the believer (5:16–18)

But I say, walk by the Spirit, and do not gratify the desires of the flesh. For the desires of the flesh are against the Spirit, and the desires of the Spirit are against the flesh; for these are opposed to each other, to prevent you from doing what you would. But if you are led by the Spirit you are not under the law.

Exposition

According to Paul, the Spirit is to be each believer's guide. Believers should take advantage of the influence of the Spirit (5:16) rather than look to the law for help (5:18). It is possible that Paul is presenting two imperatives, "Walk by the Spirit" and "Do not gratify the desires of the flesh" (5:16). It is more likely, however, and also possible according to the Greek grammar, that he is presenting an imperative followed by a promise: "Walk by the Spirit, and you will not gratify the desires of the flesh." Those who continuously walk with the Spirit will naturally develop a lifestyle that is not dominated by sinful activities because the Spirit will be their guide and empower them. Whereas the law points the person in the right direction, the Spirit enables the believer to reach the destination.

Here, Paul uses the term "flesh" to mean sinful tendencies. The Spirit is superior to the law because he empowers believers to overcome sin. Paul confirms the authority of the Spirit using a Greek double negative (*ou mē*), to be rendered, "You will *definitely not* gratify the desires of the flesh." Since sin is diametrically opposed to the Spirit in terms of both motivation and consequence, believers need to keep walking with the Spirit to ensure that they do not sin (5:17). The Spirit heralds a new era, enables believers to enter it, and empowers them to live accordingly.

Significance for the Original Readers

Paul is not advocating an undisciplined lifestyle that has no code of conduct or suggesting that it is no longer necessary for the believer to lead a sanctified life. Neither is he saying that the Spirit enables the believer to keep the law better than the person who does not have the Spirit. What he wants his readers to realize is that the law has served its purpose, and now a better guide has come in the person of the Spirit. This is not because the law was inaccurate or a mistake that the Spirit has now come to remedy. Rather, Paul affirms that the Spirit achieves that which believers could not do by trying to keep the law.

The Spirit	*The Law*
The Spirit brings a person into relationship with God.	The law only points out the barrier of multiple sins in a person's life that makes such a relationship impossible.

The Spirit acts as a guide and influence for life.	The law simply provides a code of conduct.
The Spirit is a personal friend.	The law is impersonal.
The Spirit points out sin and provides power to overcome it.	The law only points out sin and condemns the sinner.
The Spirit is able to advise the believer in innumerable situations.	The law is restricted to offering guidance concerning that which it contains, much of which is not specifically relevant to the Christian.
The Spirit acts as an ever-present guide.	The law, inasmuch as it is a collection of books, is much less immediate.

The Spirit provides fruit for the believer (5:22–6:1)

The fruit of the Spirit is love, joy, peace, patience, kindness, goodness, faithfulness, gentleness, self-control; against such there is no law. And those who belong to Christ Jesus have crucified the flesh with its passions and desires. If we live by the Spirit, let us also walk by the Spirit. Let us have no self-conceit, no provoking of one another, no envy of one another. Brethren, if a man is overtaken in any trespass, you who are spiritual should restore him in a spirit of gentleness. Look to yourself, lest you too be tempted.

Exposition

There has been a great deal of discussion over Gal 5:16–21, concerning whether these verses refer to the experience of the believer or the unbeliever. The major purpose of this passage, however, as we saw above, is to explain the significant role of the Spirit in the life of the believer. If Paul is describing the tension felt by believers who wish to do right but are tempted to do otherwise, then he is exhorting readers to appreciate the power of the Spirit to help in their internal battle. To fail to take advantage of such a powerful ally would be unwise.

Paul is probably, however, drawing a contrast between unbelievers and believers. Unbelievers have no one to help them and experience the logical consequence—lives dominated by sin (5:19–21). Believers enjoy the constant presence and power of the Spirit operating within them, which leads to lives dominated by love (5:22–23). The central point is the same in both interpretations, whether Paul is describing believers or both believers and unbelievers: The Spirit is limitless in his ability to improve the believer and in his enthusiasm to ensure that this improvement occurs. Those who start with the Spirit should continue with the Spirit (5:25).

Furthermore, the Spirit produces fruit in the believer, while the unbeliever, acting on his or her own effort, produces sinful consequences. The latter is self-initiated; the former is Spirit-initiated. The Spirit produces fruit naturally in the believer; the fruit, which is positive and beneficial for all concerned, is not the result of human effort. Sin, by its own effort, generates a lifestyle that is destructive and chaotic. Paul is not suggesting that believers need not exert any effort in ethical development; on the contrary, to walk with the Spirit anticipates a life of obedience. What Paul insists upon is that believers recognize that the Spirit is on their side, bringing about his desires for their lives. On their own, they would be very limited in their ability to improve their lives.

In 6:1, the expression *hymeis hoi pneumatikoi* ("you who are spiritual") does not refer to mature believers, but to "Spirit people" (i.e., Christians). Paul is describing the kind of lifestyle that should characterize all people in whom the Spirit resides. Thus, they will act with gentleness, a fruit of the Spirit (5:23). According to 6:2, this is equivalent to a new law: the law of Christ. The word "principle" is a more suitable translation than "law." Believers are to produce Christlikeness rather than reproduce a set of rules. Freedom from the Torah does not lead to lawlessness; indeed, Paul reminds believers that walking with the Spirit should have positive consequences (5:22). Christ himself focused particularly on love. That love is to be the route of all Spirit people, since the Spirit is their guide.

Significance for the Original Readers

The readers were in danger of lapsing into a lifestyle that confused liberty and license. They needed to be reminded that the Christian life is one of high standards (5:21). The list of sinful actions in 5:19–20 may provide a glimpse of some of their lifestyles before they became Christians. Such are human nature and peer pressure that they probably regularly experienced the temptation to revert to some of these activities. To give in to these temptations is unacceptable, Paul says—especially because it indicates that they are ignoring the Spirit, who lives in them and offers them an inexhaustible resource for improvement.

The images of fruit and growth would have been familiar to these people who made their living through agriculture. The few major cities and villages of the province were set among vast areas of countryside that produced wool, grain, and wine. Paul knows that the Galatians will identify with this way of thinking about how the Spirit's life and character are naturally developed in them.

Selected Bibliography

Dunn, James D. G. *The Epistle to the Galatians*. London: A. & C. Black, 1993.

Fee, Gordon D. *God's Empowering Presence: The Holy Spirit in the Letters of Paul*. Peabody, Mass.: Hendrickson, 1994.

Fung, Ronald Y. K. *The Epistle to the Galatians*. New International Commentary on the New Testament. Grand Rapids: Eerdmans, 1988.

Longenecker, Richard N. *Galatians*. Word Biblical Commentary 41. Dallas: Word, 1990.

The Significance for Readers Today

1. The Spirit came into your life when you began your Christian walk. What does this tell you about the Spirit's commitment to you and relationship with you (3:2–5)?
2. What does the Bible have to say about our attempts to achieve holiness or "earn" salvation by our own efforts (3:13–14)?
3. What difference does it make in your life that the Spirit validates and affirms your position as a child of God (4:6)?
4. Like the Galatians, we too live in an uncertain world. What is our hope through the Spirit, both now and eternally (5:5; 6:8)?
5. How can you listen to and walk by and with the Spirit (5:16–18)?
6. How can you know that you are walking with the Spirit (5:22–6:1)?

*e*phesians

The Setting

Paul is identified as the author in 1:1. We cannot be certain about the identity of the community that the letter addresses, because the word "Ephesus" in 1:1, while well attested in the early Greek manuscripts, is absent from some important textual witnesses. The predominant view of the early church was that the letter was sent to the city of Ephesus.

After commencing the work in Corinth, Paul went to Ephesus, where he spent three years establishing the church (Acts 19:1–6). It was a time of extraordinary miracles (Acts 19:11–12), comprehensive teaching (Acts 20:27, 31), and significant suffering (1 Cor 15:32; 16:9). When he left for Jerusalem, Paul prophesied that divisive opposition would affect the church in Ephesus (Acts 20:28–30). Tragically, by the time Timothy was sent to the church, the prophecy had been fulfilled (1 Tim 1:3–7), and when Timothy received his second letter, the consequences of the false teaching had exacerbated an already worrisome situation (2 Tim 1:15).

What Does the Author Say about the Spirit?

Paul wants readers to fully appreciate the incredible resources of the Spirit available to them. In the first three chapters he explores what the Spirit does on their behalf, and in the second three chapters he explores what the Spirit expects believers to do in response.

The Spirit

- blesses the believer (1:3)
- seals the believer (1:13)

- acts as a guarantee (1:14)

- provides wisdom and revelation (1:16–17; 3:4–5)

- provides ongoing access to God (2:18)

- forms believers into a dwelling place for God (2:21–22)

- empowers believers (3:16)

- provides unity among believers (4:3)

Therefore, the believer

- is not to grieve the Spirit (4:30)

- is to be filled with the Spirit (5:18–19)

- is to use that which the Spirit supplies (6:17–18)

The Spirit blesses the believer (1:3)

Blessed be the God and Father of our Lord Jesus Christ, who has blessed us in Christ with every spiritual blessing in the heavenly places.

Exposition

The introductory section of the letter, 1:3–14, takes the reader on a breathtaking tour from one level of wonder to the next. Paul is deeply impressed by the excellence of salvation, and he expresses his admiration for God and all that God has done for believers in a Christian version of a Jewish poem of praise to God (*berakah*).

Spiritual Blessings

Although many Bible translations use the expression "spiritual blessing" to translate *eulogia pneumatike* in 1:3, a more helpful rendering is "blessing that pertains to the Spirit" or "blessing that is mediated by the Spirit." It is not that "spiritual" people receive the blessings, but that the Spirit blesses people. Paul is not simply stating that as a result of a believer's position in Christ he or she benefits from spiritual (and thus not necessarily material) blessings. Rather, he is saying that because of what Christ has done, the Spirit becomes the resource for the believer.

Heavenly Places

With the expression *ta epourania* in 1:3, Paul describes the believer being overwhelmed with blessings normally associated with "heavenly places." Paul uses the word *epouranios* elsewhere in his letters, but this particular expression appears only here and on four other occasions in Ephesians (1:20; 2:6; 3:10; 6:12).

The blessings in question are not waiting for the believer in heaven, nor are they blessings to be anticipated later throughout one's life on earth. Rather, Paul is describing blessings from heaven that come with salvation. The verses that follow, which include explicit references to the Spirit, describe some of these benefits.

Significance for the Original Readers

The readers would have been accustomed to seeing spiritual phenomena, and Paul uses language that is familiar to them. They were used to thinking about spiritual forces that existed in heavenly places (6:12; cf. 2:2). However, the gods that they worshipped often incited fear. They identified poor harvests, fire, or other such calamities with punishment from gods who had been offended. Because of this, many people lived with an attitude of fearful servility to the gods.

Belief in the demonic also bred uncertainty among people living in the first century. Many believed that demons caused calamities including illnesses and breakdowns in relationships as well as a range of personal problems. People longed to be rescued from the instability of human existence, and they hoped to achieve this by relating to the gods who, they believed, inhabited the higher levels of the cosmos. Paul, however, reminds them that they have received the blessings associated with Christ, who himself dwells in heavenly places and has subjugated other so-called powers that the people assumed were dwelling in such environments (1:20–22).

Ephesus was one of the most important commercial centers in the Roman Empire. With a flourishing international trade, it controlled the financial affairs of western Asia Minor. Important roads from the east ended at Ephesus, where people and goods were transported to and from Rome. Ephesus enjoyed political independence as a Roman free city, as a result of which it paid no tribute to Rome and acted relatively autonomously. The city reflected the pomp and splendor that went with that privilege, and emperors often visited Ephesus. It had its own proconsul, and all governors traveling east from Rome were required to land at Ephesus before continuing farther east. It was the third largest city in the East after Antioch and Alexandria, and the third most important city in the empire after Rome and Alexandria.

Paul informs the readers that their inheritance comes not from earthly riches but from heaven. Such an inheritance is secure, in contrast to the demise of status that can occur when unforeseen events befall an earthly city, as happened in Ephesus when its river silted up so badly that the city ceased to be valuable as a commercial center. Believers experience blessings that are of a different and timeless nature.

The Spirit seals the believer (1:13)

In him you also, who have heard the word of truth, the gospel of your salvation, and have believed in him, were sealed with the promised Holy Spirit.

Exposition

The description of the Spirit as "promised" is probably a reference to Ezek 36:26–27; 37:14 and Joel 2:28–32, although the fact that the fulfillment of this promise also included Gentiles may initially have surprised many (2:11–22; 3:6). Paul also describes the Spirit as "holy"—which refers more to the fact that he is different from all other spirits than to his perfection or sinlessness. The word "holy" (*hagios*) described deities, people, and objects, within and outside of Judaism, that were different and set apart. The Spirit is not simply different, however; he is unique.

Through their faith in Christ, believers are sealed with the Spirit. This "sealing" takes place at salvation, the term "seal" acting as a metaphor for the personal imprint of the Spirit on believers' lives. There is little evidence to suggest that it refers to a subsequent experience, be it water baptism or a secondary experience of the Spirit.

This concept of being sealed with the Spirit provides Paul with an opportunity to explore the radical nature of salvation. The practice of sealing documents and even people (Rev 5:1; 7:3) was common in the ancient world. Since it is less common today, it is helpful to look at the practice in ancient society in order to appreciate the significance of this concept. The seal was symbolic in a number of ways that help to illustrate the comprehensive nature of the Spirit's involvement in the life of a believer.

First, a seal signified ownership; that which was sealed bore the seal of its owner. A believer is sealed with the Holy Spirit, therefore the one who arranged for that sealing, Christ, owns that person. In a society that was rapidly becoming inhospitable to Christians, it was of considerable encouragement to them to realize that Christ had chosen to own them and had affirmed this by the presence of none other than the Spirit.

Second, a seal signified security. In the commercial center of Ephesus, buyers secured goods that they intended to purchase by stamping them with a seal of some description, indicating that the goods were spoken for and no longer for sale. The Spirit is such a security for believers. Not only does someone own them, but this owner also happens to be the one who possesses all authority. To seek to harm a believer, therefore, would be equivalent to attempting to harm God.

Third, a seal signified a completed transaction (Esth 8:8; Jer 32:10). The Spirit is God's way of reminding believers that he has completed the act of salvation.

Fourth, a seal signified value. To a group of Christians who soon will experience persecution and be treated as worthless objects, Paul sends the reminder that they are precious to God. Their promised destiny is their future and final redemption (4:30) after the act of salvation.

Significance for the Original Readers

As we saw above, first-century devotees did not generally have favorable relationships with the gods they worshipped. They sought to placate the gods rather than enjoy them. Most people did not anticipate a personal relationship with the gods, although they believed that some gods did protect and care for the emperor and some heroic figures. Most people, however, had a very distant relationship with the gods. The mystery cults came closest to offering a social dimension to relationships with supernatural forces. Paul, however, introduces the Spirit as the one who affirms the salvation of the believer, thereby authentically establishing his or her personal relationship with God.

The Spirit acts as a guarantee (1:14)

[The promised Holy Spirit] is the guarantee of our inheritance until we acquire possession of it, to the praise of his glory.

Exposition

Paul also uses the word *arrabōn* ("guarantee, down payment") in 2 Cor 1:22; 5:5, and always with reference to the Spirit. It is a technical term for a first installment or guarantee. The Spirit is God's down payment in the believer's life, and as such, he acts as a guarantee and a taste of the future. But whose inheritance is being guaranteed? Is it the inheritance that the believer will receive in this life and the next? Or is it the inheritance of God, which consists of all those who have been sealed by him? Paul may be referring to the fact that believers will receive their full inheritance after death. However, it is more likely that he is indicating that believers themselves are God's inheritance. The phrase "acquire possession" is regularly translated "redeem" and elsewhere in the Bible, redemption is always initiated by God (Ps 111:9; Isa 43:1).

The first option is comforting; the second is remarkable. According to the first interpretation, believers will possess the inheritance graciously promised to them by God. The latter, and more likely, interpretation indicates that God will possess the inheritance of his choosing, the church, for himself. The cumulative effect is to provide readers with a sense of well-being and security; they are loved beyond their understanding.

Significance for the Original Readers

There was a great deal of uncertainty in the ancient world. Centuries before Paul, the famous Ephesian philosopher Heraclitus acknowledged the timeless fact that "No one can wash his feet twice in the same water, because everything is changing." In Ephesus, a fire was kept burning to act as a guarantee that the city would not be destroyed. Security was an important feature of Ephesian life, and a six-mile-long wall surrounded the city. Ephesians felt apprehension about the uncertainty of life most acutely in matters relating to illness and life after death. Many believed that dead people continued to exist in some form after burial in or near the tomb; thereafter, hopes grew that a pleasant afterlife awaited many.

However, what was lacking was a sense of certainty about such issues. The believer's security in God was unchanging, guaranteed by the Spirit. For Paul, Christianity was not a distant religion with an absent deity; the ascended Christ did not signal an absent Christ. The remarkable aspect of Christianity is that the Spirit has taken up residence within the worshipper. The implication of such a privileged status is that believers are encouraged to live in the knowledge that they have been chosen by God.

The Spirit provides wisdom and revelation (1:16–17; 3:4–5)

I do not cease to give thanks for you, remembering you in my prayers, that the God of our Lord Jesus Christ, the Father of glory, may give you a spirit of wisdom and of revelation in the knowledge of him. (1:16–17)

When you read this you can perceive my insight into the mystery of Christ, which was not made known to the sons of men in other generations as it has now been revealed to his holy apostles and prophets by the Spirit. (3:4–5)

Exposition

In 1:17, Paul prays that God will give his Spirit to the believers so that they can accurately and experientially know certain aspects of truth concerning God, particularly relating to their salvation. Although God grants the Spirit to give power for Christian service, the Spirit also enables the believer to explore God intellectually and experientially. Being absorbed in an examination of God is what gives the Christian life dynamism. That has been Paul's experience, and he wants his readers likewise to realize that God is to be explored and to recognize that the Spirit enables them to enjoy that journey into God.

Although many translations have "spirit of wisdom" in 1:17, it is preferable to understand that Paul is referring to the Spirit of wisdom and revelation (cf. Col 1:9). He who revealed information by his Spirit to prophets and apostles in the past (3:4–5) is now willing to offer revelation to other believers.

Significance for the Original Readers

Many people believed that Roman gods preferred anonymity, based on the assumption that the power of the god was invested in its name. If the name was known, the power of the god could be accessed, even without its acquiescence. Thus, in magical practices both gods and magicians carefully guarded the name of the god. "The God of our Lord Jesus Christ," however, chooses not to remain hidden or distant, and it is the Spirit who helps the believer to understand more about God.

Sometimes people accessed the will of the gods by oracles, dreams, or divination. Generally, oracles provided responses to requests for information given through a devotee of a god, often based at a particular shrine. Dreams sometimes were thought to reveal information and were generally interpreted or explained by priests. Divination was also a common practice. Many people believed that the gods could communicate in everyday events, such as the flight path of birds or the casting of dice. A special class of diviners identified such omens, and many took them seriously.

Paul indicates that believers have access to a much more dependable source of wisdom, mediated by the Spirit. This was also a marked improvement on the OT situation, in which the Spirit inspired only a few special people (3:5).

The Spirit provides ongoing access to God (2:18)

Through [Christ Jesus] we both have access in one Spirit to the Father.

Exposition

Starting at 2:1, Paul has been exploring the radical change that occurred in the believers' lives because of their salvation. They had been transferred from death to life (2:5), from following the prince of the power of the air to being seated with Christ (2:2, 6), and all this had been achieved by the grace of God (2:4–8). The verse now under examination concludes a section that commences with 2:14 in which Paul describes the reconciliation achieved by the Spirit between the readers and God and with each other as Jews and Gentiles. The Spirit is the common sphere of their lives together and of their life with God. The phrase "in one Spirit" (2:18) probably describes the proximity of believers to the Spirit, as a result of which they have access to God's presence. Paul's expectation is that they will realize that they are constantly in the presence of God and learn to experientially enjoy it. It is the Spirit who makes this possible.

Paul uses the term "access" (2:18) to describe what the Spirit creates. The term has been used in various ways—to refer to introducing people to others as well as to providing an open door to the presence of (often important) people. Although both interpretations are attractive, the context best suits the latter alternative. Either one describes a privileged relationship with God—unusual for Jews, rare for Gentiles. However, because they are in the Spirit, they are also in the presence of God and are enabled to enjoy a relationship with him.

Significance for the Original Readers

The heart of Ephesus was the agora (about 110 meters square), a public space where many activities took place relating to politics, entertainment, education, religion, and commerce. However, the marginalized members of society were denied entry to it. It also housed the advisory council of the city, the ecclesia—a term used in the NT for the church (nine times in Ephesians). Paul celebrates the fact that all believers are able to enjoy access to the Christian ecclesia.

In ancient religions, people had access to the gods through the priests. Over the years, the ranks and orders of priests became more complex and hierarchical, but their fundamental role was a mediatorial one between the worshipper and the gods. They officiated when a devotee brought a sacrifice to the gods and acted as the representative for the gods when advice was asked of them. Believers have been granted personal access to God on an ongoing basis, and the Spirit is the guarantee of that relationship.

Because of the work of the Spirit, all believers are granted this privilege. Previous access to God was through the temple and its cult; now, it is through the Spirit, and therefore anyone can benefit, at any time, anywhere, and continuously.

The Spirit forms believers into a dwelling place for God (2:21–22)

The whole structure is joined together and grows into a holy temple in the Lord; in whom you also are built into it for a dwelling place of God in the Spirit.

Exposition

Not only is God accessible to believers, but the Spirit also makes believers accessible to God. Paul describes the readers as being part of a "holy temple in the Lord" (2:21). The phrase "in the

Spirit" (2:22) indicates that believers become the dwelling place of God because of their relationship with the Spirit. This phrase could also be translated "by the Spirit," meaning that it is the Spirit who builds the believer into the temple. The translation "in the Spirit" affirms the significance of the act of salvation that results in the believer being the dwelling place of God, while "by the Spirit" identifies the dynamic and deliberate incorporation of the believer into the temple. Regardless of the interpretation that one prefers, and they are similar, it is clear that the Spirit consolidates believers into God's place of residence by an act of the divine will.

Significance for the Original Readers

The fact that believers are likened to a temple is significant. The temple in Jerusalem played a crucial role in Jewish history, for it was the place where God's glory was believed to dwell. God now dwells in the church, in Gentiles as well as Jews, who together make up the church. This has a twofold significance: It reminds Paul's readers of the privilege of such a position and that they should not take it for granted; it also emphasizes the fact that they are part of a wider body that includes Jews and Gentiles.

Many temples, which acted as the earthly residences of various gods, dominated the city of Ephesus. On two occasions by the beginning of the second century, Ephesus was honored by being named as the "temple warden" (*neokoros*) of the imperial cult. Chief among those venerated was the goddess Artemis (Diana, to the Romans), who was worshipped as the ruler over all and the mother of everything.

Artemis's temple was rebuilt, about four hundred years before Paul reached the city, on top of the ruins of a previous temple to her that was begun about 550 B.C.E. This latest temple measured 70 by 130 meters and featured seventy columns, each two meters wide and twenty meters tall. Given that many temples were no larger than several meters square, functioning as little more than shrines, the temple to Artemis was huge and was designated as one of the wonders of the world. The temple of God, by contrast, is not built with beautiful sculptured stones. Rather, it is formed by a community of ordinary members of society who have been transformed by the Spirit.

Significantly, temples were often used as vehicles of propaganda. Victorious emperors, triumphant generals, or newly elected politicians dedicated temples to commemorate their successes.

They were high-profile showcases and, as such, they demonstrated the status of those who instituted them. It is a marvel
that God entrusts believers to act as the base of his operations
in the world.

Temples were also used as banks for storing valuables belonging to individuals and cities. Paul encourages his readers to recognize that a commodity of inestimable value has been stored in
them: none other than God himself. The fundamental purpose of
the Greco-Roman temple was to provide a location for the image
of the god or goddess. The Ephesian believers, who had no equivalent temple in which to house their God, were themselves his
temple.

The Spirit empowers believers (3:16–19)

*[For this reason I bow my knees before the Father . . .], that accord-
ing to the riches of his glory he may grant you to be strengthened
with might through his Spirit in the inner man and that Christ may
dwell in your hearts through faith; that you, being rooted and
grounded in love, may have power to comprehend with all the
saints what is the breadth and length and height and depth, and to
know the love of Christ which surpasses knowledge, that you may be
filled with all the fulness of God.*

Exposition

Paul now prays (3:16–19) that the readers will receive power
to comprehend God's love more fully and to be filled with God,
acknowledging that this occurs because of the Spirit.

In this letter, Paul has not yet explored the charismatic power
of the Spirit that enables the believer to serve God effectively. He
is intent on first exploring with his readers the value of the Spirit,
who leads believers into God—a journey that will result in their receiving a greater revelation of the grandeur of their God and the
comprehensive nature of their salvation. Paul wants his readers to
understand that the Spirit helps believers understand the glory of
God and their value to him. Once they understand that, he will explore their role as empowered servants. For the present, Paul
informs them of their identity in God, noting that it is the Spirit's
express purpose to enlighten them in that regard.

Only Paul uses the term "inner man" (*eso anthropos*) in the NT. It refers to the central and foundational aspect of an individual, the essence or heart of a person. The power imparted is related neither to physical strength nor to prestige. It is a supernatural, motivating force intended to effect changes in character and thought. Paul anticipates that love will become a dominating force in believers' lives (3:17–19) as a result of this power.

Significance for the Original Readers

Most ancient religions and cults believed that the gods empowered some people with supernatural powers to reveal secrets, protect against tragedies, or receive answers to prayers. Thus, the concept of divine empowerment was common, and sometimes harnessed through magic. Ephesus was renowned for its magical activities (Acts 19:19). People purchased charms and special "Ephesian letters" in the city, placed them in small metal tubes or lockets, and wore them around their necks in the hope of averting disasters and fulfilling desires. The people of Ephesus were interested in supernatural spirits and their ability to empower, but Paul's desire was that they know the Holy Spirit and his empowerment. Although supernatural spirits of the secular world were expected to provide supernatural information on occasion, Paul knows not only that their source is evil but also that they are untrustworthy and insubstantial in their effectiveness. The Spirit, however, is motivated by love, is comprehensively powerful, and enables them to be empowered supernaturally, effectively, and for their benefit.

The Spirit provides unity among believers (4:3)

[Be] eager to maintain the unity of the Spirit in the bond of peace.

Exposition

Paul's statement here assumes that the Spirit has already initiated unity; the believers' responsibility is to maintain it. They are already one body; now, Paul exhorts them to experience the benefits of such unity and guard it.

The quality of this unity is defined by the word "peace"—it is a "bond of peace." It is possible that Paul is suggesting that they will display this unity by living in peace with each other, indicating the importance of such unity having a demonstrable outcome. Paul may also be saying that they will achieve this peace by allowing the fruit of peace expressed by the Spirit to be manifested through them—thereby reminding readers of the importance of ensuring that the Spirit is an active part of their development as believers. They are to emulate that unity in their fellowship because of, and with the help of, the Spirit.

Significance for the Original Readers

Except for the mystery religions, Christianity was unique in that it offered the possibility of a close-knit egalitarian society. Although the Roman Empire was a single political entity, a fragmented population inhabited it. Disunity characterized the era. Not only were there political and geographical rivalries between provinces and leaders, but also other, more common, phenomena were evidence of a society in danger of falling apart. There were huge variations in lifestyle and stark contrasts in status. Slaves existed in close proximity to wealthy folk; racial barriers divided Jews and Gentiles, Jews and Samaritans, Egyptians and Romans, indigenous people and immigrants. Paul presents a gospel that breaks down such barriers among people.

Paul's teaching about the unity that the Spirit initiates spoke to a difficult situation. His readers were the product of an economically divided city. The poorer members of the community tended to live outside the city, while the upper classes of people lived in the city precincts, with the wealthiest citizens dominating the center of the city. The quality of living accommodation reflected these differences, with the poorer members of society existing in hovels without running water while the richer citizens lived in lavish and well-built houses, often with inner courtyards with fountains.

The populace also represented different racial groupings. There was a large Jewish community at Ephesus (Acts 18:19; 19:8) that was granted freedom in the observance of the Sabbath and other religious practices. Although Gentiles dominated society, in Ephesus and some other cities Jews had won certain privileges. Nevertheless, they were still two distinctly separate groups that sometimes experienced conflict. Thus, Paul encourages his readers to maintain the unity that the Spirit has initiated.

The believer is not to grieve the Spirit (4:30)

And do not grieve the Holy Spirit of God, in whom you were sealed for the day of redemption.

Exposition

This verse highlights one of the most serious issues regarding the Spirit's presence in believers. This is the only place where Paul describes the Spirit as "the Holy Spirit of God"—a solemn and graphic reminder of the one of whom he is speaking.

In 4:17–21, Paul reminds his readers of their previous lives; then he exhorts them to develop their new lives as believers (4:22–5:20), offering a number of suggestions about how they can best achieve this. Of primary importance is that they should not grieve the Spirit, a concept recorded only here in the NT. The clearest OT parallel to this idea is found in Isa 63:10, where Israel, in rejecting God, is said to have "grieved his holy Spirit." The expression has the sense of "to hurt, cause pain" rather than "to irritate, annoy."

The parallel with the OT passage is clear. Both Israel and the church had been redeemed and brought into a relationship with God based on a covenant. Since the Spirit has sealed believers for the day of their consummated redemption, for them to hurt the Spirit is an inconceivable act. It is as if Paul is recommending that the readers consider the humiliation of embarrassing someone who vouches for them, whom they let down, and whose reputation as a guarantor they thereby bring into disrepute. It is the height of ingratitude for people to hurt the one who has authenticated them. Also, Paul is concerned that his readers not commit sins that undermine what the Spirit is seeking to achieve.

The Spirit is seeking to unite the people; if by their actions they bring about disunity and hurt within the body of believers, they will also be hurting the Spirit. Given that the Spirit, having sealed them, is committed to them until their final redemption, such behavior on their part would be all the more grievous.

Significance for the Original Readers

The readers would have been accustomed to the idea that the actions of people could offend the gods. Most public disasters were assumed to have been caused by a breakdown in relations between the gods and humanity. Thus, as far as the official religions were concerned, it was important to placate the gods by sacrifice and to obey them. Worshippers were to fulfill all vows that they offered to the gods and to avoid all offensive actions. Otherwise, the gods might become hostile.

Opportunities for grieving the Spirit abounded in Ephesus. The temples provided opportunities for idolatry and other excesses, while the secular society accommodated indulgence in many kinds of immoral practices. For example, in the center of Ephesus, opposite the library of Celsus (large enough to accommodate twelve thousand scrolls) and next to the temple of Hadrian, stood a two-story brothel.

However, the sins that appear to be particularly injurious to the Spirit are those associated with the tongue (4:29, 31; 5:4, 6). These sins break fellowship, destroy friendships, undermine unity, and therefore grieve the Spirit. Although other crimes may be particularly heinous, Paul reminds the readers of the destructive potential of the tongue. The Spirit indwells believers in order that they may be sanctified. When believers adopt an evil lifestyle instead, the objectives of the Spirit are not realized.

Paul is saying that the Spirit can feel. Trying to describe in human terms what the Spirit feels is fruitless, but believers need to recognize that their behavior affects the Spirit and has consequences. The Spirit is affected by the spiritual journey of believers when it does not lead to the destiny planned from the start. The Spirit is not an impersonal deity but is impacted by the sins of believers.

The believer is to be filled with the Spirit (5:18–19)

And do not get drunk with wine, for that is debauchery; but be filled with the Spirit, addressing one another in psalms and hymns and spiritual songs, singing and making melody to the Lord with all your heart.

Exposition

Paul encourages believers to ensure that the Spirit is the dominating force in their lives, rather than to allow a sinful agenda to control their lives. Paul locates the outworking of being "filled with the Spirit" in corporate worship and life. The evidence of being filled with the Spirit is a corporate life characterized by worship (5:19), thanksgiving (5:20), and mutual submission (5:21–6:9).

As with the command not to grieve the Spirit (4:30), Paul employs an imperative here: "be filled with the Spirit." Because the Greek imperative verb translated "be filled" (*plerousthe*) is in the present tense, it indicates a continuing filling. Thus, Paul does not exhort them to be full of the Spirit, but rather to be continuously filled with the Spirit. The potential consequences of such a Spirit-controlled life are radically important for the individual and corporate lives of the believers.

Significance for the Original Readers

The command "Do not get drunk on wine, . . . but be filled with the Spirit" may be understood in a number of ways. It is unlikely that Paul is concerned about a problem with drunkenness in the church, as he does not refer to it anywhere else. He may, however, be seeking to draw out the consequences of being filled with wine versus being filled with the Spirit. Whereas the former inevitably leads to excess and potential debauchery, the latter automatically leads to harmonious communal worship and thanksgiving to God (5:19–20). Thus, Paul contrasts a foolish action with a wise one (5:15), or their old lives with their new ones (5:8).

In addition, one of the major effects of drunkenness is losing one's self-control; the drink becomes the controlling force. It is possible that Paul is drawing a parallel with the Spirit by indicating that the Spirit must be the dominating force in their lives. Being filled with the Spirit will not result in debauchery, but rather in the Spirit's beneficial influence on their worship, thanksgiving, and personal living. Paul encourages readers to allow the Spirit to exercise this force that will benefit them individually and communally.

The believer is to use that which the Spirit supplies (6:17–18)

And take the helmet of salvation, and the sword of the Spirit, which is the word of God. Pray at all times in the Spirit, with all prayer and supplication.

Exposition

Paul's final two references to the Spirit are found in his description of the armor with which believers are to clothe themselves (6:10–20). The statements concerning the Spirit relate to his provision in situations of conflict. Paul encourages the readers to use "the sword of the Spirit." This may refer to the idea that the Spirit gives the sword, or that the Spirit provides power to use it effectively, or that it belongs to the Spirit. Given the activity antici-pated on the part of the believer, a combination of the first two options is preferable.

The sword is not to be equated with the Spirit; the sword is identified as the "word" (*rhēma*). Although *rhēma* and *logos* are sometimes used synonymously, Paul may be emphasizing the role of the Spirit in inspired speech at a given point in time rather than referring to the Scriptures as the sword of the Spirit. Thus, while the Spirit is ready to impart wisdom, it is incumbent on believers to be sensitive to his guidance so that they may speak authoritatively when he leads them. Paul uses the word *rhēma* to describe the good news of the gospel (5:26), and so he is perhaps reminding the readers that although they may not be confident in sharing the good news, the Spirit ensures that the presentation of the gospel will be supernaturally supported.

The second reference to the Spirit is in the context of "praying in the Spirit" (this may be another imperative, but the Greek does not require it). It is possible that Paul is offering another weapon to the believer, although no military parallel is linked to prayer. The meaning of the sentence must relate, at least in part, to the empowering of the Spirit in prayer. This may include praying in tongues, but it more likely refers to the practice of praying in co-operation with the Spirit, when the Spirit assumes a central role. Thus, Paul is probably reminding readers that the Spirit initiates prayer. Prayer is not an opportunity to instruct or advise God as to the best outcome, but rather an opportunity to listen to the Spirit, who will advise the believer how best to pray.

Significance for the Original Readers

Paul is not reprimanding his readers, nor is there a crisis of dis-cipleship. It is more likely that they are experiencing a crisis of confidence. In the face of the inhospitable community surround-ing them and the hostile forces arrayed against them (6:11–12), God has made spiritual resources available to them, and Paul en-courages his readers to access them. He acknowledges the exis-tence of malevolent supernatural forces (1:21; 2:2; 6:12). Gentile readers were familiar with the concept of supernatural rulers who held authority over large areas of the world. Ancient astrological schemas also assumed the existence of such powers. Similarly, Jewish readers were acquainted with spiritual powers in the heavens (Job 1:6; Dan 10).

The imagery of armor would have been familiar to readers because it was similar to that worn by the Roman legionnaires. In addition, the OT presents God as a warrior who dons armor (Isa 42:13; 59:17).

The Spirit promises to impart wisdom in communicating the gospel and/or the revelation of God to others and to help in prayer. In the ancient religions, one of the most commonly accepted ways of securing help from a deity was through prayer. Worshippers often offered prayers in association with sacrifice or other rituals. Paul presents prayer for believers as a privilege that God grants to them, and not as associated with any formulaic or mechanistic setting. A major difference is that believers are encouraged not simply to pray, but also to recognize that the Spirit helps them to pray.

Selected Bibliography

Best, Ernest. *A Critical and Exegetical Commentary on Ephesians.* International Critical Commentary. Edinburgh: T&T Clark, 1998.

Fee, Gordon D. *God's Empowering Presence: The Holy Spirit in the Letters of Paul.* Peabody, Mass.: Hendrickson, 1994.

Hoehner, Harold W. *Ephesians. An Exegetical Commentary.* Grand Rapids: Baker, 2002.

Lincoln, Andrew T. *Ephesians.* Word Biblical Commentary 42. Dallas: Word, 1990.

O'Brien, Peter T. *The Letter to the Ephesians.* Pillar New Testament Commentary. Grand Rapids: Eerdmans, 1999.

The Significance for Readers Today

1. What are some of the blessings that the Spirit provides for you today (1:3)?
2. How does the Spirit provide security for you (1:13)?
3. Does the Spirit guarantee your inheritance, or God his inheritance, which is the church (1:14)? How does your answer make you feel?
4. For what personal issues do you need wisdom (1:16–17; 3:4–5)?

5. What does it mean, practically speaking, to have access to God (2:18)?
6. What are the implications of knowing that you are the dwelling place of God (2:21–22)?
7. In what ways does the Spirit empower your life (3:16)?
8. How can you maintain the unity initiated by the Spirit (4:3) in your family, church, and other spheres of influence?
9. In what ways is it possible for you to grieve the Spirit? What steps can you take to ensure that you don't do this (4:30)?
10. Is the Spirit the dominating influence in your life? If not, what do you need to do so that you can be filled with the Spirit on an ongoing basis (5:18–19)?
11. What difference does the Spirit's empowering make in your witness and in your prayer life (6:17–18)?

chapter 10

*P*hilippians

The Setting

Paul wrote this affectionate letter while in prison, probably in Rome, to people who were part of the first church established in Greece (Acts 16:11–40). He had first spoken to the Jews in Philippi at the place of prayer. One of the first converts was Lydia, and her home became their base. The only recorded exorcism in Acts occurred in Philippi and was followed by Paul's arrest, flogging, imprisonment, miraculous release, and the subsequent conversion of the jailer and his family. After being released from prison, Paul returned to Lydia's home and then moved on to Thessalonica. Most of Paul's original readers were probably Gentiles.

What Does the Author Say about the Spirit?

The Spirit

- is the resource for the believer (1:19)

- provides unity and fellowship (1:27; 2:1–2)

- enables worship (3:3)

The Spirit is the resource for the believer (1:19)

Yes, and I shall rejoice. For I know that through your prayers and the help of the Spirit of Jesus Christ this will turn out for my deliverance.

Exposition

Paul refers to "the Spirit of Jesus Christ." Although modern readers may wonder whether he is referring to Jesus or the Spirit or both, such questions are less important to Paul. His understanding of God is quite fluid and dynamic. While he appreciates the distinctive nature of the members of the Godhead, he also recognizes their interactive interdependency. He often identifies one characteristic or function as belonging to more than one of the members. He probably associates the Spirit with Jesus Christ in the context of his numerous references to the latter in 1:1–18.

Paul begins here to reflect on his own situation in prison (1:13–14). In particular, he is confident that he will continue to rejoice and be positive in his circumstances because of the prayers of the Philippians and supernatural help. He recognizes that this help, coming from the Spirit, is of the same quality as that which Jesus, to whom he has just been referring, had experienced when he was on earth.

It is not certain what specific form this help took. Paul anticipates deliverance (*sōtēria*), though he does not specify whether it refers to deliverance from prison (2:24), from a situation of humiliation and disgrace (1:20),[1] or from a position of helplessness and weakness to one characterized by boldness (1:20). Regardless of the form of deliverance, three conclusions may be drawn:

- Paul is aware that prayer makes a difference. Indeed, it is possible that he assumes a link between their prayers and the outpouring of supernatural help on his behalf. In the Greek, a single definite article governing both "prayers" and "help" suggests their close association. While the Spirit is not only activated through the prayers of others, this fact does identify prayer as an important part of the process.

- Paul is certain that the resources of the Spirit are available to him, though he appears to be indicating that it is

---

[1] In 1:20, Paul is not concerned about being embarrassed or humiliated by his experiences. Rather, when he speaks of not being "ashamed," he uses the word in its Jewish sense, whereby he, as the representative of God, does not want his present context to somehow reflect negatively on the one who sent him. His thoughts are not egocentric, but theocentric, centered not on his personal pride but on the majesty of God, which must not be demeaned.

not so much the resources of the Spirit that are made available to him as the Spirit himself. Although it is unnecessary to try to separate the Spirit from the help he provides, here is another helpful reminder that Paul is less interested in downloading the resources granted by the Spirit than he is in developing a relationship with the Spirit. Both are necessary for, and available to, the believer, but Paul's emphasis is always on the latter. The Spirit is the fundamental gift (Gal 3:5) who also gives gifts.

• As a consequence of the prayers of the readers and the help the Spirit provided, Paul is confident that he will not be shamed by this experience. He will experience sufficient courage to do what is necessary, with the result that Jesus will be exalted. He is confident that, although he is unable to fulfill his normal apostolic ministry because of his confinement in prison, God is still in charge and will ensure not only that his plans are achieved but also that the Spirit will support his messenger.

Significance for the Original Readers

Acts 16 explains the context of opposition in which the church in Philippi was established, with the leaders being imprisoned prior to their leaving the city. The believers are also aware of supernatural and civic opposition. It is no surprise, therefore, that suffering is a major theme in Paul's letter to the Philippians (1:29–30; 3:10). He encourages his readers to have confidence that the same resources of the Spirit that were available to him, and to Jesus before him, are also available to them. This same Spirit is theirs also. Paul refers to vindication, courage, and the exaltation of Jesus, and these concepts take on new significance for the readers as they apply them to various circumstances. They are also to look forward to exalting Jesus in their lives and among their contemporaries, with supernatural backing and courage.

The Spirit provides unity and fellowship (1:27; 2:1–2)

Only let your manner of life be worthy of the gospel of Christ, so that whether I come and see you or am absent, I may hear of you that you stand firm in one spirit, with one mind striving side by side for the faith of the gospel. (1:27)

Exposition

Although the term *pneuma* here is translated as "spirit" and thus interpreted as an internal attitude of mutual determination among the addressees to stand together, it is also possible that Paul is referring to the Spirit, especially because likely translations of *pneuma* to mean "spirit" are difficult to locate in Pauline literature. Paul is therefore recommending that the readers stand together in the Spirit, with his resources. They are different from any other group of people; they are not like a guild or group of like-minded artisans. There is a different dimension to their relationships with each other—a spiritual one. Not only do they function in relationships on a horizontal level, but they add to this a vertical dimension as they relate to God. It is the Spirit who makes the latter possible and who also enables them to experience horizontal relationships that can be stronger and deeper than those among all other groups of people.

So if there is any encouragement in Christ, any incentive of love, any participation in the Spirit, any affection and sympathy, complete my joy by being of the same mind, having the same love, being in full accord and of one mind. (2:1–2)

Exposition

Paul here continues the theme of unity that he referred to a few verses earlier in 1:27. He emphasizes his desire for this unity in four expressions, one of which relates to fellowship in the Spirit. Here, as in 1:27, it is possible that *pneuma* refers to "spirit," or an internal attitude of people committed to being united, but it is much more likely that Paul is referring to the Spirit. It makes sense, then, that Paul is appealing to the fellowship associated with the Spirit as an incentive for the readers to be united. Since the Spirit is committed to unity within the Godhead, Paul assumes that he also initiates unity among believers. He therefore encourages believers to emulate the Spirit by being like-minded with one another.

The word "participation" (*koinōnia*) that Paul uses here is regularly used for two-way conversation. He anticipates a dialogical rather than a hierarchical relationship between the believers—a partnership of friends who talk and listen to each other. If this mutuality did not characterize their relationships it would be strange, if not bizarre, and certainly a cause for concern, since they are a community of the Spirit, who manifests himself in love and who empowers believers to do the same. If love is not present in relationships between believers, it begs the question as to why not.

Participation in the life of the Spirit could relate to fellowship with other believers, fellowship between Paul and the Philippians, or fellowship with the Spirit. Although the last option is more likely, it is possible that Paul prefers not to specify, since all are applicable. What is more important is that, in their striving for unity, they are to note the Spirit's example and empowering activity on their behalf.

Significance for the Original Readers

Not only is this verse a reminder of an integral element of the Spirit's person and ministry, that of unity, but it also focuses on the fact that true fellowship is not possible among believers unless they appreciate its importance to the community. Furthermore, they need to understand that the Spirit provides the resources to maintain this unity.

This stress on unity is particularly important in a context where believers are a minority in a multicultural city. They are strongest when they are able to maintain good relationships with each other (1:27; 2:1–4; 4:2–3). Not only is this a useful defensive measure, but it also functions as a telling testimony in a city that was fragmented along lines of culture, religion, wealth, and language (1:27). Paul emphasizes that the Spirit is committed to unity and enables believers to develop it.

The Spirit enables worship (3:3)

For we are the true circumcision, who worship God in spirit, and glory in Christ Jesus, and put no confidence in the flesh.

Exposition

There seems to be little reason not to translate the Greek *pneuma* as "Spirit" (many translations prefer to follow early manuscripts that read "worship in/by the Spirit of God"). This verse is set in the context of a warning, that believers should not attempt to please God by human activity (3:3b). It appears that Paul is referring to Jews who are advising the believers to adopt Jewish practices, including circumcision (3:2). In response, he affirms that believers already worship and serve God whether they are circumcised or not. Physical characteristics are inconsequential; what matters is the authenticity of the worship, and this is determined by spiritual, not physical, issues. Jews and Christians used the term "worship" (*latreuō*) for service to God (Deut 6:13; Rom 1:9), and "service" is probably the more appropriate translation, since service can also include worship.

Significance for the Original Readers

The citizens of Philippi were proud of their heritage and wealth gained from mining precious metals, and also of their status as citizens of Rome (Acts 16:12, 21, 37–38). They were pleased to serve Caesar and to oppose those who served any other. Paul reminds his readers that their higher citizenship is in a heavenly kingdom (3:20) and that the Spirit gives them supernatural help to enable them to serve their God. The majority may exclude them, but they have an exclusive resource in the person of the Spirit.

Jews, who were offering the OT as support for their contention that the people of God must be circumcised, were badgering the believers. In response, Paul refers the readers not to a literary prescription, the OT, but to a living person, the Spirit. It is not a static guideline that is to influence their lifestyles, but a dynamic guide. Whereas the Scriptures can give some guidelines, the Spirit is essential to authentic worship. Paul wanted the believers to recognize the superior form and communication of revelation available through the Spirit, who dynamically lives in each believer, enabling him or her to fulfill the agenda the Spirit sets for a godly life.

In particular, Paul's contention is that circumcision does not enable a person to serve or worship God; rather, the Spirit enables the believer to worship. Divine activity, not human activity, determines acceptable service to God—not what people achieve, but what the Spirit achieves. Initially, it is what the Spirit does for people, not what people do for God. The Spirit makes service possible, enabling believers to do that which only he himself is able to do. Indeed, the term once used to describe the Jews' service and worship of God has now been transferred to that of the Christians.

Selected Bibliography

Fee, Gordon D. *God's Empowering Presence: The Holy Spirit in the Letters of Paul*. Peabody, Mass.: Hendrickson, 1994.

Hawthorne, Gerald F. *Philippians*. Word Biblical Commentary 43. Waco, Tex.: Word, 1983.

O'Brien, Peter T. *The Epistle to the Philippians: A Commentary on the Greek Text*. New International Greek Testament Commentary. Grand Rapids: Eerdmans, 1991.

The Significance for Readers Today

1. How can a focus on the Spirit and his resources help you through times of trial and suffering (1:19)?
2. Given that unity is one of the Spirit's top priorities, what can you do, in your sphere of influence, to improve unity among believers (1:27; 2:1–2)?
3. In what ways does the Spirit stimulate you to serve God, and how can you be more open to his influence (3:3)?

chapter 11

*C*olossians

The Setting

Paul wrote this letter mainly in response to a heresy that undermined the person of Jesus. Consequently, although there are few references to the Spirit in the letter, there are many references to the person of Christ. Apparently, Paul himself did not establish the church at Colossae. It may have formed as a result of the evangelism of Epaphras (1:7; 4:12). Although once a major city with a thriving woolen industry, by Paul's time Colossae had lost much of its prominence.

What Does the Author Say about the Spirit?

The information that Paul presents concerning the Spirit focuses on his association with love, wisdom, and worship. The Spirit is the one who inspires and enables believers to love others and to praise God, while also providing them with the wisdom they need to live godly lives.

The Spirit

- inspires love (1:8)

- provides wisdom (1:9)

- inspires praise (3:16)

The Spirit inspires love (1:8)

[Epaphras] has made known to us your love in the Spirit.

Exposition

The love that the Colossians demonstrate for other believers encourages Paul (1:4). It is possible that he is referring to that same love here in 1:8, although he may be referring more specifically to their love for him. Perhaps he feels able to write such an authoritative letter to them because of their love for him. While he may be referring to their love for all the believers, including himself in particular, his main point is that this love indicates the presence of the Spirit in their lives. It is because they have received the Spirit that they are able to manifest this quality of love.

Significance for the Original Readers

The majority of the readers were Gentiles (1:21; 2:13). Before they became believers, they would have participated in some of the various worship activities of the city. This may have included worship of the emperor and local deities as well as the major gods and goddesses of Greco-Roman society. Mystery religions met in small groups, offering an intimate relationship with the deity concerned as well as occult activities. None of these, however, were likely to have motivated the worshippers to live ethically upright lives. In 1:21, Paul specifically refers to the previous evil behavior of the readers.

However, as a result of their coming to faith in Christ, a new force, the Spirit, has entered their lives and has stimulated them to love others. Through the Spirit, they have been able to transform their lifestyles by initiating love for others instead of exhibiting egocentric behavior. Paul presents the same information to the smallest city to which he writes as he does to the largest (Rom 5:5). The role of the Spirit is to establish love in the lives of believers and to empower them to love.

Whereas false teachers present mystical beliefs and carefully crafted propositions, Paul directs the attention of the readers to the tangible evidence of the work of the Spirit in their lives. There is no comparison between the Spirit and those who provide intellectual arguments or academic treatises. The Spirit makes a real difference in the lives of those whom he inhabits as he enables them to act, not just think, differently. The wisdom of the false teachers leads their followers to a false humility (2:18); the wisdom of the Spirit leads believers to the humility of loving others. The Spirit provides the inclination and power to love, not the intellectual prowess that leads to pride (2:18). The Spirit brings not the love of knowledge, but the knowledge of love and how to practice it.

The Spirit provides wisdom (1:9)

And so, from the day we heard of it, we have not ceased to pray for you, asking that you may be filled with the knowledge of his will in all spiritual wisdom and understanding.

Exposition

A better translation of the last part of this verse is "that you may be filled with the knowledge of his will in all wisdom and understanding by the Spirit." Paul is saying that the presence of the Spirit in the lives of believers will result in their being able to discern his will for their lives—in ways that he will outline in the verses that follow. It is not that the wisdom is simply spiritual; more accurately, it comes from the Spirit.

Significance for the Original Readers

Although it is difficult to determine precisely what Paul was combating in his letter to the Colossians, clearly he was responding to a belief that strongly emphasized wisdom (2:8). The danger that the peddlers of this philosophical thinking will deceive the believers concerns him (2:8). He responds by talking about the Spirit, and in particular he reminds the believers that he, too, has a resource of wisdom available to him. In fact, he describes this wisdom that resides with the Spirit as full, or complete, knowledge (1:9).

In this regard, Paul is, in effect, contrasting those who do have the Spirit with those who do not. Those who have no relationship with the Spirit are not privy to this comprehensive wisdom, but Paul is.

Human wisdom	*The wisdom of the Spirit*
Their wisdom is based on human reasoning (2:22).	The wisdom of Paul springs from divine revelation.
It appears to be related to wisdom (2:23).	It is rooted in the source of wisdom.

| It comes from spiritual forces of the universe (2:8). | It comes from the Spirit who owns the universe. |
| Their wisdom fails to restrain sexual indulgence (2:23). | The wisdom offered by the Spirit leads to ethically upright lifestyles (3:1–4:6). |

Paul here informs his readers of his regular prayer that they also will increasingly be recipients of this same wisdom, available to them because of the presence of the Spirit.

The Spirit inspires praise (3:16)

Let the word of Christ dwell in you richly, teach and admonish one another in all wisdom, and sing psalms and hymns and spiritual songs with thankfulness in your hearts to God.

Exposition

A more suitable translation of the expression "spiritual songs" is "songs of the Spirit." Paul is not referring to Christian choruses as opposed to secular songs of the theater or folk songs. He is describing an outpouring of the Spirit, through the believers, of worship to God. One of the Spirit's roles is to inspire new songs and motivate believers to sing praise to God. As elsewhere, Paul presents the Spirit in an all-encompassing way, showing that he supports believers at all times, including in their worship.

Significance for the Original Readers

One element of the heretical teaching that entices the believers is related to the worship of angels (2:18). Paul reminds them that true worship is given to God through Jesus Christ (3:17), and the Spirit leads them in that direction. Believers can trust the Spirit, unlike the false teachers, to inspire their praise properly. Before they became believers, they were aware of the influence of evil spirits on them (2:20). Now, he states, their spiritual guide is the Spirit, who knows how and where to direct their worship aright.

The characteristics of joy and happiness expressed in song are of the Spirit, while the false teaching is associated with self-harm (2:23). Instead of a harsh regime of self-imposed worship (2:23), the Spirit inspires elation fueled by gratitude. This is not a solemn and somber worship, but one characterized by exhilaration and delight. It leads not to emptiness (2:18), but to overflowing. It is not about submission to rules (2:20), but about a relationship with the Spirit, whose presence brings joy.

Selected Bibliography

Dunn, James D. G. *The Epistles to the Colossians and to Philemon*. The New International Greek Testament Commentary. Carlisle: Paternoster Press, 1996.

Fee, Gordon D. *God's Empowering Presence: The Holy Spirit in the Letters of Paul*. Peabody, Mass.: Hendrickson, 1994.

O'Brien, Peter T. *Colossians, Philemon*. Word Biblical Commentary 44. Waco, Tex.: Word, 1982.

The Significance for Readers Today

1. How can you be a more effective channel of the Spirit's love (1:8)?
2. How does your wisdom, which comes from the Spirit, differ from the wisdom of those in the world around you (1:9)?
3. How does the Spirit enable you to worship God more effectively (3:16)?

chapter 12

*1–2 T*hessalonians

The Setting

The letters to the Thessalonians are perhaps the first NT letters to have been written, dating from around twenty years after the death of Jesus. The first verses of both letters identify Paul, Silvanus, and Timothy as the ones sending the letter, though for convenience, the name of Paul will be used to designate the writer. Thessalonica was a seat of administration for the Romans in Macedonia. The city's significant Jewish community had its own synagogue. When Paul preached there for about three weeks (Acts 17:1–3), some notable Greeks and leading women also became believers (Acts 17:4; 1 Thess 1:9).

What Does the Author Say about the Spirit?

The first letter focuses on encouraging believers to recognize that they are secure in their newly found faith in Jesus. Paul emphasizes the certainty of their salvation by reminding them of all that they have experienced thus far, especially through the ministry of the Holy Spirit. The Spirit's involvement in their lives and their experience of him are evidence of their conversion. The Spirit is proactive and dynamic, but he is also sensitive and gentle, and believers need to allow him to operate in their lives and community as he wishes. The second letter focuses on concerns relating to the return of Jesus.

The Spirit

- is associated with power (1 Thess 1:5)

- is associated with joy (1 Thess 1:6)

- is a gift from God to believers (1 Thess 4:8)

- is quenchable and testable (1 Thess 5:19–22; 2 Thess 2:1–2)

- sanctifies the believer (2 Thess 2:13)

The Spirit is associated with power (1 Thess 1:5)

For our gospel came to you not only in word, but also in power and in the Holy Spirit and with full conviction. You know what kind of men we proved to be among you for your sake.

Exposition

Building on the fact that God chose them (1:4), this verse reminds readers that they experience their salvation internally, with evidence of a power that comes from the Spirit. The apostles did not convince them through their intellect or rhetoric. The Spirit had supernaturally enabled their response to the message. Although the reference to power may allude to miracles that occurred at the time, the text does not specify any such miracles, and it makes more sense in the context to understand the power as defining the act of salvation. The power of the Spirit is such that the speaker was able not only to present the gospel, but also to convict and convince the listener. The fact that this power comes from the Holy Spirit allays any fears that the supernatural force was illegitimate or untrustworthy.[1]

The word translated "conviction" (*plerophoria*) can mean "assurance" or "fullness." Adopting the latter meaning would result in a description of the Spirit coming into their lives in "much fullness," though this language is redundant and clumsy. It is preferable, therefore, to recognize that the writer is identifying the Spirit as the one who assured them of their salvation. Although the word may be describing the fact that preachers are convinced of the validity of their message, it is more likely that it describes the Spirit assuring listeners that the message is authentic. It is not certain how they experienced this assurance, but it is

---

[1] The lack of a definite article in the Greek does not mean that the reference is to "a holy spirit." The NT often refers to the Holy Spirit without a definite article (Rom 5:5; 9:1; 15:13, 16).

clear that some emotional and/or intellectual response to the gospel occurred, as a result of which the hearers were convinced without a doubt that the gospel was true. The Spirit's manifestation of himself experientially is important. The Spirit is not a creed, but a creator; not a vacuum, but a validator; not distant, but dynamic. He made it possible for them to be fully convinced of the message of the gospel.

Significance for the Original Readers

After hearing Paul preach on three Sabbaths (Acts 17:2), the Jews in Thessalonica reacted to his message, and with a mob they attacked Jason's house and dragged him and some other believers to the authorities, claiming that they had committed treason (Acts 17:5–9). By night, the believers had dispatched Paul and his fellow missionaries from the city. The believers probably experienced great anxiety in the absence of the apostles, not the least with regard to the validity of their salvation. Since the believers were a minority group in the city, they may have felt vulnerable to further attack.

Thessalonica was no different from any other city of the time in that it was home to a variety of religions. For at least eighty years it had served as a base for the emperor cult. The cult of Cabirus, identified as "the mother of the gods," was also dominant, and the richest and most powerful people of the city supported it. Both of these cults were linked to the civic life of the city, and most people viewed failure to support them as treachery against the emperor and the city itself. The Christians were vulnerable and fearful on a number of levels, and the apostles needed to support them. They chose to assure the believers by describing the quality of their salvation experience. The apostles reminded them that the message of salvation is not simply a verbal declaration. Rather, the power of the Holy Spirit accompanies the message, resulting in their complete certainty of its validity and veracity. Against powerful people and cults, that same Spirit is invincible.

The welcome reminder of the Spirit's power also brought a much-needed message of security to the believers. The emperor himself had described Christians a few years earlier as "a general plague that infests the whole world." This reminder of the truth that a force superior to the most powerful man in the world was on their side was a timely assurance to the Thessalonian believers.

The Spirit is associated with joy (1 Thess 1:6)

And you became imitators of us and of the Lord, for you received the word in much affliction, with joy inspired by the Holy Spirit.

Exposition

The word translated "affliction" (*thlipsis*) is rare in classical Greek, though it occurs more frequently in the Septuagint. It originally referred to pressing grapes until they burst, and the association extended to pressure or trouble. The point here is not simply to encourage readers to recognize that the Spirit brings joy in times of trouble or when people suffer for the gospel. Rather, the purpose of the reference is to encourage readers to recognize that such joy is not natural or self-initiated. It occurs because of the Spirit. Their experience of joy demonstrates that the one who initiates it is in them. This joy, then, is further evidence that they have been chosen (1:4). Their friends, neighbors, and fellow citizens may have rejected them, and they may even have felt abandoned without the apostles. But God has chosen them, and his Spirit will never desert them and will provide them with what they need at all times. On this occasion his gift to them is joy, a natural fruit of his presence in their lives.

Significance for the Original Readers

Acts 17:5–6 records the early suffering that the Thessalonians experienced, which probably continued after the apostles left. This letter commends the believers for imitating the apostles and Jesus in receiving the word in the context of affliction. It is not that they are deliberately seeking affliction in order to imitate them, but the fact that they are joyful in their suffering is evidence of the presence of the Spirit (cf. 1 Pet 4:13–14), which is proof that their salvation is authentic. They are not in control of their own destinies. The Spirit has become involved, and his role is to inspire them supernaturally, an example of which is that despite their affliction, they still express joy. Such an incongruous emotion in times of suffering indicates a deeper force working within them. Joy was not a pervasive feature of first-century life for many people and was even less associated with the gods. The gospel has introduced a startling new kind of joy that they can experience in the most disagreeable circumstances because it is supernatural.

The Spirit is a gift from God to believers (1 Thess 4:8)

Therefore whoever disregards this, disregards not man but God, who gives his Holy Spirit to you.

Exposition

The context of this statement that the Spirit is a gift from God is an exhortation to godly living (4:1–7). An unusual triple-compound particle, *toigaroun* ("therefore"), used in the NT only here in 4:8 and in Heb 12:1, immediately follows this exhortation.

The effect of this particle is to emphasize the importance of this exhortation—to disregard it would be to disregard God. It is God who gives the Holy Spirit to believers. The purpose of giving the Spirit in this context is to enable believers to adopt wholesome lifestyles. Although it is not a major point, it is nevertheless of interest to note that the Spirit is literally described as being given "into" (*eis*) them. He is not simply a passing guest; he has taken up residence in their lives. His presence is a constant challenge to do better and a continuous reminder that because of his resources and commitment to them, they can do better.

Significance for the Original Readers

The implication of this verbal picture is challenging. The danger is of disregarding not an inanimate list of instructions but the Spirit who has feelings and sensitivities. God delegates the Spirit to believers so that he can help them please God by living holy lives. To ignore his help is absurd. Because the one delegated to help them has all the power they need, any rejection of that help is quite perverse. Because the one placed within them is holy, any resistance to him is offensive. Because the one given is none other than the Spirit of God himself, any refusal to benefit from his help is heinous.

Furthermore, the severe warning in 4:8 indicates the complete illegitimacy of sexual sin (the issue presented in 4:1–7). The first-century Greco-Roman world accommodated sexual immorality and irregularities without too much difficulty, especially among men. Although ethical norms for women were generally strict, the sexual attitudes of men were generally quite lax (though there were exceptions in some cultures, including Judaism, and some groups followed high moral codes). Most people had very ambivalent and even cynical views about marriage. People often indulged in unbridled prostitution and extramarital sexual relations. Both male and female prostitution was a generally accepted feature of life, this lax attitude also being common among the rich and powerful. The Spirit safeguards and empowers believers against temptations to follow the immoral norms of society.

The Spirit is quenchable and testable (1 Thess 5:19–22; 2 Thess 2:1–2)

Do not quench the Spirit, do not despise prophesying, but test every-thing; hold fast what is good, abstain from every form of evil. (1 Thess 5:19–22)

Exposition

These four verses issue five imperatives. It is not clear whether Paul is addressing current behaviors or presenting good practice for the future. He employs a metaphor that identifies the concept of fire with the Spirit. The message is clear. The Spirit is crucially important, and so he must not be stifled or stopped as a fire or lamp might be extinguished.

Paul also warns believers not to underestimate the value of prophecy. It is possible that this is a clarification of what it means to quench the Spirit and that the following exhortations relate to the same topic. Thus, believers are to test every prophecy, retaining that which is deemed good and rejecting the rest. It is also possible that the final two injunctions have a wider significance for all forms of behavior, including prophecy.

Now concerning the coming of our Lord Jesus Christ and our as-sembling to meet him, we beg you, brethren, not to be quickly shaken in mind or excited, either by spirit or by word, or by letter purporting to be from us, to the effect that the day of the Lord has come. (2 Thess 2:1–2)

Exposition

It is better to translate *pneuma* here as "Spirit" rather than "spirit," as Paul is probably referring to messages purporting to be from the Spirit as well as messages supposedly from him. The Thessalonians have received misinformation concerning the return of Jesus. As in 1 Thess 5:19–20 (and 2 Thess 2:15), Paul encourages believers to test everything and cling to the truth.

Significance for the Original Readers

The believers found themselves, after just a few weeks, without their new leaders. In a city of conflicting beliefs and aspirations, it was difficult for them to remain unshaken. Loneliness can lead to feelings of being out of control. Suffering has been their experience, and although Paul commends them for their testimony, he recognizes their vulnerability. He warns the believers that a claim to be representing the Spirit is no guarantee that the claim is true, especially when the claimant opposes the teaching of the apostles. What the believers must do is develop a sensitive framework of consideration for prophecies. Paul does not provide the readers with a list of guidelines whereby they would be able to authenticate prophecies. Instead, the emphasis of his words suggests that what is important is that all apparent prophecies should be carefully assessed to determine veracity.

The Spirit sanctifies the believer (2 Thess 2:13)

But we are bound to give thanks to God always for you, brethren beloved by the Lord, because God chose you from the beginning to be saved, through sanctification by the Spirit and belief in the truth.

Exposition

Paul describes the Spirit's role as a sanctifying agent in the salvation of the Thessalonians (see also Rom 15:16; 1 Cor 6:11). As a result of their conversion, believers have been set apart and can function ethically, benefiting from the resources of the Spirit.

Significance for the Original Readers

Thessalonica was a cosmopolitan city, as Greeks and Jews alike had joined the original Macedonian population. Because of its large harbor and importance as a trading center, it attracted speculators and the upwardly mobile. At the same time, its agricultural and forestry products ensured that it did not lose its rural influence in the urban sprawl. With Thessalonica's complexity of religious groups and social, civic, and political emphases, one could easily become lost in the city. Paul reminds the believers that the Spirit has come into their lives in order to, among other things, establish them as different. He has set them apart from the beginning of their Christian journey. It is a challenge to be worthy of that calling, as well as a privilege to function as a distinct group in a dangerous world. The Spirit desires to help them in this challenge to live differently from those around them.

Selected Bibliography

Bruce, F. F. *1 & 2 Thessalonians*. Word Biblical Commentary 45. Waco, Tex.: Word, 1982.

Fee, Gordon D. *God's Empowering Presence: The Holy Spirit in the Letters of Paul*. Peabody, Mass.: Hendrickson, 1994.

Wanamaker, Charles A. *The Epistles to the Thessalonians: A Commentary on the Greek Text*. New International Greek Testament Commentary. Grand Rapids: Eerdmans, 1990.

The Significance for Readers Today

1. What did you experience of the Spirit's power when you became a Christian (1 Thess 1:5)?
2. How do you experience the joy of the Spirit in your life (1 Thess 1:6)?
3. How does the Holy Spirit empower you to overcome temptation and live a godly lifestyle (1 Thess 4:8)?
4. What practical guidelines can you follow when trying to accurately discern messages from the Spirit (1 Thess 5:19–22; 2 Thess 2:1–2)?
5. What difference does it make in your life that the Spirit has set you apart (sanctified you) (2 Thess 2:13)?

chapter 13

*T*he *P*astoral *E*pistles

The Setting

Although there is ongoing discussion about whether Paul is the author of the Pastorals, and who might be the author, if Paul is not, it is safe to say that the Pastoral Epistles contain a great deal of information that is reminiscent of Paul. There is enough in the content of the letters, as well as in the external evidence, to make a strong case for Paul as the likely author. The letters 1–2 Timothy were written to Timothy, whom Paul left in Ephesus to combat false teachings (1 Tim 1:3), including those on asceticism. Timothy was born in Lystra, son of a Gentile father and a Jewish mother (Acts 16:1–3). His mother taught him from the OT from childhood. It is possible that he converted to Christianity under Paul's ministry (1 Tim 1:2), and we know that Paul mentored him (1 Cor 4:16–17). Timothy joined Paul on his missionary journeys in Galatia (Acts 16:3–5), partly because the believers in Lystra recommended him so highly (Acts 16:2). It appears that he also shared imprisonment with Paul (Phil 1:1; Col 1:1) and acted as his representative in Macedonia (Acts 19:22).

The letter to Titus focuses on his responsibility in Crete to complete unfinished business (1:5). Titus, who also perhaps converted under Paul's ministry (Titus 1:4), traveled with him to Jerusalem for the important council (Gal 2:1), represented Paul in Corinth (2 Cor 7:6, 13), collected money for the poor on Paul's behalf (2 Cor 8:6), and ministered in Dalmatia (2 Tim 4:10). Paul also describes him as his partner and fellow worker (2 Cor 8:23). We do not know who established the church in Crete. Cretans had a poor moral reputation, and Paul describes them graphically by quoting a Cretan, Epimenedes, who stated, "Cretans are always liars, evil beasts, lazy gluttons" (Titus 1:12).

What Does the Author Say about the Spirit?

These letters highlight the Spirit's supportive role on behalf of believers. Drawing encouragement from how the Spirit affirmed Jesus in the completion of his mission on earth, Timothy and Titus are to take advantage of the resources that the Spirit generously makes available to them. These letters also describe the Spirit's continuing commitment to transform them in their personal lives as well as in their ministries.

The Spirit

- vindicates Jesus (1 Tim 3:16)

- inspires prophecy (1 Tim 4:1)

- empowers the believer (2 Tim 1:6–7)

- lives in the believer as a guard (2 Tim 1:14)

- renews the believer (Titus 3:5–6)

The Spirit vindicates Jesus (1 Tim 3:16)

Great indeed, we confess, is the mystery of our religion: He was manifested in the flesh, vindicated in the Spirit, seen by angels, preached among the nations, believed on in the world, taken up in glory.

Exposition

This verse may be part of an early hymn or creedal statement that focuses on Jesus. Although the use of the term "flesh" (*sarx*) here may suggest a parallel translation of *pneuma* as "spirit," referring to the human spirit, it is more likely that Paul is describing the Spirit's affirmation of Jesus as the Savior on earth. It is difficult to see how the human spirit (as we have seen, a concept infrequently used by Paul) could affirm the person and mission of Jesus.

More important is the question of how the Spirit validated the person of Jesus. The Spirit is active in Jesus' birth (Luke 1:35), baptism (Luke 3:21–22), the beginning of his ministry and his temptation (Luke 4:1–2), the setting of his ministry agenda (Luke

4:18–19), and his resurrection (Rom 8:11). Paul perhaps has all of these key moments (and others) in mind. The focus is not on the Spirit's affirmation of Jesus on one particular occasion, but rather on the fact that such affirmation was characteristic of the relationship between the Spirit and Jesus on earth. While Paul may be referring to the new context of Jesus in heaven, after his resurrection, that does not fit the chronology of the events in this verse, which presents Jesus' vindication by the Spirit before he was taken up in glory.

Significance for the Original Readers

One of the major problems that motivated Paul to write to Timothy was the false teaching that was beginning to permeate the church in Ephesus. Starting in the Jewish community, the opposition sought to impose Jewish practices, including circumcision, on the Gentile believers while encouraging both Jewish and Gentile believers to retain or adopt the Mosaic law (1 Tim 1:3–11). Inevitably, this resulted in diminishing the person and message of Jesus.

To combat this trend and to ensure that the believers recognized the true, exalted nature of their Savior, Paul succinctly highlights the major elements in the life of Jesus. As part of this presentation, he identifies the Spirit as the one who affirmed Jesus. It was not Jesus who looked for affirmation, but the Spirit who provided it. The message to the readers is clear. In assessing the messages offered, they must first inspect the quality of the lifestyles of the messengers and, in particular, whether they bear the hallmark of the Spirit in their lives.

The Spirit inspires prophecy (1 Tim 4:1)

Now the Spirit expressly says that in later times some will depart from the faith by giving heed to deceitful spirits and doctrines of demons.

Exposition

It appears that this prophecy has already come to pass (1:19–20). It is possible that Paul is writing to Timothy what the Spirit is currently inspiring him to say or that he is referring to a prophetic revelation of the Spirit that Timothy is also aware of, in which case Paul simply mentions it by way of reminder. It is also possible that it reflects the prophecies of Jesus (Mark 13:6) and Paul (2 Thess 2:9–12) concerning such matters.

Significance for the Original Readers

Readers may glean a number of lessons from the role of the Spirit here:

- The Spirit wants to warn, and thus prepare, believers concerning some future problems.

- The opposition has not taken the Spirit by surprise.

- The decision to leave one's faith in Christ is not the result of the Spirit's inadequate commitment to the believer.

- The source of the false teaching is not natural or the result of human reasoning; it is supernatural and demonic.

- The same Spirit who affirms the truth of the message of Jesus also exposes the error of the false teachers. He is trustworthy and reliable in both assessments.

- Both the Spirit (*pneuma*) and deceiving spirits (*pneumata*) are capable of providing revelation and offering guidance. It is essential that the readers discern which is which.

In Ephesus, a city accustomed to supernatural phenomena, these warnings were astute because the danger of deception was acute.

The Spirit empowers the believer (2 Tim 1:6–7)

Hence I remind you to rekindle the gift of God that is within you through the laying on of my hands; for God did not give us a spirit of timidity but a spirit of power and love and self-control.

Exposition

It is possible that these verses relate to the issue that Paul mentions in 1 Tim 1:18 and 4:14. There, he reminds Timothy that he has received prophecies that were accompanied by the laying on of hands by the elders. The latter occasion probably was when

Timothy was commissioned for his ministry (see Acts 13:1–3 where Paul and Barnabas were similarly commissioned).

The text here specifies that Paul also laid hands on Timothy. There is no suggestion that a gift, or a portion of a gift, was transferred from Paul to Timothy. Paul was involved not because he was able to transfer supernatural properties but because of his position as a leader in the church. As such, he was able to affirm that which the Spirit had initiated. He affirms the action of the Spirit and guides the gifted person in the use of the gift. He does not determine which gifts are to be administered, for that is the purview of the Spirit (1 Cor 12:4–7, 11).

Paul says in 1:6 that this gift is within Timothy, though he does not identify it. Paul may be referring to Timothy's salvation, to his commission to ministry, or to a particular gift of the Spirit that enables him to function in ministry. Since Paul, alluding to fire within the word "rekindle," says that God gave this gift to Timothy, it is possible that he is referring to the Spirit himself, who is associated with power, love, and self-control.

Significance for the Original Readers

The significance of this verse is to encourage Timothy not to neglect what has been given to him. Timothy's timidity should not restrict him, but instead he should use his gift—a theme that appears elsewhere when Paul encourages believers to be diligent in the use of their gifts and not be indolent (Rom 12:4–8). In addition to the exhortation to Timothy to function in the gift that he has received, the description of the Spirit may be instructive. For all believers must use their gifts with power, love, and self-control—all of which are possible under the influence of the Spirit, and all of which ensure that gifts will not be used in an insensitive, tentative, or undisciplined manner. The Spirit functions in the believer not in weakness or cowardice but in authority and integrity.

Timothy is being asked to rely not upon his gift but upon the Spirit who gave him the gift and who enables him to use it. As he often does, Paul is calling for a relationship with the giver of the gift above any reliance on the gift itself.

The Spirit lives in the believer as a guard (2 Tim 1:14)

Guard the truth that has been entrusted to you by the Holy Spirit who dwells within us.

Exposition

Paul is probably talking about the importance of Timothy guarding the gospel, which he described in 1:8–13. Paul has referred to this task before (1 Tim 6:20). As God has invested in Timothy, so now Timothy must guard that investment. God does not, however, expect him to take on this responsibility on his own; as Paul reminds him, it is a task that he is to undertake by means of, and with the help of, the Spirit. The preposition *dia* followed by an object in the genitive case means "with, by means of." Furthermore, the Spirit who is to empower his guardianship actually dwells within him. The Spirit is closer to Timothy than he can imagine, and the present participle *enoikountos* ("dwelling") reminds him that this is a continuous indwelling.

Significance for the Original Readers

In all of Timothy's responsibilities, the Spirit does not simply observe, but enables; he does not just encourage, but ensures; he not only undergirds Timothy's strength, but he also supplies him in his weakness; he not only declares his ability to help Timothy guard, but he also demonstrates his authority to guard. Timothy has a part to play, but he needs to rely on the Spirit in order to fulfill it. The Spirit is not observing him from a distance, but he is dynamically moving him; his help is not far removed, but closer than a whisper.

The Spirit renews the believer (Titus 3:5–6)

[God] saved us, not because of deeds done by us in righteousness, but in virtue of his own mercy, by the washing of regeneration and renewal in the Holy Spirit, which he poured out upon us richly through Jesus Christ our Savior.

Exposition

These verses present the central role of the Spirit in the process of salvation. Though some suggest that the washing refers to water baptism, this seems unlikely, given the absence of supportive evidence in the letter and the limited references to water baptism in Pauline literature. More problematic for this view, however, is that Paul does not associate the Spirit with water baptism anywhere else, though he does elsewhere identify the Spirit's role in salvation.

The word Paul uses here for "regeneration" (*palingenesia*) appears only one other time in the NT (Matt 19:28), where it refers to the new world to come. The word translated "renewal" (*anakainosis*), likewise, is found in only one other place in the NT (Rom 12:2), where Paul encourages the Romans to renew their minds with the help of the Spirit. It appears that Paul is encouraging Titus to remember that the Spirit has cleansed him, made him a new person, and will also refresh him throughout his life. Titus is realizing the fulfillment of the prophecy of Ezek 36:25–27. Ezekiel promised not only cleansing but also the imparting of a new Spirit.

Titus, like all believers, is a recipient of both. In addition, the Spirit has been lavishly poured into his life. This promise echoes Paul's final words to Timothy in the first letter (1 Tim 6:17). The generosity of God to his children is what Paul wishes them to remember as they work as God's servants. They are not on their own; the supernatural waterfall of the Spirit is continually refreshing them.

Although the believer experiences regeneration and renewal at salvation (Titus 3:5), there is no reason for Titus not to experience further refreshings of the Spirit throughout his life. There is no need to restrict these activities of the Spirit to only a second blessing. Rather, he should recognize them as part of the ongoing support of the Spirit in his life.

Significance for the Original Readers

Titus is ministering in a situation in which there are a number of hurdles to be overcome. It appears that some people are advising believers to adopt an ascetic ritualism. Titus also has to deal with several strong characters who are prepared to oppose and destabilize him (1:10; 2:15), who teach error (1:11), who reject the truth (1:14), who waste time in senseless controversies (3:9), and whose lifestyles are inappropriate (1:16). Paul's advice is that Titus be firm in his response and his actions, rebuking error wherever he sees it (1:9, 11, 13; 2:15; 3:10), teaching the truth instead (ch. 2), and establishing leaders throughout the island (1:5–8). These are arduous tasks, but Paul reminds Titus that he is not alone. The Spirit who founded a relationship with him by cleansing him has made a commitment to stay with him, renewing him from an inexhaustible, immeasurable, and magnanimous source.

Selected Bibliography

Fee, Gordon D. *God's Empowering Presence: The Holy Spirit in the Letters of Paul*. Peabody, Mass.: Hendrickson, 1994.

Knight, George W. III. *The Pastoral Epistles*. The New International Greek Testament Commentary. Carlisle: Paternoster Press, 1992.

Marshall, I. Howard, with Philip H. Towner. *A Critical and Exegetical Commentary on the Pastoral Epistles*. International Critical Commentary. Edinburgh: T&T Clark, 1999.

The Significance for Readers Today

1. How did the Spirit vindicate Jesus when he was on earth (1 Tim 3:16)?
2. What are some reasons for the Spirit inspiring predictive prophecy (1 Tim 4:1)?
3. How does the Spirit empower you in your life and ministry (2 Tim 1:6–7)?
4. How does the Spirit help you to guard the truth of the gospel (2 Tim 1:14)?
5. What does it mean to you that the Spirit is renewing you, and how does this renewing affect you and your witness (Titus 3:5–6)?

chapter 14

*H*ebrews

The Setting

The unknown author of this letter wrote to Jewish Christians, some of whom are in danger of drifting away from the gospel (3:6, 14; 10:23, 25), while others have been very slow to grow (5:11–13; 6:12; 10:25). They may have become lethargic because of persecution from other Jews or hostility from Gentiles or government leaders. It is possible that they were disappointed because Jesus had not returned and they had begun to wonder whether they had opted for an alternative path to God that was deficient. These feelings may have been compounded by heretical teachings or by teachings from Jewish protagonists seeking to modify the beliefs of the believers in a Jewish direction.

What Does the Author Say about the Spirit?

The references to the Spirit in the letter to the Hebrews fit under the two main headings of revelation and salvation. These are both important issues, given the serious danger of these readers losing their attachment to Christianity and adopting Judaism.

The Spirit

- inspires revelation (3:7–8; 10:15)
- is associated with the process of salvation (2:4; 6:4; 9:8, 14; 10:29)

The Spirit inspires revelation (3:7–8; 10:15)

Therefore, as the Holy Spirit says, "Today, when you hear his voice, do not harden your hearts. . . ." (3:7–8)

Exposition

Having noted the preeminence of Jesus in comparison to Moses (3:1–6), the writer presents here the letter's first major warning about the consequences of not following Jesus. It is in this respect that the reference to the Spirit is significant. Given the importance of the Spirit, his words are to be recognized as being very important. It is none other than the Holy Spirit who declares that believers should retain their faith in Jesus.

The writer mentions the Holy Spirit here in the context of this quotation from Ps 95:7–11 (which continues through 3:11). Although written centuries earlier, these words are still relevant for this generation. Thus, the writer uses the present tense for the communication of the Spirit: "the Holy Spirit says . . ."

Significance for the Original Readers

The readers are concerned that they have precipitously departed from the religious framework of the OT, the temple, the sacrificial system, the law, and some of the greatest heroes of Jewish history. In order to stabilize them, the writer to the Hebrews reminds his readers of the example of the Jews who demonstrated unbelief and the resulting dire consequences. To emphasize the significance of what is happening, he begins the OT reference by identifying the author: the Holy Spirit.

The OT portrays the Spirit as one who functions powerfully and authoritatively. Thus, the Spirit is responsible for creation (Gen 1:2) and for eschatological renewal (Isa 32:15). He also inspires prophecy (2 Sam 23:2; Ezek 11:5) and provides revelation (Isa 11:2; Dan 4:8–9). He has a proven track record, and it is important for the readers to bear this in mind when they consider anything that he says. When the Spirit speaks, the people are expected to listen and obey. It is vital that these particular readers recognize that they are not simply being reminded of an event in Israel's history. Rather, they are being reminded of a message from the Spirit then, which he is reiterating now. This is a message from the Spirit today.

The Holy Spirit also bears witness to us. (10:15)

Exposition

This text introduces the conclusion to the argument concerning the inability of the sacrificial system to completely cleanse the worshipper, in contrast to the sacrifice of Jesus, which achieved a comprehensive and perfect cleansing. Again, to provide a final affirmation for his argument, the writer refers to OT Scripture (Jer 31:33–34). He introduces this quotation as well with a present-tense reference to the Holy Spirit, to remind readers that the Spirit is speaking today. He is the Spirit not only of prophecy past but also of prophecy now.

Significance for the Original Readers

As in 3:7, this text confronts readers with the fact that the Spirit's communication is not confined to the past; he is speaking to them now in their situation, which mirrors the experience of former generations. The message of the Spirit is consistent, and they are to remember who is speaking to them. The words are ancient, but the message is contemporary. Because the Spirit speaks to us, a prompt response is expected.

The Spirit is associated with the process of salvation (2:4; 6:4; 9:8, 14; 10:29)

God also bore witness by signs and wonders and various miracles and by gifts of the Holy Spirit distributed according to his own will. (2:4)

Exposition

The book of Hebrews presents a carefully constructed case for the authenticity and supremacy of the person and message of Jesus over Judaism. The writer refers to the Spirit at crucial points to enhance this claim. Although this verse records the authority of the Spirit to distribute gifts to people, its more fundamental message concerns the Spirit's role in confirming the salvation initiated by Jesus (2:3). The purpose is not to identify the Spirit as the one who assigns gifts, but to emphasize that the gifts he assigns are affirmations of the veracity of the gospel that Jesus presented. Signs and wonders themselves are less important than what they point to: the truth of the gospel and the presence of the Spirit.

The Jewish readers would have been familiar with several of the Holy Spirit's roles. They would not have been surprised that the Holy Spirit distributes these miracles, for in the OT the Spirit endows people with power, including strength (Judg 14:6, 19), skills (Exod 31:1–5), wisdom (Dan 5:14), and even supernatural travel (2 Kgs 2:16). He not only commissions, but he also empowers the one commissioned to fulfill the objective. In particular, the Messiah is thus empowered (Isa 11:2; 42:1). The one who affirmed the OT heroes—including Moses (Num 11:17), Joshua (Num 27:18), Gideon (Judg 6:34), and David (1 Sam 16:13)—is the one who witnessed to the authenticity of the salvation wrought by Jesus. The Spirit in the OT also provided the key to the eschatological destiny of the people of God (Ezek 11:19; 18:31) and to the Messiah (Isa 59:21; 61:1). Finally, the Jews understood that the Spirit indicated the presence of God himself (Isa 63:10–14). What more evidence did they need to recognize the superiority of Jesus than the consistent witness that the Spirit offered, in the OT and in their time? The Spirit, who is associated with God, who anointed only worthy recipients, witnesses to the truth of the salvation message of Jesus.

Significance for the Original Readers

This presentation is valuable for Jewish readers because their knowledge of the Spirit enables them to recognize a powerful argument for the exaltation of Jesus. It is not so important that Jesus achieved miracles. What matters is that believers recognize that Jesus functions with the authoritative support of the Spirit. The Spirit provided evidence of the authenticity of God's chosen leaders and their missions in the OT. The Jewish readers understand and appreciate this equation. The Spirit affirms people by providing supportive testimonials in the form of supernatural phenomena that act as signposts to the one commissioned by God. The Spirit affirmed Jesus in this way to a superlative degree. Therefore, if the Spirit affirms him, the readers must also do so. Signs and wonders were probably still occurring in the church—and these continuous reminders of the work of the Spirit in their midst served as further evidence for the authenticity of Jesus' message, the implications of which they were still working out in practical terms.

For it is impossible to restore again to repentance those who have once been enlightened, who have tasted the heavenly gift, and have become partakers of the Holy Spirit. (6:4)

Exposition

This verse is found in the letter's third major warning to the readers against abandoning their faith in Jesus (6:1–12). To emphasize the drastic nature of such a step, the writer outlines the severe consequences. Becoming a believer means entering into a relationship of friendship, partnership, and camaraderie with the Spirit. To disavow one's relationship with Jesus is also to reject this relationship with the Spirit. To accept the gift of salvation is not to commit to a creed or a list of rules, but to embrace a relationship with the Holy Spirit.

Significance for the Original Readers

The author clearly describes the calamitous consequences of any believer forsaking Christianity. He presents his case forcefully by concentrating on the relationship between the Spirit and the believer. To reject salvation is to reject the benefits of a relationship with the Spirit. It is possible that the author is indicating the potential of a complete breakdown of any relationship between the believer and the Spirit or anticipating the removal of the empowering nature of the Spirit from the person concerned. However, he is probably simply seeking to emphasize the inappropriate and illegitimate nature of rejecting such a privileged position of being in such a intimate and beneficial relationship with the Spirit.

By this the Holy Spirit indicates that the way into the sanctuary is not yet opened as long as the outer tent is still standing. (9:8)

Exposition

The larger context of this verse (9:1–10) is a discussion concerning the significance of the tabernacle to the worship of the Jews, and in particular the role of the high priest entering the holiest place annually to request forgiveness for the peoples' sins. The writer to the Hebrews explains here that the Spirit had demonstrated that this system was only temporary, for it prepared the way for Jesus' framework for salvation (9:11–28), which is superior to that offered through the tabernacle (9:9–10). Although the writer is not referring to any specific texts here, he is speaking of the Spirit as the one who inspired the Scriptures that he has just referred to.

Significance for the Original Readers

As part of his argument for the supremacy of Jesus over everything that Judaism can offer, the author finally turns his attention to the significance of the Jewish sacrificial system. His desire is to demonstrate that although this system had value, it was intended, at least in part, to declare itself as incomplete; it prefigured something else that would complete what it had started.

To clarify his point, the writer argues that the tabernacle distanced the people from the presence of God. Only the high priest could enter God's presence in the tabernacle, and only once a year, after completing a complex, detailed preparation ritual. Women, children, physically weak or diseased people, and Gentiles were excluded from the inner court of the temple. All of this, the writer argues, indicates that a better route to God must still be available. While the tabernacle existed, the supposition was that it was the way to God, albeit through the representative high priest. The message of the Spirit, however, is that a new way to God is available and believers are to take full advantage of it since Jesus, the one whom they are thinking about rejecting, has provided it.

How much more shall the blood of Christ, who through the eternal Spirit offered himself without blemish to God, purify your conscience from dead works to serve the living God. (9:14)

Exposition

Like many other passages, this verse highlights the superiority of Jesus' sacrifice over that of the Jewish sacrificial system. The focus here is not on the role of the Spirit as the means whereby Jesus lived a pure life. Rather, it is on Spirit as the one who raised Jesus from the dead (Rom 8:11), having demonstrated his blamelessness.

Significance for the Original Readers

The readers' knowledge of the OT was sufficient for them to appreciate the significance of the reference to the Spirit. Jesus did not simply offer himself as a sacrifice, but he did so after leading a completely faultless life. The mission of Jesus was undertaken in association with the Spirit. As well as functioning in the power of the Spirit, he was also affirmed and endorsed by the Spirit in his life and mission. As such, he achieved his divine agenda faultlessly.

The reference to the Spirit does not undermine the exalted nature and authority of the incarnate Jesus, nor does it suggest that Jesus was weak and needed the supportive aid of the Spirit, like a disabled person might need a crutch. On the contrary, Jesus and the Spirit are both totally committed to fulfilling Jesus' mission.

How much worse punishment do you think will be deserved by the man who has spurned the Son of God, and profaned the blood of the covenant by which he was sanctified, and outraged the Spirit of grace? (10:29)

Exposition

In the letter's final warning section (10:19–31) the writer refers to the Spirit again, this time identifying him as "the Spirit of grace." In order to help his readers step back from the precipice of rejecting Jesus as their Savior, the writer asks them to consider the consequences of outraging the Spirit. The presence of the Spirit in their lives demonstrates grace on a number of levels. Not only was the Spirit involved in the preparation of the gift of salvation (9:8), but he was also involved both in the life of the one who was to bring salvation (9:14) and in the act of salvation for the believer (6:4). He is, indeed, the Spirit of grace.

For the believer to diminish the significance of these actions or to lose sight of the gracious work of the Spirit would be outrageous and disgraceful. Here, then, is the climax of the writer's exhortation to the believers to maintain their relationship with Christ. The fact that the writer uses a word to describe this sense of "outrage" (*enybrizo*) that is unique in the Bible perhaps indicates the strength of his feelings.

Significance for the Original Readers

Once more, the writer refers to the Spirit to emphasize the heinousness of believers rejecting one who has done so much for them. To insult a person is bad enough (cf. Ps 69:20), but to insult the Spirit is appalling.

Selected Bibliography

Ellingworth, Paul. *The Epistle to the Hebrews: A Commentary on the Greek Text*. New International Greek Testament Commentary. Grand Rapids: Eerdmans, 1993.

Hagner, Donald A. *Hebrews*. New International Biblical Commentary 14. Peabody, Mass.: Hendrickson, 1990.

Lane, William L. *Hebrews*. 2 vols. Word Biblical Commentary 47A, 47B. Dallas: Word, 1991.

The Significance for Readers Today

1. How are we to respond to the Spirit (3:7–8; 10:15)?
2. What has the Spirit done for you? How can the Spirit's involvement in your salvation help you maintain your faith in Christ (2:4; 6:4; 9:8, 14; 10:29)?

chapter 15

1 Peter

The Setting

This epistle introduces its author as the Apostle Peter, who wrote to believers in Pontus, Galatia, Cappadocia, Asia, and Bithynia—regions that covered a wide expanse in what is now western, northern, and southern Turkey. The population was highly cosmopolitan, with many different races, religions, and cultures. The Christian communities probably reflected this diversity as well. It is likely that the believers met in small, close-knit fellowships (2:17; 5:9). Most, though not all of them, had pagan backgrounds (1:18; 2:10; 4:3) and were poor. A number of slaves were included among them.

What Does the Author Say about the Spirit?

Peter has several purposes in writing this letter. It appears that the readers were being persecuted (1:6–7; 2:12; 3:13–17; 4:4, 12–19), and consequently he wants to encourage them and offer practical guidance (2:11–12; 3:13–18; 4:1–6, 12–19; 5:6–11) while helping them to make sense of their suffering. He presents Christ as their example and also teaches them about maintaining proper relationships with others (1:22; 2:11–3:13; 4:7–11; 5:1–5) in order to ensure that they do not jeopardize their testimony to the unbelieving society (2:9).

In this context the Spirit's role is crucial, for the Spirit has set them apart to God, and as a result they are able to know him. Rather than suggest that they withdraw from their situation, Peter stresses that the Spirit is there with them. Given the extent of the suffering that these believers were apparently experiencing, they must have found his assurance of an immediate source of strength and support most welcome. Such encouragement helped them to put their earthly suffering into eternal perspective.

The Spirit

- sets the believer apart (1:2)
- inspires prophecy (1:11)
- motivates the preaching of the gospel (1:12)
- resurrected Jesus from the dead (3:18)
- provides life for the believer (4:6)
- is identified with glory and rests on the believer (4:14)

The Spirit sets the believer apart (1:2)

[To the exiles] chosen and destined by God the Father and sanctified by the Spirit for obedience to Jesus Christ and for sprinkling with his blood: May grace and peace be multiplied to you.

Exposition

The reference to the Spirit here emphasizes his work in setting the believer apart to God as a member of his family. This is not the ongoing ethical development of the believer, but the initial act of consecration at the moment of salvation when the believer is transferred from one kingdom to another. The continuous presence of the Spirit in the lives of believers is an ongoing reminder of that transferal.

Significance for the Original Readers

In 4:12, Peter encourages his readers not to be surprised at the painful trial that they are experiencing. Although this may indicate that they are experiencing persecution of significant proportions, the likes of which they have not known before, it is more likely that he is referring to their sense of bewilderment that they should suffer persecution for their faith. This has come as a complete shock to them, apparently, and so Peter teaches them that suffering is a part of the Christian life.

He emphasizes that their predicament has not come as a surprise to God. On the contrary, since the Spirit has set them apart, he knows about everything that happens to them, including this affliction. Suffering is not necessarily illegitimate for the believer. Indeed, Peter underscores the potential value of suffering for believers (1:7; 2:19; 3:14; 4:13, 14).

Many people in the first century perceived that the gods took no interest in the situations of individuals and did not bother to get involved in their lives. Peter's message to his readers was that the Spirit holds their destiny in his hands, whatever it might be—life or death, miracle or martyrdom. In the absence of answers to many of their questions, what is certain is that the Spirit is still in charge.

The Spirit inspires prophecy (1:11)

They inquired what person or time was indicated by the Spirit of Christ within them when predicting the sufferings of Christ and the subsequent glory.

Exposition

This verse highlights that the Spirit inspires prophecy, here specifically in regard to predictive prophecy. It is helpful to compare a text from Peter's second epistle: "No prophecy ever came by the impulse of man, but men moved by the Holy Spirit spoke from God" (2 Pet 1:21). Peter is referring to OT prophets who, while inspired to prophesy about the good news to come, also sought to investigate its contents. The expression "the Spirit of Christ" is found one other time in the NT, in Rom 8:9, where Paul helps the readers identify the Spirit, and in doing so associates the Spirit closely with the person of Jesus. In a similar way here, the Spirit of Christ is the one who predicts the sufferings of Christ. It is unnecessary to speculate whether the term refers to the spirit of Christ in his preincarnate state or to the Holy Spirit. To Peter (and Paul) there is little difference between the two. Peter is not seeking to muddle their identities but to harmonize their intentions. The reference in 2 Pet 1:20–21 to the prophetic authority of the Holy Spirit with regard to the inspiration of the Scriptures affirms this conclusion.

Significance for the Original Readers

Although the message of both 1 Pet 1:11 and 2 Pet 1:21 affirms the Spirit's role in initiating prophecy, the former offers an underlying message pertinent to the readers in their suffering. The Spirit's capacity to offer prophecy concerning future events includes his ability to predict future sufferings in particular. The Spirit was aware of the sufferings that Jesus was to experience. The suffering of these believers, likewise, has not taken the Spirit by surprise.

Furthermore, the one who knew the final outcome of Jesus' sufferings also knows the outcome of the believers' suffering. In Jesus' case, suffering preceded glory; the intimation is that a similar prospect awaits the believers, as 1:7 expresses.

The Spirit motivates the preaching of the gospel (1:12)

It was revealed to them that they were serving not themselves but you, in the things which have now been announced to you by those who preached the good news to you through the Holy Spirit sent from heaven, things into which angels long to look.

Exposition

As part of his supportive comments to the readers in the midst of their suffering, Peter reminds them of the nature of their salvation, which came through the Holy Spirit. Not only did the Spirit inspire the message, but also, Peter adds, the Spirit was sent from heaven. Peter is not concerned to identify who has sent the Spirit from heaven (God is the sender in Gal 4:6, Jesus in John 16:7, and both in John 15:26). What matters is that he has come from heaven. Therefore, the message that he brings has also come from heaven. Since the good news is divinely initiated, we know that it is accurate. Because of this heavenly provenance, even angels long to explore the content of the gospel.

Significance for the Original Readers

Peter encourages his readers by reflecting on the quality of their salvation (1:3–5, 8–9) and by affirming that their sufferings are evidence of the authenticity of their faith (1:6–7). Although prophets and angels longed to investigate the good news, the Holy Spirit alone can comprehend such depths of wonder. Those who preached the gospel to these believers did so through this very Spirit, who also affirms the integrity of the message. Although they may be tempted to think that their suffering suggests God's absence, the Spirit points to God's presence.

The Spirit resurrected Jesus from the dead (3:18)

For Christ also died for sins once for all, the righteous for the unrighteous, that he might bring us to God, being put to death in the flesh but made alive in the spirit.

Exposition

Once again, the context here relates to the sufferings of the readers. Peter advises them how to respond when they suffer as a result of doing good, quoting from Ps 34:12–16 in 3:10–12 and from Isa 8:12 in 3:14 to emphasize his point. He then points out that Jesus is an example for them to follow. Not only did Jesus suffer, but the suffering resulted in his death. Although the believers' sufferings are not of the same intensity, remembering Jesus' suffering enables them to see their own experiences in perspective.

Peter is interested in exploring one of the consequences of Jesus' death, but before he does that, he states that the Spirit was involved in raising Jesus from the dead. It is preferable here to understand *pneuma* as referring to the Spirit rather than to the spiritual component of the person of Jesus. Thus, one possible interpretation of the text says not that Jesus was made alive spiritually (in the spirit) versus humanly but that the Spirit enabled Jesus to function when disembodied. In other words, it is incorrect to think that the Spirit was present with Jesus in his incarnate state but not in his disembodied existence. On the contrary, Jesus and the Spirit are eternally intertwined in life and death. It is in relationship with the Spirit that Jesus preached to the spirits in prison (3:19). To note that Jesus functioned spiritually or immaterially after his death does not reveal anything significant, although it does make clear that the lack of a human body does not restrict the activities of Jesus. The recognition that his activity after death was in the same sphere of the Spirit as before death, however, provides a powerful message to the readers.

Significance for the Original Readers

The believers have experienced suffering, and although it does not appear that any had been martyred, that is a possibility in the future. Peter meets this reality head-on and reminds them of the death of Jesus. Although Jesus left his body, the Spirit did not leave him. On the contrary, when Jesus' human body perished, the Spirit continued to be with him.

In their times of suffering, which may lead to death, these believers have the assurance that the Spirit is with them as they progress through death to what comes next on their eternal path. For Jesus, it was to preach a sermon to people who had lived in the time of Noah (3:19–20). The substance of the next step after death is less important than the fact that the Spirit will supervise it. Believers can trust the Spirit, who has overseen and directed their lives before death, to continue to do so after death. As the Spirit did with Jesus, so also he will do for them. Whereas the Jews believed that angels took care of the righteous after death (Luke 16:22), Peter identifies none other than the Holy Spirit as the one who undertakes this responsibility for believers.

Though for a short while subjugated under the constraints of his earthly body, Jesus, now resurrected and in the place of supreme authority above his adversaries, continues his relationship with the Spirit. Believers must remember that their foes, though presently in a position of dominance, are destined for subjugation as a result of the life-giving, role-reversing work of the Spirit. The Spirit has done it once for Jesus; he will do it again for them.

The Spirit provides life for the believer (4:6)

For this is why the gospel was preached even to the dead, that though judged in the flesh like men, they might live in the spirit like God.

Exposition

The context of this promise is the surprise that unbelievers express and the abuse they dispense when believers do not join in their sinful activities. Here again Peter reflects on the role of the Spirit in this situation of suffering. Again, it is better to translate *pneuma* as "Spirit" rather than "spirit," which more generally denotes an immaterial life-form. Peter's concern is to elevate the reward of the believer's pilgrimage as a life associated with the

Spirit, not simply a life without a body. He is pushing his readers to adopt an eternal perspective.

Peter contrasts the negative judgment of believers by unbelievers with the Spirit's positive assessment of believers. This approval by the Spirit is not just eschatological. The Spirit approves the believers in the presence of God; it is in this context that they accept human disapproval.

The expression "like God" (*kata theon*) may be interpreted "according to God's values/standards" or, more simply, "in the presence of God." Although unbelievers denigrate them, the believers are in fact operating by God's standards, and therefore any opposition directed toward them is directed toward God as well. This parallels Jesus' experience also, for although unbelievers rejected him, he was chosen by and precious to God (2:4).

Significance for the Original Readers

The unbelieving community was incensed by the refusal of the Christians to join in their debauchery, but Peter points out that the Spirit affirms them in their stance, will continue to do so in the future, and is their constant support. They should recall the Spirit's warm approval of them when their unbelieving neighbors disparage them.

The Spirit is identified with glory and rests on the believer (4:14)

If you are reproached for the name of Christ, you are blessed, because the spirit of glory and of God rests upon you.

Exposition

Peter makes this final reference to the Spirit, again, in the context of the believers' suffering (4:12–13). As he advises them in their response to this suffering, Peter continues to point to the Spirit. In particular, he says that bearing reproach for being a Christian is a blessing. Whenever a believer endures such disapproval, Peter promises that the Spirit will be with him or her.

Peter perhaps has in mind Jesus' promise that the Holy Spirit will inspire believers to speak appropriately at their arrest and trial (Mark 13:11). The reference to the Spirit of glory probably should be interpreted in light of the preceding verse, which speaks of a future occasion when the glory of the ascended Christ is revealed to the believers. The Spirit who will demonstrate the glory of Jesus is the one who is with them in times of suffering. The same Spirit who rested on the Messiah (Isa 11:2), who will reveal his glory, also rests continuously on them.

Significance for the Original Readers

In this final passage relating to the experience of suffering, Peter again refers to the Spirit, emphasizing that he is an invaluable resource for anxious believers. Not only does Peter recall Jesus' promise that the Spirit will be their constant director and inspirer, but he also encourages them again by comparing the work of the Spirit in Jesus with the work of the same Spirit in their lives. Although presently they are experiencing verbal abuse and ridicule, the Spirit will reverse that humiliating, inglorious situation. The same Spirit who will reveal the glory of Jesus in the presence of all, including those who demeaned him, continually rests with them to refresh them and to remind them to maintain a perspective that is eternal. While the future may disclose the reasons for present sufferings, it will certainly provide a revelation of God that will put those sufferings into perspective.

Selected Bibliography

Davids, Peter H. *The First Epistle of Peter.* New International Commentary on the New Testament. Grand Rapids: Eerdmans, 1990.

Elliott, John H. *1 Peter.* Anchor Bible 37B. New York: Doubleday, 2000.

Michaels, J. Ramsey. *1 Peter.* Word Biblical Commentary 49. Waco, Tex.: Word, 1988.

Skaggs, Rebecca. *The Pentecostal Commentary. 1 Peter, 2 Peter, Jude.* London: T&T Clark, 2004.

The Significance for Readers Today

1. How has the Spirit set you apart from the moment of salvation (1:2)?
2. Why might the Spirit prophesy certain future events (1:11)?

3. What is the significance of the Spirit being involved in the presentation of the gospel (1:12)?
4. How would you describe the intimate relationship between the Spirit and Jesus (3:18)?
5. How does the Spirit support persecuted believers (4:6)?
6. Why is it important that we have the present assurance that the Spirit of God rests on believers (4:14)?

chapter 16

1 John

The Setting

The author of this epistle is presumed to be John, the beloved disciple, who wrote to believers meeting in house churches in and around Ephesus. This group was apparently a mixture of Jewish and Gentile Christians who were, among other things, struggling to achieve a balanced perspective on the identity of Jesus. In conjunction with this, they were dealing with ethical issues and relational matters arising from the difficulty of sharing fellowship with those who held different opinions.

What Does the Author Say about the Spirit?

The Spirit is crucial to the message of 1 John, even though he is mentioned only a few times. The Spirit's presence in the believers is what assures them that they have a relationship with God, and the Spirit also affirms the incarnation of Jesus.

The Spirit

- assures believers that they are in relationship with God (3:24; 4:13)

- affirms Jesus' incarnation (4:2, 6; 5:6–8)

The Spirit assures believers that they are in relationship with God (3:24; 4:13)

All who keep his commandments abide in him, and he in them. And by this we know that he abides in us, by the Spirit which he has given us. (3:24)

Exposition

Having encouraged his readers to love each other (3:11–18), John comments on their confidence before God. He reminds them that their obedience is proof of the authenticity of that confidence and of the Spirit in their lives. It is, of course, because of the Spirit that believers are able to obey God's commands, since he is their spiritual resource and guide.

God Is in the Believer; the Believer Is in God

The concept of believers dwelling in God is found elsewhere in 1 John (2:5–6, 24, 27–28; 3:6; 4:13, 15–16; 5:20), as is the description of God dwelling in the believer (2:14; 3:9; 4:12). Both pictures indicate the intimate nature of the relationship between the believer and God. This is more than an awareness of God. The word "abide" (*menō*) is commonly used to communicate the concept of "remaining with." The fact that this verb is in the present tense in 3:24 supports the idea that this is a continuous relationship.

The Spirit Is Evidence of a Relationship with God

God gives the Spirit to believers. The aorist tense of the verb "has given" (*edoken*) indicates the certainty of that gift at salvation. The presence of the Spirit in the lives of believers, however, does not simply indicate their interconnection with God. Because God indwells them and the Spirit has been given to them, the expectation is that believers will obey God. The Spirit enables them to do what God expects of them. The Spirit is a gift to believers, and he seeks to function through them, to authenticate and empower them.

By this we know that we abide in him and he in us, because he has given us of his own Spirit. (4:13)

Exposition

John has been exploring the fact that God exists in a context of eternal and continuous love, which he demonstrated by sending Jesus to resolve the problem caused by sin. In response to God's love, John expects the believers to love one another, and he goes one step further by declaring that mutual love is evidence of God's presence in their lives. It is at this point that he introduces the Spirit as further evidence that God abides in the life of a believer. Furthermore, the Spirit enables believers not only to be more aware of God's love but also to love others.

John again declares that God gives the Spirit, but on this occasion he uses the perfect tense of the verb "give" (*dedoken*). This tense generally refers to something that happened in the past but has ongoing effect. Thus the Spirit, given at salvation, continuously manifests his presence with the believer. John's previous encouragement to them to love one another takes on greater import when it is set in the context that God does not ask them to perform this in their own strength. The Spirit of love is their constant resource; they have no excuse for not sharing God's love with others, because the Spirit dwells in them and wishes to manifest this love through them. To make the point more forcibly, John reminds the readers that it is none other than God's Spirit who resides within them—which brings both privilege and responsibility.

Significance for the Original Readers

It is clear that there is some sort of dissension among the readers over matters of doctrine and behavior. To help them, John reminds them of the Spirit, who not only affirms them as believers but also empowers them to live in accordance with godly principles. Because of the differences in opinion concerning the person of Christ, John uses the touchstone of behavior as the guiding principle to help determine who is speaking the truth concerning Jesus.

Because of the presence of the Spirit in the believers' lives, John is convinced that they will live upright lives if they listen to the Spirit. Believers are to look to people who live in this godly way as valid teachers of the truth. Their lifestyles demonstrate the indwelling presence of the Spirit and thus the authenticity of their relationship with God. For John, pure doctrine is closely associated with an unpolluted lifestyle—not because the lifestyle necessarily proves the doctrine, but because a supernatural source enables such a lifestyle. The Spirit who inspires and empowers godly living is the one who initiates truth.

The Spirit affirms Jesus' incarnation (4:2, 6; 5:6–8)

By this you know the Spirit of God: every spirit which confesses that Jesus Christ has come in the flesh is of God. . . . We are of God.

Whoever knows God listens to us, and he who is not of God does not listen to us. By this we know the spirit of truth and the spirit of error. (4:2, 6)

Exposition

In the section in which these verses are found, John is warning of the danger of being deceived by false spirits. He is aware that alternative supernatural modes of revelation exist, and so he offers guidance to enable readers to determine which prophecies they are to believe (4:1). In particular, he identifies the Spirit who comes from God as the one who will always affirm that Jesus became incarnate. When people acknowledge these facts, it indicates that the Spirit is inspiring them. Those who reject these facts reveal that the Spirit is not present in their lives. Similarly, the fact that people will listen to these truths is evidence for the presence of the Spirit in their lives. Although in 4:6 it is uncertain whether John is referring to the Spirit of truth or to a person who has been inspired by the Spirit to speak truthfully, the difference between the two is not significant. What is important is that the readers discern the different sources of revelation concerning the person of Jesus. John indicates that a readiness to acknowledge Jesus' incarnation is an authentic means of identifying whether or not the source is the Spirit.

This is he who came by water and blood, Jesus Christ, not with the water only but with the water and the blood. And the Spirit is the witness, because the Spirit is the truth. There are three witnesses, the Spirit, the water, and the blood; and these three agree. (5:6–8)

Exposition

Having reiterated the importance of love and obedience as evidence of being a child of God (5:1–5), John refers back to the incarnation of Jesus. He again identifies the Spirit as the witness of the incarnate Jesus, affirming him as the Spirit of truth and therefore dependable. He also explains that the Spirit, along with water and blood, is proof of Jesus' incarnation.

The phrase "the water and the blood" can be interpreted in a number of ways: (1) Some suggest that it refers to water baptism and the Lord's Supper; (2) others argue that it may refer to the flow of water and blood from Jesus' side at the crucifixion (John 19:34); (3) many maintain that it refers to the water baptism of Jesus and his crucifixion; (4) it is also possible that John is alluding to birth, which involves the elements of water and blood, as evidence of the human nature of Jesus. Regardless of which interpretation is closest to the truth, John is dealing here with the issue of Jesus' nature, for some people apparently were questioning the reality of his incarnation. All but the first of these interpretations attest to the genuineness of Jesus' humanity. Together with the testimony of the Spirit, the water and the blood are abundantly clear attestations that Jesus' incarnation was real. John concludes that the person who chooses not to believe this thereby casts God as a liar (5:10).

The role of the Spirit is to witness to Jesus, in particular to the fact that he became human. The present tense in 5:7, stating that the Spirit "is" the witness, indicates that this is not just true in the historical life of Jesus or in the life of the Johannine community. Rather, the Spirit continues to witness to these truths in the life of every believer. Thus, as the Spirit witnessed to the humanity of Jesus in his incarnate state throughout his life, so also the Spirit testifies to that truth in the life of every believer.

Significance for the Original Readers

Some readers emphasized Jesus' divinity, while others stressed his humanity. Both perspectives have value. It is important to stress the divinity of Jesus because we need to recognize that Jesus is God and therefore worthy of worship and obedience. It is also important to stress the humanity of Jesus because we need to recognize that Jesus was fully able to identify with the human condition. Difficulties arise when we push either perspective too far while ignoring the other, resulting in an unbalanced or heterodox view of Jesus Christ. Such tensions and dangers have existed throughout church history as people have sought to understand the inexplicable. On one point, however, John is adamant that there is no debate: He and the Spirit testify that Jesus truly was incarnate.

Selected Bibliography

Marshall, I. Howard. *The Epistles of John*. New International Commentary on the New Testament. Grand Rapids: Eerdmans, 1978.

Smalley, Stephen S. *1, 2, 3 John*. Word Biblical Commentary 51. Waco, Tex.: Word, 1984.

Thomas, John Christopher. *The Pentecostal Commentary. 1 John, 2 John, 3 John*. London: T&T Clark, 2004.

The Significance for Readers Today

1. How does the Spirit affirm that a believer is a child of God (3:24; 4:13)?
2. Why is it so important for the Spirit to affirm the humanity of Jesus (4:2, 6; 5:6–8)?

chapter 17

Jude

The Setting

Jude, the brother of Jesus, probably wrote this letter. He became a believer after the resurrection of Jesus (Acts 1:14) and was possibly an early missionary (1 Cor 9:5). It is very difficult to determine the identity of the letter's original recipients, though the fact that the author is a Jew and the Jewish nature of the contents suggest a Jewish Christian audience. It is unlikely that Jude established the church, since he refers to earlier teaching that these believers had received from the apostles (17).

What Does the Author Say about the Spirit?

Although there are only two references to the Spirit in this letter, they provide important information. Jude addresses a problematic situation in which a serious heresy has affected the believers. In order to combat this teaching, he refers to the Spirit in two fundamentally important ways: (1) the presence of the Spirit in a person's life is the defining marker identifying those who are of the truth; (2) an important counteracting action that believers need to undertake is to pray in the Spirit.

The Spirit

- identifies the true believer (19)
- is associated with prayer (20)

The Spirit identifies the true believer (19)

It is these who set up divisions, worldly people, devoid of the Spirit.

Exposition

Jude refers to the Spirit here as he describes a heresy that is affecting the Christian community. Jude's assessment of the propagators of this false teaching is succinct and scathing. He portrays them as "worldly" (*psychikoi*) people who are unspiritual because they do not have the Spirit. It is impossible to be spiritual without the Spirit, and Jude focuses on the Spirit to clearly identify the difference between believers and those who peddle heresies.

Significance for the Original Readers

The heresy has serious theological and practical consequences. Jude 4 suggests that the false teaching offered an abased view of the person of Christ, in particular distorting the doctrine of grace, which resulted in immorality. Jude 8–9 reveals that the heretics claimed ecstatic revelations and rejected the orthodox doctrine of angels, which also led to physical defilement. The moral shortcomings of the heretics cause Jude the most concern (4, 7–8, 10, 16, 23), for not only are they immoral, but they engage in unnatural practices, acting like animals, being controlled by lust, yet arrogantly claiming this to be normal behavior.

Jude is adamant about the error of their conduct. Their behavior is not of the Spirit, because they do not have the Spirit. They are not able to express the life of the Spirit, because the Spirit does not live in them. It is possible that the false teachers claimed to be of the Spirit because of their visionary experiences and their ability to practice unbridled liberty, unchecked by any rules. Jude is clear that this cannot be the case because their lifestyle is opposed to the Spirit's agenda. Charismatic excesses provide no evidence of a Spirit-filled believer.

The Spirit is associated with prayer (20)

But you, beloved, build yourselves up on your most holy faith; pray in the Holy Spirit.

Exposition

The writer recommends two responses to the activities of the heretics. First, believers should engage in self-development in matters related to the Christian faith. Second, they should engage in prayer in the Spirit. Whereas the former will result in their being strengthened through their own activity in particular, the latter will result in their being strengthened through the Spirit's activity. Consequently, Jude recommends that they continuously engage in both activities (the Greek words for "build up" and "pray" are both in the present tense).

Significance for the Original Readers

As a defense against the unspiritual doctrine of the false teachers and their profligate lifestyles, Jude recommends that his readers pray in the Spirit. It is unclear whether Jude is describing the Spirit's role in inspiring prayer or in supporting the person who is praying, though it could be both. What is important is that the Spirit's presence in believers, which identifies them as God's people, is not static but dynamic, involving relationship and empowerment regardless of the circumstances. They occupy a privileged position, and they should engage in every opportunity to benefit from it.

Selected Bibliography

Bauckham, Richard J. *Jude, 2 Peter.* Word Biblical Commentary 50. Waco, Tex.: Word, 1983.

Skaggs, Rebecca. *The Pentecostal Commentary. 1 Peter, 2 Peter, Jude.* London: T&T Clark, 2004.

The Significance for Readers Today

1. How can you discern the difference between believers and those who peddle heresies (1:19)?
2. Besides increasing the frequency of your prayer, how can you be more open to the influence of the Spirit in your prayer life (1:20)?

chapter 18

Revelation

The Setting

The first verse of Revelation identifies the author as John (1:1). He wrote this circular letter to seven churches in Asia that were in need of direction, exhortation, or rebuke. After addressing particular issues in each of the seven churches (chs. 2–3), John addresses the plight of the churches existing in an antagonistic society. Persecuted Christians needed encouragement, and John provides this encouragement by graphically portraying the inevitability of Christ's ultimate victory over evil, the certainty of divine judgment on the enemies of the church, and the invincible sovereignty of God.

What Does the Author Say about the Spirit?

John mentions the Spirit a number of times throughout the book, and several of these references relate to his association with believers on earth.

The Spirit

- speaks to the church (2:7, 11, 17, 29; 3:6, 13, 22; 14:13)
- provides revelation (1:10; 4:2; 17:3; 21:10)
- is associated with the church (19:10; 22:17)

The Spirit speaks to the church (2:7, 11, 17, 29; 3:6, 13, 22; 14:13)

He who has an ear, let him hear what the Spirit says to the churches. (2:7, 11, 17, 29; 3:6, 13, 22)

Exposition

This phrase appears seven times—at the end of each message to the individual churches. These words emphasize the importance of the messages, though a deeper meaning may be available to those who read the text with the help of the prophetic Spirit. In the Gospels Jesus offers similar words to emphasize his own teaching (Matt 11:15; Mark 4:9, 23; Luke 8:8), and it is possible that John expects his readers to identify Jesus and the Spirit as joint speakers with him. Thus, while the introductory remarks in each letter refer to Jesus, the concluding comments relate to the Spirit. The ascended Jesus, who spoke when he was on earth, is still speaking, but now through the Spirit.

Significance for the Original Readers

John relays a specific message to each of the churches, much of which is unique to each particular church. To ensure that the readers are not indolent in their reactions, John reminds them of the one who is associated with the proclamation of the messages. The Spirit who is present with them is the one speaking. The exhortation to listen is best understood as a command to respond. John was encouraging them not simply to listen but to heed and obey.

And I heard a voice from heaven saying, "Write this: Blessed are the dead who die in the Lord henceforth." "Blessed indeed," says the Spirit, "that they may rest from their labors, for their deeds follow them!" (14:13)

Exposition

A heavenly voice, assumed to reflect the voice of God, introduces this prophecy concerning the death of believers in the future. The Spirit appears to affirm the message. This may reflect the Jewish legal practice of requiring at least two witnesses to affirm an act or speech, or it may be drawing attention to the fact that the Spirit works in harmony with God.

The words of the Spirit provide extra information—in particular, that the believers will be able to rest because their (good) deeds have eternal significance. The Spirit is affirming that actions undertaken in this life have ongoing implications in the next life. Believers should anticipate a positive response from God, who is mindful of what they have done. To believers who are experiencing harassment or persecution and are facing the prospect of martyrdom, the message of the Spirit is that death will bring relief and refreshment from these burdens.

Significance for the Original Readers

At first glance, this does not seem to be a very encouraging prophecy, since it proclaims that while believers can expect hard labor, they are not to expect rest and refreshment before death. The Spirit, however, is reflecting the reality of the situation of first-century readers. It is preferable to state the truth about suffering and hardship, thereby preparing them for what is to come, than to conjure an illusion of peace. What is important for the believers to recognize is that the Spirit is aware of their destiny in this life and the next. He also affirms that the good they have achieved in this life has not gone unnoticed. Though there is no explicit indication of a reward, it is encouraging to know that hardship is confined to this life and that good deeds have eternal significance.

The Spirit provides revelation (1:10; 4:2; 17:3; 21:10)

I was in the Spirit on the Lord's day, and I heard behind me a loud voice like a trumpet. (1:10)

At once I was in the Spirit, and lo, a throne stood in heaven, with one seated on the throne! (4:2)

And he carried me away in the Spirit into a wilderness, and I saw a woman sitting on a scarlet beast which was full of blasphemous names, and it had seven heads and ten horns. (17:3)

And in the Spirit he carried me away to a great, high mountain, and showed me the holy city Jerusalem coming down out of heaven from God. (21:10)

Exposition

In each of these verses the phrase "in the Spirit" is in the context of revelation received by John. Indeed, the presentation assumes that the Spirit is the appropriate sphere for revelation—John receives revelation as a result of being in the Spirit's presence. It is possible that John is describing a spiritual experience such as a vision or prophecy, but as we have seen elsewhere, there is little reason to separate the experience from the Spirit who has inspired it. Given that a case may be made for the believer always existing in the presence of the Spirit, it is better to identify this particular phrase as a description of those specific occasions when the Spirit inspired revelation. These references to the Spirit invite the reader to pause and consider the role of the Spirit before rushing on to read the revelation itself.

It is noteworthy that John is passive in each of these settings, neither actively preparing himself nor manipulating the situation. Indeed, on two of the occasions, he describes the Spirit carrying him away, a phenomenon we see also in Ezek 3:14 and Acts 8:39. Whether John was literally moved from one location to another or simply experienced a shift in vision is less important than the fact that the Spirit was in control. The Spirit takes him where the Spirit wants him to be. Although three of the four revelations are of positive scenes, 17:3 records the Spirit taking John to the desert, a place of emptiness and, for the Jews, demonic infestation. While there, he is shown a scarlet beast, representing Rome (17:18). This is a sobering, even frightening, revelation because of the blasphemy and innocent blood associated with the beast. In 21:10, by contrast, the Spirit takes John to a great, high mountain—an allusion to Ezek 40:2, where Ezekiel is taken to a very high mountain from which he sees a city. In this revelation, John sees the new Jerusalem coming down from heaven—a radiant and joyful scene.

Significance for the Original Readers

The believers in the seven churches would have been well acquainted with the concept of the Spirit and his capacity to inspire revelation from the OT and the teachings of the apostles. It was therefore natural that John should mention the Spirit's role as he described his revelations to them. These references to the Spirit further helped his readers to acknowledge the revelations as divinely inspired. In a world rife with various spirits, occult oracles, and philosophical revealers of knowledge, it was crucial that the believers have evidence that these revelations were authentic.

John does not describe the Spirit as forcing him in an inappropriate or frightening way. John presents himself as rational and lucid in each of these narratives. The fact that the Spirit can function in a revelatory capacity in the life of a believer need not cause alarm or concern. At the end of each revelation and at the end of the book itself, John functions no differently than any other prophet in the Bible, despite the detailed nature and content of his revelations.

It is also important for readers to recognize from these verses that the Spirit is in charge of any revelation. Sometimes he may lead believers to the wilderness (17:3) for a challenging encounter, as he did Jesus. On other occasions he may lead them to the high mountain (21:10) for an encouraging experience. Time in the wilderness is not necessarily the result of a believer having moved away from or sinned against God. As with John, the Spirit may lead believers to various encounters for reasons that may or may not be clearly understood. The journey demands trust on the part of the believer. By the same token, occasions of blessing are not necessarily a reward for positive achievements, but may be an opportunity to receive a revelation to be shared with others.

The Spirit is associated with the church (19:10; 22:17)

Then I fell down at his feet to worship him, but he said to me, "You must not do that! I am a fellow servant with you and your brethren who hold the testimony of Jesus. Worship God." For the testimony of Jesus is the spirit of prophecy. (19:10)

Exposition

After a revelation describing the climactic conclusion of the redemption of the church, John is so overcome that he falls at the feet of the angel who has introduced this scene to him. He is told to worship God. The words "the testimony of Jesus is the spirit of prophecy" are difficult to interpret. The "testimony of Jesus" probably refers to testimony about Jesus as identified in the lives of the readers, as referred to elsewhere (6:9; 11:7; 12:11). In particular, this same expression earlier in the verse describes the activities of John's fellow believers. A more helpful translation of *to pneuma* in this verse is "the Spirit," the one who initiates prophecy through believers.

The testimonies of believers, including their lifestyles, words, and deeds, result from the Spirit's activity. The Spirit of prophecy communicates through them as his mouthpieces. It is he who in-

spires them to act and react as they do. He who initiates prophecy
also initiates testimony.

*The Spirit and the Bride say, "Come." And let him who hears say,
"Come." And let him who is thirsty come, let him who desires take
the water of life without price. (22:17)*

Exposition

The joint invitation of the Spirit and the Bride comes in response to the declaration that Jesus is to come soon (22:12), and
22:20 then reaffirms this declaration. The phrase "I am coming [to
you] soon" is found elsewhere in Revelation (2:16; 3:11; 22:7) and
is the promise of Jesus. Here, the Spirit and the Bride articulate
their desire that he come.

The term "the Bride," also found in 21:2 (cf. 21:9), personifies
all believers throughout time who are destined to live eternally in
the closest relationship imaginable with Jesus: as his bride. That the
Bride should request the arrival of her bridegroom is understandable. That the Spirit should do likewise is less understandable, since
the Spirit and Jesus are in eternal relationship as members of the
Godhead. However, this coupling of the Spirit and the Bride has
some implications that explain better why John writes thus.

The joint request of the Spirit and the Bride graphically identifies the close relationship of the Spirit with the church. They both
look to the return of Jesus. Indeed, the Spirit is so closely identified with believers that he even seems less identified with Jesus.
Now, in partnership, the Spirit and the church eagerly anticipate
the return of Jesus. Together, they invite Jesus to come.

The role of the Spirit here is to affirm the validity of the
request and thus confirm that the return of Jesus is part of the will
of God. The Spirit also affirms that it is acceptable for believers to
be in such close relationship to the exalted Jesus, to be his bride.
The Spirit enables the church to articulate its heartfelt desire (cf.
Rom 8:26–27). Finally, the Spirit here assures that the request will
be granted.

Significance for the Original Readers

These verses offer valuable encouragement. First, John reminds the readers that they are not alone in testifying in the face of
rejection. Theirs is a pathway trodden by others who were accompanied by the Spirit. As the testimonies of the others have been,

theirs is not a mixture of self-inspired words and actions; it is not merely human or meager in terms of its impact. The Spirit of prophecy inspires and affirms it. It has the stamp of authenticity, validated and provided by the Spirit himself.

Second, John addresses the suffering that his readers are experiencing in various forms. He is not able to promise that this suffering will end immediately or that it will diminish in intensity. What he is able to promise, however, is that this suffering will end when Jesus returns, although the timing of the return is uncertain. John records that the Spirit, who prays the same prayer with the church, shares this desire with the church. The Spirit's close relationship with the church is such that he suffers with believers, longs for their release, and articulates their heartfelt desires. If the Spirit prays with believers, they can be assured that although the timing of the answer is uncertain, the answer itself is not.

Selected Bibliography

Aune, David E. *Revelation.* 3 vols. Word Biblical Commentary 52A, 52B, 52C. Dallas: Word; Nashville: Nelson, 1997–1998.

Beale, Gregory K. *The Book of Revelation: A Commentary on the Greek Text.* New International Greek Testament Commentary. Grand Rapids: Eerdmans, 1999.

Osborne, Grant R. *Revelation.* Baker Exegetical Commentary on the New Testament. Grand Rapids: Baker, 2002.

The Significance for Readers Today

1. What should be the believer's response to words from the Spirit (2:7, 11, 17, 29; 3:6, 13, 22; 14:13)?
2. In what ways, and for what purposes, does the Spirit reveal himself to believers (1:10; 4:2; 17:3; 21:10)?
3. How would you describe the relationship between the Spirit and the church (19:10; 22:17)?

chapter 19

Listen to What the Spirit Says to the Church

The NT explores many aspects of the Spirit that have timeless relevance. The list below identifies the most important of these. Let us learn to appreciate the Spirit for who he is and for what he wishes to do in us and through us.

- The Spirit is, by definition, set apart. That means not only that he is sinless but also that he is unique.

- The Spirit exalts Jesus and inspires the believer to worship and belief in Jesus.

- The Spirit is a personal, immediate, dynamic, and perfect guide. He speaks, and so we must listen to him. This means developing a personal relationship with him, walking with him, learning to recognize his voice, and responding to his guidance.

- The Spirit is committed to setting believers apart, proactively transforming them ethically and spiritually, and inspiring and empowering them to follow his guidance.

- The Spirit is a comprehensive, limitless resource for the believer with regard to salvation. He is the one who, with Jesus, makes it possible for people to enter the kingdom of God; to recognize that they are adopted by God with all the pertinent privileges and responsibilities; and to relate to God as Father, experiencing eternal life from the inception of that relationship as a son or daughter of God. The Spirit's presence is the evidence that believers are authentic children of God, sealed and guaranteed for time and eternity.

- The Spirit provides resources and gifts for all believers and expects them to use them sensitively. He provides all the resources necessary to complete every task he sets. He diversely distributes gifts for believers to use for the benefit of all in the development of the church, inspiring and initiating evangelism, preaching, prophecy, and miracles. He brings liberty, inspires joy, and offers wisdom, faith, truth, and revelation, among other gifts, and believers must ensure that such a fountain of good gifts is continually appreciated, accessed, and enjoyed.

- The Spirit expects transformation in the believer, who needs to learn the daily experience of being controlled by him. The believer will then experience the influential presence of the Spirit and see his or her lifestyle increasingly reflect the character of Jesus.

- The Spirit is committed to unity. Believers are therefore to work to maintain unity, to guard it as a priceless treasure, and to recognize that the aim of the Spirit is to welcome folk from all people-groups and backgrounds and to pour out the love of God through each believer.

- The Spirit is committed to a relationship with all believers both individually and corporately. Believers are to experience and enjoy the Spirit, recognizing that such closeness has profound implications, including the possibility that they may hurt him.

- The Spirit is eternal and, being omniscient, is available to guide believers as they gaze at God, who beckons them to come ever closer to enjoy the benefits of a remarkable salvation with the help of the remarkable Spirit.

*I*ndex of *S*ubjects

Agabus, 70–71

Barnabas, 68

Cornelius, 59–61

devil, 12–14
dove, 10–11

Elizabeth, 24, 26, 28–29

Holy Spirit
  access to God, 148–49, 218–20
  adoption for believers, 88–91
  affirmation, 25–26, 66–69,
    85–88, 93–96, 106–7, 151–52,
    173–74, 183–85, 211–12
  baptism with/filling with, 24,
    41–45, 52–63, 155–56
  baptism with the Holy Spirit
    and fire, 6–9
  believers, 41–45, 116–18, 133,
    76–77, 110–13, 128, 149–51,
    176–79, 184–85, 197–98,
    202–3
  birth of Jesus, 3–6, 23, 29–31
  blasphemy, 19–20
  Counsellor, 42–43, 46–49
  empowerment, 25–26, 66–69,
    85–88, 93–96, 106–7, 151–52,
    173–74, 183–85, 211–12
  evangelism, 38–41, 71–73,
    199–200
  exorcism, 17–18
  fellowship, 152–53, 162–64
  "first fruits" for believers, 91
  flesh, 85–88
  fruit, 138–40
  grieved, 153–55
  guarantee, 145–47, 205–7
  gifts, 77–79, 99–106, 142–44
  godhead, 20–21, 76–77
  Jesus, 9–14, 35–38, 181–82,
    200–201, 207–9
  joy, 175
  law, 79–83, 136–38
  love, 83–85, 167–69
  prayer, 23, 31–34, 91–93,
    212–13
  preaching, 23, 24–26
  prophecy, 23, 26–29, 69–71,
    182–83, 198–99
  quenchable and testable,
    177–78
  salvation, 38–41, 113–16,
    123–24, 131–33, 135–36,
    190–94, 201–2
  seals the believer, 121–23,
    144–45
  sin, 65–66
  sovereignty, 40
  speech, 14–17
  transforms the believer, 124–28,
    185–86
  wisdom and guidance, 63–65,
    107–10, 136–38, 147–48,
    169–70, 188–90, 214–18
  worship, 45–46, 164–65, 170–71,
    218
  xenolalia, 54

John the Baptist, 6–7, 24, 36, 61–63

Maccabees, 16
Mary, 26, 30
messiah, 8

Moses, 125–27
mystery religions, 6

Nicodemus, 39–40

Pentecost, 12, 53–55
Peter, 52
Philip, 67

Samaritans, 46, 56–58
Simeon, 27–28
Stephen, 65–66

temple, 110–13, 118, 149–51

Zechariah, 24, 27, 29

*J*ndex of *A*ncient *S*ources

OLD TESTAMENT

Genesis
1:2 5, 10, 30, 189
2:7 43
6:3 5
8:8–12 10
31:1 126
45:13 126

Exodus
3:2 8
13:21–22 8
16:8 20
17:1–6 42
19:14 76
19:22 76
23:16 55
23:19 91
28:41 25
29:33–37 76
31:1–5 191
31:18 123
33:15–16 11
34:22 55
34:34 125
40:34 126
40:34–35 30

Leviticus
2:14 91
5:7 10
5:11 10
23:34–36 42

Numbers
11:17 191
11:26–27 69
11:29 9, 11
27:18 191
28:26 55

Deuteronomy
6:13 165

Judges
6:34 11, 191
13:5 24
14:6 191
14:9 191

1 Samuel
10:1 25
10:10 24, 34, 69
16:13 11, 191
16:14 24

2 Samuel
23:2 189

1 Kings
9:3 76
18:12 67
19:16 25

2 Kings
2:16 67, 191

1 Chronicles
16:27 32
16:33 32

Esther
8:8 145

Job
1:6 157

Psalms
2:7 12
34:12–16 200
69:20 194
91:4 30

95:7–11 189
110:1 15, 17
111:9 146

Song of Songs
1:15 10
2:14 10

Isaiah
4:4 8
6:9–10 66
8:7 126
8:12 200
11:2 5, 8, 189, 191, 203
12:3 42
29:6 8
32:15 30, 189
32:15–20 30
42:1 9, 12, 191
42:1–4 15
42:13 158
43:1 146
44:2 24
44:3 42
44:3–4 5
49:1 24
59:17 158
59:21 191
61:1 191
61:1–2 25
61:1–3 30
63:10 65, 154
63:10–14 191
63:17 89

Jeremiah
1:5 24
10:16 89
31:3–34 79
31:33 123

31:33–34 190
32:10 145

Ezekiel
1:1 10
3:14 217
11:5 189
11:19 79, 134, 191
18:31 191
36:25 39, 115
36:25–27 186
36:26–27 144
37:9 43
37:14 43, 144
47:1–12 42

Daniel
4:8–9 189
5:14 191

Hosea
7:11 10

Joel
2:28 11, 84
2:28–29 28
2:28–32 55, 70, 144

Zechariah
13:9 8
14:8 42

Malachi
3:10 84

NEW TESTAMENT

Matthew
1:18   4, 5, 22, 29
1:20   4, 22, 29
2:16   16
3:11   4, 6, 22
3:12   7
3:16   4, 5, 9, 22
4:1   4, 5, 9, 12, 22
4:7   11
7:7–11   32
7:11   33
10:5–6   21
10:16   10
10:20   4, 14, 15, 22
11:15   215
11:25   31
12:18   4, 14, 15, 16, 22
12:22   18
12:27   18
12:28   4, 17, 18, 22
12:31–32   4, 19, 22
12:39   19
12:45   19
16:19   44
19:28   186
22:43   4, 14, 15, 17, 22
28:19   4, 5, 20, 22

Mark
1:8   4, 6
1:10   4, 6
1:12   4, 9, 13
3:29   4, 19
4:9   215
4:23   215
9:38–40   18
12:36   4, 14, 15, 17
13:6   183
13:11   4, 14, 15, 202

Luke
1:1–4   23
1:6   24
1:13   29

1:15   24, 34
1:15–17   23, 33
1:16–17   24
1:31   30
1:35   4, 5, 23, 29, 30, 34, 181
1:41   24, 26, 34
1:41–45   23, 33
1:47   31
1:67   24
1:67–69   23, 26, 27, 33, 34
2:10   29
2:25–32   23, 26, 27, 33, 34
2:29–31   23, 33
2:34–35   23, 26, 33, 34
3:16   4, 6
3:21–22   181
3:22   4, 9, 10
4:1   4, 9, 12
4:1–2   181
4:14–15   23, 25, 33, 34
4:16–30   25
4:18   25, 34
4:18–19   23, 33, 182
4:21   25
8:8   215
9:2   44
9:6   44
10:17   31
10:21   31, 34
10:21–22   23, 31, 33
11:5–13   33
11:9–13   32
11:13   23, 32, 34
12:1–3   20
12:2   19
12:4–5   19
12:4–7   20
12:4–10   16
12:8–9   20
12:8–10   19
12:10   4, 19, 20
12:11–12   20
12:12   4, 14, 15
12:13–21   16
16:22   201
24:49   52, 53

John
1:7–8   38
1:15   38
1:32–33   10, 35, 36, 37, 50
3:3   39
3:5–6   35, 38, 50
3:8   35, 38, 40, 41, 50
3:11   38
3:22   39
3:23   39
3:26   38
3:34   35, 36, 37, 50
3:36   41
4:1   39
4:2   39
4:10   115
4:14   39, 41, 115
4:23–24   35, 39, 45, 50
4:24   43
5:24   41
5:31–39   38
6:47   41
6:54   41
6:63   35, 40, 41, 50
6:68   40
7:2   42
7:37–39   115
7:39   35, 39, 41, 50
10:25   38
14:2–3   42
14:16–17   35, 41, 42, 46, 47, 50
14:26   35, 42, 43, 46, 47, 50
15:26   35, 37, 38, 42, 46, 47, 50, 62, 199
16:7   35, 44, 46, 47, 48, 50, 199
16:7–15   42
16:8   47
16:8–11   47
16:13   43, 47
16:14   47
19:34   208
20:21   43

20:22   35, 41, 43, 50
20:23   44
20:31   35, 37

Acts
1:2   51, 63, 74
1:4   52, 53
1:4–5   7
1:5   51, 52, 74
1:8   12, 44, 52, 54, 57, 60, 71, 72, 74
1:14   211
1:16   51, 55, 63, 74
2:1   53
2:4   7, 24, 51, 52, 53, 54, 74
2:6–8   54
2:11   54
2:13   54
2:17   70
2:17–18   52, 69, 70, 74
2:18   70
2:23   55
2:26   31
2:33   51, 52, 53, 54, 55, 74
2:38   51, 52, 53, 56, 74
2:39   53
4:8   24, 52, 54, 71, 74
4:13   72
4:25   51, 54, 63, 74
4:28   55
4:31   24, 52, 54, 66, 71, 72, 74
5:1–11   66
5:3   52, 65, 66, 74
5:9   52, 65, 66, 74
5:29   53
5:32   51, 52, 53, 74
5:38–39   55
6:3   52, 57, 66, 67, 74
6:5   52, 66, 67, 75
6:10   52, 54, 66, 71, 72, 74

6:15 72
7:2–53 66
7:51 52, 65, 74
7:55 24, 52, 54,
   66, 71, 74
7:55–56 72
7:56 10, 54
8:5–13 56, 57
8:9–13 57
8:14–19 51, 52,
   56, 74
8:25 57
8:29 51, 63, 64,
   74
8:39 52, 66, 67,
   74, 217
8:40 68
9:17 24, 51, 52,
   56, 58, 74
9:20–21 59
9:31 52, 71, 74
10:3 60
10:9–16 59
10:11–24 61
10:19 51, 63, 64,
   74
10:19–20 60
10:22 59, 60
10:38 52, 66, 67,
   68, 74
10:43 68
10:44 56, 60
10:45 60
10:45–47 51, 52,
   59, 74
11:1 60
11:2–3 60
11:12 51, 63, 64,
   74
11:15 60
11:15–16 51, 52,
   59, 74
11:23–24 54
11:24 52, 71, 72,
   74
11:28 52, 69, 74
11:29 70
12:25 3
13:1–3 184
13:2 52, 65, 66,
   67, 68, 74
13:4 51, 63, 64,
   65, 74

13:9 52, 71, 72,
   74
13:9–10 54
13:9–11 72
13:12 72
13:29 55
13:33 55
13:50–52 72
13:52 52, 71, 72,
   74
15:8–9 60
15:28 51, 63, 64,
   74
15:37–40 3
16:1–3 180
16:2 180
16:3–5 180
16:6 130
16:6–7 51, 63,
   64, 65, 74
16:11–40 160
16:12 165
16:16–18 114
16:21 165
16:37–38 96, 165
17:1–3 172
17:2 174
17:4 172
17:5–6 175
17:5–9 174
18:1–18 98
18:2 72
18:7 112
18:19 153
18:23 130
18:24–25 61
19:1–6 61, 141
19:2 51, 52, 61,
   62, 74
19:3 62
19:6 51, 52, 61,
   69, 74
19:8 153
19:11–12 141
19:19 152
19:21 70
19:22 180
20:22–23 51, 63,
   64, 74
20:27 141
20:28 52, 66, 67,
   68, 74
20:28–30 141

20:31 141
21:4 52, 69, 70,
   74
21:11 52, 69, 70,
   74
21:14 55
21:28 94
22:25 70
22:25–29 96
22:29 70
23:16 70
25:24 92
28:25 51, 52, 54,
   63, 65, 66, 74

Romans
1:1 75
1:3 86
1:4 75, 76, 97
1:7 76
1:9 165
1:11 75, 77, 97
1:11–15 77
1:16 75
1:21 79
2:9–10 75
2:15 79
2:29 75, 79, 81,
   97
3:9 75
3:29 75
5:3 84
5:5 75, 76, 79,
   83, 84, 97, 168,
   173
6:1–23 81
6:17 79
7:6 75, 79, 80,
   81, 97
7:14 75, 79, 81,
   97
8:1–13 88
8:2 75, 79, 82, 97
8:3 83
8:4 75, 79, 84, 97
8:5 86
8:5–13 75, 85, 97
8:6 86
8:7 86
8:8 86
8:9 86
8:10 87
8:10–11 87

8:11 182
8:12 87
8:12–13 87
8:13 193
8:14–17 75, 88,
   97
8:15 76, 88, 90
8:15–16 8, 32
8:17 89
8:18–22 91
8:19–25 88
8:23 55, 76, 88,
   91, 97
8:26–27 75, 91,
   97, 219
8:27 92
8:34 92
9:1 173
9:4 88
9:8 194
9:14 194
9:24 75
10:12 75
10:19–31 194
10:29 194
11:13–32 75
12:1 94
12:2 186
12:3 78
12:3–5 78
12:4–8 184
12:6–8 75, 77,
   78, 97, 101
14:5 94
14:13 94
14:13–16 94
14:14–23 94
14:17 76, 93, 94,
   97
14:18 94
15:7 95
15:7–12 75
15:8–18 94
15:13 76, 93, 95,
   97, 173
15:16 76, 93, 94,
   97, 113, 173,
   178
15:18–19 76, 93,
   95, 97
15:19 75
15:23 75
15:25 75

15:30   75, 83, 84,
   97
16:5   75
16:10–11   75
16:14–15   75

1 Corinthians
1:4   100
1:4–7   100
1:5   99
1:7   98, 99, 119
1:10–13   104
1:11   98
1:14   98
1:17–31   106
1:18   107
1:18–25   106
1:22–24   98
1:26–29   98, 100
1:27   107
2:2   109
2:2–4   107
2:4   98, 106, 119
2:5   107
2:6   108
2:6–9   109
2:6–16   106
2:7   109
2:9   109
2:10   109
2:10–15   99, 107,
   108, 119
2:12   109
2:13   109
2:14   108
2:15   109
2:16   109
3:3   104
3:10   110
3:11   110
3:12–15   110
3:16–17   99, 110,
   116, 119
3:21   104
4:6   104
4:6–7   102
4:16–17   180
5:6   110
6:1–6   104
6:2   110
6:2–8   113
6:3   110
6:9   110

6:11   99, 113, 119,
   178
6:13   117
6:15–16   110, 117
6:19   110
6:19–20   99, 116,
   119
7:7   101
7:18   98
7:21–23   98
7:40   99, 107,
   108, 109, 119
8:1–13   104
9:5   211
9:13   110
10:2   115
11:21   104
12:3   99, 113, 114,
   119
12:4–6   101
12:4–7   98, 99,
   100, 119, 184
12:4–11   115
12:5   100
12:6   100
12:6–7   101
12:7   101, 104
12:8–10   101
12:9–10   102
12:11   98, 99,
   100, 101, 119,
   184.
12:12–26   104
12:12–31   115
12:13   99, 113,
   115, 119
12:27–31   98, 99,
   102, 119
12:28   101, 104
12:30   93
12:31   103, 105
13:1–3   101
14:1   98, 99, 105,
   119
14:2   93
14:3–5   70
14:6   101
14:12   98, 99, 105,
   119
14:14   93
14:14–15   93
14:26   101
14:29   71

15:32   141
16:9   141

2 Corinthians
1:5   121
1:6   121
1:7   121
1:8–9   121
1:10   121
1:12–14   121
1:15–16   121
1:17–20   121
1:21–22   120, 121,
   122, 129
1:22   146
2:17   120
3:1   120
3:3   120, 123
3:3–6   55
3:6   120, 123
3:12   125
3:16   124
3:16–18   120, 125,
   129
3:17   125
4:2   120
5:1–4   122
5:5   120, 121,
   122, 129, 146
6:4–5   127
6:6–7   120, 127,
   129
6:8–10   127
7:6   180
7:13   180
8:6   180
8:23   180
13:14   120, 128,
   129

Galatians
1:1   130
2:1   180
3:2   131
3:2–5   130, 131,
   140
3:3   86, 131
3:5   131, 132, 162
3:6   133
3:13–14   130, 133,
   140
3:14   133
3:17–18   81

3:19–4:7   130
4:4   134
4:5   88
4:6   130, 131,
   133, 134, 140,
   199
5:5   130, 135, 140
5:16   137
5:16–18   130, 136,
   140
5:16–21   138
5:17   137
5:18   81, 137
5:19–20   139
5:19–21   139
5:21   139
5:22   139
5:22–23   139
5:22–6:1   130, 138,
   140
5:23   139
5:25   139
6:1   139
6:2   139
6:8   130, 135, 136,
   140

Ephesians
1:1   141
1:3   141, 142, 143,
   158
1:3–14   142
1:5   88
1:13   141, 144,
   158
1:14   142, 145,
   158
1:16–17   141, 147,
   158
1:17   147
1:18   126
1:20   143
1:20–22   143
1:21   157
2:1   148
2:2   148, 157
2:4–8   148
2:5   148
2:6   143, 148
2:14   148
2:18   143, 148,
   159
2:21   149

2:21–22 110, 143, 144, 149, 159
2:22 143, 150
3:4–5 142, 147, 158
3:5 148
3:6 144
3:10 143
3:16 142, 159
3:16–19 151
3:17–19 152
4:3 142, 152, 159
4:11 101, 104
4:17–21 154
4:22–5:20 154
4:29 155
4:30 142, 145, 153, 155, 159
4:31 155
5:4 155
5:6 155
5:8 156
5:15 156
5:18 24
5:18–19 142, 155, 159
5:19 155
5:19–20 156
5:20 155
5:21–6:9 155
5:26 157
6:10–20 156
6:11–12 157
6:12 143, 157
6:17–18 143, 156, 159

Philippians
1:1 180
1:1–18 161
1:13–14 161
1:19 160, 166
1:20 161
1:27 160, 162, 163, 164, 166
1:29–30 162
2:1–2 160, 162, 163, 166
2:1–4 164
2:24 161
3:2 165
3:3 160, 164, 165, 166

3:10 162
3:20 165
4:2–3 164

Colossians
1:1 180
1:4 168
1:7 167
1:8 167, 168, 171
1:9 147, 167, 169, 171
1:11 126
1:21 168
2:8 169, 170
2:13 168
2:18 168, 169, 170, 171
2:20 170, 171
2:22 169
2:23 169, 170
3:1–4:6 170
3:16 167, 171
3:17 170
4:10 3
4:12 167

1 Thessalonians
1:4 173
1:5 172, 173, 179
1:6 172, 175, 179
1:9 172
4:1–7 176
4:8 172, 176, 179
5:19–20 178
5:19–22 173, 177, 178
5:21 20, 71

2 Thessalonians
2:1–2 173, 177, 179
2:9–12 183
2:13 173, 178, 179
2:15 178

1 Timothy
1:3 180
1:3–7 141
1:3–11 182
1:18 183
1:19–20 182
3:16 181, 187

4:1 181, 182, 187
4:14 183
6:17 186
6:20 185

2 Timothy
1:6–7 181, 183, 187
1:8–13 185
1:14 181, 184, 187
1:15 141
4:10 180

Titus
1:4 180
1:5 180
1:5–8 186
1:9 186
1:10 186
1:11 186
1:12 180
1:13 186
1:14 186
1:16 186
2:15 186
3:5 113, 186
3:5–6 181, 185, 187
3:9 186
3:10 186

Hebrews
2:3 190
2:4 188, 190, 195
3:1–6 189
3:6 188
3:7 190
3:7–8 188, 195
3:11 189
3:14 188
6:1–12 192
6:4 188, 190, 191, 195
9:1–10 192
9:8 188, 190, 192, 195
9:9–10 193
9:11–28 193
9:14 188, 190, 193, 195
10:15 188, 189, 195

10:23 188
10:25 188
10:29 188, 190, 195
12:1 176

1 Peter
1:2 197, 204
1:3–5 199
1:6–7 196, 199
1:7 198, 199
1:8–9 199
1:11 197, 198, 204
1:12 197, 199, 204
1:18 196
1:22 196
2:4 202
2:9 196
2:10 196
2:11–12 196
2:11–3:13 196
2:12 196
2:17 196
2:19 198
3:10–12 200
3:13–17 196
3:13–18 196
3:14 198, 200
3:18 197, 200, 204
3:19 200
3:19–20 201
4:1–6 196
4:3 196
4:4 196
4:6 197, 201, 204
4:7–11 196
4:12 197
4:12–13 202
4:12–19 196
4:13–14 175, 198
4:14 197, 202, 204
5:1–5 196
5:6–11 196
5:9 196
5:13 3

2 Peter
1:20–21 198
1:21 198

1 John
2:1   47
2:5–6   206
2:14   206
2:24   206
2:27–28   206
3:6   206
3:9   206
3:11–18   206
3:24   205, 206, 210
4:1   208
4:2   205, 207, 208, 210
4:6   205, 207, 208, 210
4:12   206
4:13   205, 206, 210
4:15–16   206
5:1–5   208
5:6–8   205, 207, 208, 210
5:7   209
5:10   209
5:20   206

Jude
1:4   212

1:7–8   212
1:10   212
1:16   212
1:17   211
1:19   211, 213
1:20   211, 212, 213
1:23   212

Revelation
1:1   214
1:10   214, 216, 220
2:7   214, 220
2:11   214, 220
2:16   219
2:17   214, 220
2:29   214, 220
3:6   214, 220
3:11   219
3:13   214, 220
3:22   214, 220
4:2   214, 216, 220
5:1   144
6:9   218
7:3   144
11:7   218
12:11   218

14:13   214, 215, 220
17:3   214, 216, 217, 218, 220
17:18   217
19:10   214, 218, 220
21:2   219
21:9   219
21:10   214, 216, 217, 218, 220
22:7   219
22:12   219
22:17   214, 218, 219, 220
22:20   219

OTHER ANCIENT WRITINGS

b. Pesahim
57a   111

b. Sukkah
5:55a   45

Josephus
Jewish Antiquities
8.100   42

Leviticus Rabbah
15:2   36

m. Qiddushin
4:14   122

Philo
On the Sacrifices of Cain and Abel
69–71   122

Polybius
Histories
2.22   135
2.23   135
2.33   135

Testament of Levi
18:6–11   8